FROM THE HEART OF ANCIENT IRELAND

Even today, the sabbats of Ireland are rich with the pagan lore of their past. Witta, the Old Religion, offers all pagans a trove of wisdom and practice to enrich the tradition of any follower of Earth religions.

Most books on Irish paganism focus solely on Celtic mythology, without examining how those heroic myths shaped the Irish religion. *Witta: An Irish Pagan Tradition* supplies the missing link essential to understanding the Irish religion in a cultural context.

Here, you will find a comprehensive framework for practicing and understanding the Old Religion of Ireland, including specifics on magickal practice and the Celtic Tree system ... practicing Irish spells and magick ... constructing traditionally inspired Wittan rituals ... symbology for each tool used in Wittan religious practice ... guidelines for contacting spirits and faery folk, and more. Also provided are detailed appendices on Irish gods and goddesses, Irish terminology, magickal herbs, and traditional Irish music, as well as a bibliography for further reading.

If you are of Irish descent, Witta will put you in touch with your heritage—although the knowledge of *both* Irish and non-Irish pagans will be enhanced by access to Witta's abundant body of lore.

Witta is more than an obscure religion buried in Ireland's past; it represents a way of life, the way every Irish clan and community once viewed their world and the forces that shaped it. The beauty and simplicity of that world is alive today. If you choose to take the life-affirming path of Witta, you will find that piece of ancient Ireland which lives in your heart.

About the Author

Edain McCoy was born in South Bend, Indiana to parents from diverse ethnic and religious backgrounds who always encouraged her to explore the history of religious thought. As a teenager she began seeking the roots of her birth religion. That search, and her increasing feminist outlook, eventually brought her back to the Old Religion. A chance meeting with a hereditary Wittan at a ceilidh (Irish dance) in Houston led her to study the Irish Tradition of the craft. Though she prefers to practice as a solitary, she was initiated into a large San Antonio coven, and has since been active in several other Texas covens, most of them following the Irish Tradition. A graduate of the University of Texas, Edain now lives in the Midwest where she is continuing her formal graduate studies in cultural history. She is also active with the local Irish Arts Association. Her other interests include country decorating, needle crafts, aerobic and Irish dancing, music, and her beloved Shetland sheepdogs.

To Write to the Author

If you wish to contact the author or would like more information about this book, please write to the author in care of Llewellyn Worldwide, and we will forward your request. Both the author and publisher appreciate hearing from you and learning of your enjoyment of this book and how it has helped you. Llewellyn Worldwide cannot guarantee that every letter written to the author can be answered, but all will be forwarded. Please write to:

Edain McCoy
c/o Llewellyn Worldwide
P.O. Box 64383, Dept. 732-4, St. Paul, MN 55164-0383, U.S.A.

Please enclose a self-addressed, stamped envelope for reply, or $1.00 to cover costs.
If outside the U.S.A., enclose international postal reply coupon.

Free Catalog from Llewellyn

For more than 90 years Llewellyn has brought its readers knowledge in the fields of metaphysics and human potential. Learn about the newest books in spiritual guidance, natural healing, astrology, occult philosophy and more. Enjoy book reviews, new age articles, a calendar of events, plus current advertised products and services. To get your free copy of *Llewellyn's New Worlds of Mind and Spirit*, send your name and address to:

Llewellyn's New Worlds of Mind and Spirit
P.O. Box 64383, Dept. 732-4, St. Paul, MN 55164-0383, U.S.A.

LLEWELLYN'S WORLD MAGIC SERIES

WITTA

AN IRISH PAGAN TRADITION

❧ EDAIN McCOY ❧

1997
Llewellyn Publications
St. Paul, Minnesota 55164-0383, U.S.A.

FIRST EDITION
Fourth Printing, 1997

Cover Painting by Lissanne Lake
Interior Illustrations by Alexandra Lumen

Library of Congress Cataloging-in-Publication Data
McCoy, Edain, 1957-
    Witta : an Irish pagan tradition / Edain McCoy.
    p.   cm. — (Llewellyn's world magic series)
    Includes bibliographical references and index.
    ISBN 0-87542-732-4
    1. Witchcraft—Ireland. 2. Paganism—Ireland.
3. Magic, Celtic—Ireland. I. Title. II. Series.
BF1581.M44   1993
299'.162—dc20   93-26366
                                    CIP

Llewellyn Worldwide does not participate in, endorse, or have any authority or responsibility concerning private business transactions between our authors and the public.

    All mail addressed to the author is forwarded but the publisher cannot, unless specifically instructed by the author, give out an address or phone number.

Llewellyn Publications
A Division of Llewellyn Worldwide, Ltd.
P.O. Box 64383, St. Paul, MN 55164-0383

LLEWELLYN'S WORLD MAGIC SERIES

At the core of every religion, at the foundation of every culture, there is MAGIC.

Magic sees the world as alive, as the home which humanity shares with beings and powers both visible and invisible with whom and which we can interface to either our advantage or disadvantage—depending upon our awareness and intention.

Religious worship and communion is one kind of magic, and just as there are many religions in the world so are there many magical systems.

Religion and magic are ways of seeing and relating to the creative powers, the living energies, the all-pervading spirit, the underlying intelligence that is the universe within which we and all else exist.

Neither religion nor magic conflict with science. All share the same goals and the same limitations: always seeking truth, forever haunted by human limitations in perceiving that truth. Magic is "technology" based upon experience and extrasensory insight, providing its practitioners with methods of greater influence and control over the world of the invisible before it impinges on the world of the visible.

The study of world magic not only enhances your understanding of the world in which you live, and hence your ability to live better, but brings you in touch with the inner essence of your long evolutionary heritage and most particularly—as in the case of the magical system identified most closely with your genetic inheritance—with the archetypal images and forces most alive in your whole consciousness.

OTHER BOOKS BY EDAIN McCOY

A Witch's Guide to Faery Folk

Celtic Myth and Magick

How to do Automatic Writing

In a Graveyard at Midnight

Lady of the Night

The Sabbats

Entering the Summerland

Inside a Witches' Coven

FORTHCOMING

Making Magick

TABLE OF CONTENTS

❧ INTRODUCTION ☙

As the twentieth century (and perhaps the entire Piscean Age) draws to a close, more and more people are finding their way back to the Old Religion, the aboriginal faiths of the people of our earth long before our experiment with patriarchy and its attendant rules of obedience and conformity. Recent awareness of nature in peril, conservation, and environmentalism have aided waxing interest in paganism, as have the feminist movements and the failure of the patriarchal religions to satisfy their adherents' need to feel a connection with the earth and a balance between the feminine and masculine forces which govern the laws of the universe.

In the United States many people have turned to Native American spirituality to satisfy this missing feeling of connection. We nonnatives have been here a long time now and it is only natural that we seek to understand the spiritual system indigenous to the land. Others seek out the old pathways of their forebears. Norse, Teutonic, Polynesian, and Caucuses magickal ways are being written about and sought out amid growing popularity. Hispanics are returning to the knowledge of their curanderos (Mexican shamans) to recapture the lost knowledge of their people, and those of us of Celtic descent also are quite naturally attempting to rediscover the ancient ways of our people.

Reconstructing a religion which was forced underground and kept alive by small, secretive pockets of believers for hundreds of years is a daunting task. Through academic study, meditation, good teachers, and dubious regressions, fragments of the Old Religion are reclaimed and fitted into the framework of modern pagan pathways. But just as people evolve, so do religious systems, and many of the ways of ancient Ireland, such as the past practice of living sacrifice, are repugnant to the modern pagan who is likely to be so set against the taking of life as to be a vegetarian. We take what seems right and good from our past and we adapt it to the neo-paganism of today. And we cherish those old secret ways which have been painstakingly unearthed from old texts, and revealed to us by the descendants of those brave seekers who guarded the ancient ways of Ireland's past through whatever onslaughts the patriarchal world sent them.

Witta, the Irish Gaelic term for the Anglo-Saxon word Wicca, is one of the Irish names of the craft. The word means "wise one," and was often applied specifically to women, the traditional healers in ancient Europe, to whom people came for medicinal herbs and spells. Both terms eventually evolved into the common English word "witch" which has from time to time caused widespread outbursts of hysteria among the patriarchal faiths.

The term "pagan" is more broad in its definition. It is from the Latin paganus meaning "people of the earth." It is a word used to define followers and practitioners of earth religions everywhere. But the terms witch and pagan are not entirely synonymous. All witches are pagans, but not all pagans are witches. Some follow non-Celtic or non-Anglo-Saxon traditions which are pagan but not Wittan or Wiccan, though the basic beliefs and practices are very similar. Still other pagans use different labels to identify themselves in conformity with their heritage.

Irish witches were luckier than most in Europe. Their remoteness left many of their ways and monuments untouched by the Christian witch hunters. Pagans, Jews, and other non-Christians fled to the west of Ireland during the years of the Spanish Inquisition, a period of history known to pagans as "The Burning Times." The west of Ireland was literally the end of the earth in 1492, and a seemingly safe refuge from those legions of Rome who would cry "convert or die."

Even Saint Patrick, who first brought Christianity to Ireland in the fourth century C.E. (common era) instructed his scribes to commit to paper as much of the mythology of Ireland as they could in order to preserve the history of the Irish people. Though he eventually destroyed much of the original pagan writing, his early efforts had the blessed side effect of preserving many of the ancient myths and old religious teachings for later generations. However, as we shall see, he later reversed his benevolent feelings for the folktales of Ireland and set out on a rather successful campaign to eradicate much of what his monks and scribes had saved.

There is a popular misconception that the early Celts left no writings of their own, but there is much historical evidence to the contrary. The Druids were credited with much of that Celtic writing, or so that was the claim of a twelfth century scribe who diligently copied a book known as *Tain Bo Cuailagne*, a compendium of old Irish folktales written in beautiful lyric poetry. In order to save his neck should the Mother Church discover his heretical deed, he carefully refuted the veracity of his own work by calling it a "fable" for "the delight of fools."

Despite Ireland's factual reputation as a deeply Catholic country, Witta flourishes there both in its cities and in its remote mountains and dells. And through the large exporting of its people to the rest of the West, Wittan traditions have flowed with them, especially to North America. Since more than one-quarter of all Americans have some roots in Ireland, it is not surprising to find that American pagans are displaying a growing interest in Wittan ways.

Remember that Witta, like Wicca and other forms of paganism, is first and above all a RELIGION. The honoring of the deities is the main focus and function, as it is within any religion. Magick is a part of Witta, but magick can be worked by anybody with the knowledge and energy to do so. As a religion, and as an earth religion, Witta was viewed as a threat to the new religion, and subjected to harsh persecutions and purging by the patriarchal Church of Europe.

One of the basic tenets of paganism is that all paths to the creative life force are valid and are to be respected. No one has the corner on the truth. While some of the historical events I write about seem to pick particularly on the old Roman Church, my comments are intended only as historical insight and not as evidence of any personal discord with that institution. I also write disparagingly of the patriarchy, the 6000-year-old system of male domination under which our world labors. I do not mean to speak ill of all men, in fact some of the most staunch defenders of the current status quo are women. But the facts are that patriarchal thought and patriarchal religions have spent the past 6000 years trying to eradicate paganism, its old gods, and most of all, its veneration of the Great Mother Goddess. The Roman Church gets trounced on here not because it was in any way worse in its crusade than Judaism, Buddhism, Hinduism, or Islam, but because it is the major patriarchal religion of Ireland. The fact cannot be denied that for almost a millennium the Roman Church ruled, and often terrorized, western Europe. Its legions spread out over Europe, including Ireland, and stamped out vestiges of the Old Religion like an advancing plague.

Though this text touches upon the subjects of Irish mythology and basic witchcraft, that is not its focus. For those who wish to further explore those topics, please check the bibliography and suggested reading list for names of books and authors who cover those subjects in depth. *Witta: An Irish Pagan Tradition* is intended for those with or without some basic knowledge of pagan thought and pagan practice who wish to explore the beliefs and practices of this special tradition of the craft.

Witta can be divided into five distinct periods of practice during which it was influenced by various factors. These periods are:

❧ The pre-Druidic period which dates up to the second century B.C.E. (before common era). During this time the Celts were the predominant ethnic group of Ireland and Witta was born from their land, incorporating many elements which had been dragged with them across Europe from India many centuries before.

❧ The Druidic period, which lasted from the second century B.C.E. until about 400 C.E. During this time the Druids were the real power in Ireland, and they made many changes to the Wittan faith, often serving as a bridge between the matrifocal and patriarchal periods. Also during this time Rome was in control of nearby England, and though Ireland lay just outside the official boundaries of pagan Rome, its influence was greatly felt on Witta.

❧ The period when the early Church ran Ireland lasted from the second to the twelfth centuries. During this time Irish paganism was at first allowed to flourish uneasily alongside Christianity, and then it was decimated. During this period the Vikings invaded Ireland and left much Nordic pagan influence on Witta. Also the Norman invaders came with their hard-line Christian fundamentalism, and their very different ideas about government.

❧ The period known as "The Burning Times" lasted from the twelfth century until quite recently. These were the years of persecution and death for European pagans. And while this torment was not so widespread in Ireland, it did exist. Witta was forced underground, kept alive by a few hardy souls who valiantly refused to give up their beliefs.

❧ The late twentieth century has seen a renewed interest in paganism of all types worldwide. Most of the antiquated anti-witchcraft laws have been repealed, and many formerly ignorant people have allowed that paganism has the right to be practiced freely. Within this new framework, interest in and practice of Witta has expanded greatly.

Please be aware that many different scholars can read the same material and come to several different conclusions. The same is true in the study of Witta. I have written here my interpretation of the teaching I have received and of the material I have read. I do not claim to be the final authority on this matter and I welcome any and all comments, corrections, and additions for later revisions. Please feel free to write me in care of the publisher.

There are many expressions of paganism, and differing interpretations are often found even when delving into a single culture—Irish paganism included. Some are older, some are newer, and others combine the influences of many other traditions. No one of them is greater or lesser than any other—only different.

What is presented here is a Celtic interpretation of the Irish tradition with allowances being made for the undeniable impact which has been made on it by many other cultures while still maintaining its Irishness. It is by no means the only view of the Irish pagan tradition, though it is perhaps the most common one utilized today in the United States and Canada. Also notable among Irish traditions practiced today around the globe are the Tuatha De Danann, who presumably take their practice from the culture of this ancient race of invaders, and the Irish Pagan Movement, headquartered in County Wexford, Ireland, who claim a very ancient practice which predates the Celts. Any student of Irish paganism is encouraged to delve into the subtle nuances of these Irish traditions both to enrich and expand his or her own knowledge and understanding of this complex path, and to ensure that he or she finds that one interpretation of the Irish tradition which is just right for him or her.

For those of us who are pagans of Irish descent, reclaiming the ways of our ancestors is a way to link ourselves to past generations, to connect with our Mother Earth in the same way our forebears might have. To seekers of the Old Religion, Witta offers another dimension to be added to our growing knowledge and appreciation of our world's earth religions. It is to these seekers, from all traditions, to whom this book is lovingly dedicated.

Blessed Be!

E.M.
1992

1

History and Mythology, Deities and Druids

One of the first things a pagan writer finds out when seeking to impart wisdom on one particular tradition of the craft is that he or she will be deluged with letters from disappointed readers wanting to know why they weren't shown the authentic, pure, and unadulterated old path. Be assured that there is no such thing. Just as language reflects the influence and inbreeding of various cultures of people, so do religious and magickal practices.

Ireland has never existed in a vacuum. Though many of its pagan traditions were kept alive by its position on the far western edge of the known world, each invader and conqueror contributed to the native culture, and each had a profound influence on the predominant religious practice of the time.

The Celts, the majority ethnic group of Ireland past and present, were fierce warriors much feared throughout Bronze Age Europe. Even powerful Rome looked upon the Celts with fear and awe at the terror these large, hairy, tribal people inspired.

Like most early societies the Celts were matrifocal. That is they divided their society and households into families by mother blood relationships. Fatherhood had no significance to their early society. Children grew up in the maternal grandmother's household, and their mother's brothers acted as their male role models and teachers. Men and women had equal status in all matters of community life. Women were trained as warriors and fought alongside the men in battle.

According to archaeological evidence the Celts arrived in Ireland in the Iron Age, as early as 1200 B.C.E. Metalcrafting, especially in gold, was one of the primary skills of these people who wove intricate, knotted designs into their jewelry and armaments. Celtic art is quite beautiful, and if one looks closely at it, one can see the snakes and other sacred animals whose images have been skillfully interwoven into the drawings and carvings.

The Celts, like other pagan civilizations, developed a rich body of mythology and a large pantheon of deities. This body of oral knowledge stayed with the Irish people until long after Christian missionaries arrived to convert the populace. Celtic religion was pantheistic, meaning that there were a variety of goddesses and gods, but all were one in the sense that they were merely aspects of the one creative life source and its power. Interestingly, many ethnologists and anthropologists now believe that there has never been a truly polytheistic religion, one which asserts that there are many unrelated deities all stemming from distinctly different origins. Most pagans have expressed the belief that all things were born of one divine source. In Witta this one power was the Great Mother from whose womb all things were born, and it is into that womb that all things will return to await rebirth.

The early Irish belief in the Great Mother as the supreme and only being lasted long into the period where many other cultures were also worshiping male deities whom they viewed as the consort and child of the Goddess. This practice eventually came into Witta long after the discovery of the male role in reproduction. The early Irish Celts were a herding society, not an agricultural one, and the imagery of the Father Sky fertilizing the Mother Earth was not a relevant archetype for them until a much later period. The ancient Irish could see lunar influence in the cycles of women and in the birth process just as they would later see the inclusion of the male principle in an agricultural society. The moon represented the Goddess and it was around her that their society marked its time.

The Celts reigned supreme in Ireland for many centuries, their power virtually unchallenged from the sixth century B.C.E. to the fourth century C.E. Their artwork, stone carvings, metallurgy, and hillforts remain as a testament to their entrenchment and talents.

Writing came late to Ireland, around the second century B.C.E. It was used by only a select few because writing was considered a sacred undertaking, and what little writing remains of pre-Christian Ireland was recorded sparsely by the Druids in their sacred ogham alphabet. This secret alphabet was not perfected nor in common usage until around the third century C.E.

When the legions of pagan Rome began expanding themselves northwestward into England and Scotland in 55 B.C.E., Ireland remained largely untouched by them. Roman pagan practice therefore had a greater impact on Wicca (Anglo-Brythonic witchcraft) than on Witta, as can be seen in the way the sabbats are handled by each tradition even today. However, the Latin name for Ireland, Hibernia, remains in usage. Mutual colonization efforts between Scotland and Ireland did bring some pagan Roman influence into Witta.

The first invaders who impacted the religious life of the Irish Celts were the early missionaries of the Roman Church. It was these invaders who first began to change the basic social structure of the Celts. The early Christians were appalled at the Irish lack of concern for biological fatherhood, and by the ease with which most Celtic women took whatever lover they wished. Like other matrifocal cultures the emphasis was on blood relationships—meaning tied by the menstrual blood of the mother's clan. Reacting to the "horror" of Irish family life, the early Christian intruders broke up the old clan system, instituted the nuclear family as it has come down to us, and demonized all those who would violate this principle. It is this concept of guaranteed paternity which even today is the glue holding together the fabric of patriarchal religions.

Around the fourth century C.E. a young monk named Patrick arrived in Ireland and successfully managed a conversion campaign on the native populace. Saint Patrick ordered his monks to preserve Irish history and lore, and thanks to him much of Irish mythology was preserved. But Saint Patrick also began a systematic undermining of the Druidic priest class, and of the rulership of the high kings of Ireland.

In the ninth century the Norse Vikings invaded from the north, interrupting the progression of the Christian grip on Irish political and religious life. Many of the Norse pagan religious concepts were adopted readily into Irish life, including the observance of the Mabon and Ostara sabbats, and the movement of the Celtic new year from Samhain to Yule. Eventually many of these people became absorbed into the gene pool of Ireland, and the rest were expelled by King Brian Boru.

By the twelfth century the Church would no longer tolerate Witta living side by side with Christianity. The Wittan deities were diabolized, particularly the Great Horned God who became a model for Satan. Women's community roles as healers and goddesses incarnate were now deemed wicked, and harsh anti-witchcraft laws were enacted and brutal persecutions became the norm throughout Europe. The simple act of healing another person or assisting in childbirth was to do the Devil's work, as the ill was not left to live or die at the Christian God's whim.

Irish witches fared a little better than those in England or on the continent by virtue of their great distance from Rome and the rest of Europe. Ireland was mostly rural, as it still is today, and the monks went about their own business ignoring much of the paganism surrounding them. In some monasteries elaborate poetry was found glorifying nature, some of it bordering on open veneration for the old gods. That monks would cherish the old ways was a hidden fact, but not an isolated one. The famous epic poem *Carmina Burana* was a manuscript found in an Italian monastery which clearly glorifies the Mother Goddess. It has since been made into a beautiful classic choral work.

In 1066 William the Conqueror, the great Norman leader, invaded and conquered England bringing with him the laws and philosophies of continental Europe. In 1155 England took possession of Ireland and as a result some of their harsh anti-witchcraft laws went into effect. Many Irish witches, both falsely and rightly accused, were burned or hanged. As in England and the United States, the majority of these victims were elderly women.

Despite efforts to stamp out pagan practice, Witta in Ireland still flourished due to the isolation of many of the practitioners. And many of the rural monasteries chose to ignore all but the most flagrant infractions of the anti-witchcraft laws.

By the fourteenth century Witta had gone underground and Irish pagans met in secret, relegating the remnants of their religious lore to nursery rhymes and faery tales to keep them alive.

The Irish Myth Cycles

The mythology of a people is of central importance to its religious life. It is from myths that we derive our attitudes towards people and nature, form our models of heroes and heroines, and understand our deities. The heroic and shameful deeds of a people's past, both human and divine, provide a culture with a sense of continuity and oneness, and display lessons to be learned and pitfalls to be avoided.

Irish mythology recognizes five major myth cycles. Within each of these five myth cycles are more cycles, and each of the four ancient provinces of Ireland has some of their own mythology. This rich lore is the main source of the goddesses, gods, and celebrations endemic to Wittan religious practice. The ordinary human beings who invaded the island also put their stamp on the lives of the Irish people. Each in their turn, the Celts, the Norse, the early Roman Church, and refugees from the Spanish Inquisition all contributed their beliefs and practices to the indigenous religion.

Most of the Irish myths were recorded between 500 and 800 C.E., though they were in fact many centuries older. Many of them, surprisingly enough, were recorded by Christian monks seeking to preserve Irish history. Others were written by native Irish pagans. Many of the stories were adulterated by the men—or rather by the patriarchy—who recorded the stories, and their patriarchalization is apparent in the style and content of some of the myths. Other legends survived through an oral tradition and were not recorded until many centuries later. Even today in modern Ireland the role of the traveling storyteller is very much a part of rural community life. And many of the native myths, like society itself, have undergone editing by the dominant cultures who have had much to gain from these alterations. Wherever a god is dominant over a goddess, or where a hero has power independent of a heroine, it is usually indicative of a later story or an alteration in the original tale. Wittans saw a balance between maleness and femaleness, and stories which do not recognize this balance are to be suspect.

The Book of Armagh, the Book of the Dun Cow, the Yellow Book of Lechan, and the Book of Leinster are the primary writings in which the Irish myths were recorded. Occasionally these can be found in translation in college libraries or through Irish booksellers. Books on Irish mythology abound and condensed forms of the myths can be purchased most anywhere there are books for sale.

Even more easy to find are collections of stories translated from these books, and several good ones are listed in the bibliography. Be prepared to do some thinking about each tale. Many of them are told differently depending upon when the original Irish Gaelic material was written, and these differences can reflect later adulterations as well as regional variations on the myths.

The Irish invasion myth cycles have five components. They involve a series of invader races of faery-like folks and deities who conquered the island. They are the Partholans, the Nemed, the Firbolgs, the Tuatha De Danann (who had the most profound influence on the Wittan religion), and the Milesians, a relative of the Celts.

The Celts believed themselves to be descendants of the Goddess and God of the Underworld, Dealgnaid and her consort Partholan. They came to Ireland from the west, the acknowledged home of the dead. The Partholans were believed to have carved the face of Ireland out of barrenness and created the lakes, rivers and green groves, and they brought with them all the animals and the fish.

Then came the Formorians who brought a pestilence to Partholan and his legions. The Formorians, who were essentially sea creatures, soon left Ireland empty for further occupation. Part of the reason they left was that they were in conflict with Finn MacCool, a giant who inhabited and protected Ireland. Today the Formorians are sea monsters or faeries who prowl the Irish coast.

The second of the invader races were the Nemed, named for their leader who was a cousin of Partholan. The Nemed were a dark people who came to Ireland from the south, and many scholars believe that there indeed may have been some would-be invaders from the Iberian Peninsula in what is now Spain. But sadly for the Nemed, they were not successful warriors and the Formorians killed all but thirty men, including Fergus, their war chief. Those survivors left Ireland only to return later when the Firbolgs attempted to reclaim the island.

The greatest contribution to Irish paganism made by the Nemed was the belief in the Morrigu, a fierce triple goddess which consisted only of crone aspects. The names of the Morrigu are Badb, Nemain, and Macha.

The Firbolgs came next. They were another faery race invader who play a very little role in the mythological history of the island, and are even made out to be characters of inferiority. The Firbolgs tried to be warriors, but from all accounts they failed so miserably that even the few remaining Formorians did not bother with them.

Then came the Tuatha De Danann, the last faery race of Ireland, and with them came most of the goddesses and gods of the Irish pantheon. They arrived at Bealtaine and by the Summer Solstice had easily defeated the remaining Formorians and the inept Firbolgian fighters. Their name means "people of the goddess Dana," the first Great Mother goddess of Ireland. Dana, later renamed Brigid, was the goddess of childbirth, poetry, music, creative endeavors, smithing, crafting, metallurgy, animal husbandry, and later of agriculture.

Unlike the Partholans, Nemed, and Firbolgs, the Tuatha De Danann came not from an earthly direction, but from the heavens—though some myths say they came from all four directions at once—the direction of the elusive fifth element, spirit. In the manner of a magick circle the Tuatha created four great cities, each presided over by a separate race of faery folk: Falias, Finias, Gorias, and Murias. Eventually, after a long reign, they too were defeated and went underground where they remain today as the faery folk of Ireland.

Divine intervention and will has been the justification for royal rule from the beginning of time. It was the Tuatha who gave the right of rulership to the high kings. The Lia Fail, or Stone of Destiny, was stood upon by the kings as they were crowned. This stone did exist, and was used in Scotland as late as the tenth century to crown Scottish royalty. It can still be seen if one travels to Perth. This myth probably leaves out the much earlier idea that it was Dana who was the true giver of royal authority. The idea that a king must have a queen to rule comes from the ancient belief that all things, living or inanimate, were born of a Great Mother deity.

The last of the invaders were the Milesians, a cousin-race of the Celts. From them were born the first human legends of Ireland which culminated in the heroic tales of the warrioress Queen Madb of Connacht and of the most revered high king of all Ireland, Brian Boru.

It is highly recommend that anyone serious about the Wittan path study these tales. They are neither brief nor few. But they are highly engrossing stories of the exploits of heroes, heroines, and deities which will provide you with a greater insight into Wittan practice and belief. The bibliography supplies information on books which contain these heroic tales which can be purchased at most large bookstores.

THE IRISH DEITIES

In the beginning there was the Goddess, the primal Great Mother who gave birth to all the universe. For centuries the Goddess was the only deity of ancient Ireland. Her name was Dana or Brigid and she was maiden, mother, and crone, the giver of life and bringer of death. This association was obvious. All living things are born of a mother—period. The early Celts were a herding people, not agriculturalists, and anthropological studies have shown that a male-god concept was of less importance to herders. As Ireland became more agricultural and multiethnic a god evolved into the myths. This was the powerful sword-wielding god Lugh, for whom the sabbat of Lughnasadh (August 1) is named.

As in all pagan religions the idea of the deities being part of a polarity, not a duality, is an accepted part of the belief system. Polarity means that all aspects of good, evil, and indifference are manifest in one central power. It is up to us to determine which of these energies we draw from and work with. Therefore the Goddess and God are truly one being who manifest as two different beings depending on which aspect we call upon. Paganism is also pantheistic, meaning that there are many manifestations of the one creative life force called by many names and worshiped in many ways.

In Witta the Goddess and God have some attributes which are theirs alone and are not shared with the opposite gender deity. The Goddess is daughter, mother, and grandmother. She is the cosmic womb where all life begins, and she is the passive principle in all creation. She is comforting, protection is given in her enfolding arms, she is loving and gentle, she is harsh only to teach her children a needed lesson, and she is powerful to the point of holding the key to life and death. The Goddess is eternal, never being born and never dying. Her colors are silver, white, red, and black.

The God is both playful and stern. As a protector he is like a strong shield which guards his people. He is the active principle in all creation, that which plants the seed of life in the fertile cosmic womb of the Goddess. The God is not eternal. He lives and dies and is reborn throughout the Irish year. His colors are gold, yellow, orange, and brown.

The primary deity of Witta, or of virtually any pagan religion, is the eternal Triple Goddess. Throughout the wheel of the year she goes from being maiden to mother to crone, but she never dies. She gives birth to the God at Yule, grows up with him, takes him as a lover, watches him die at Samhain, and then gives birth to her son-lover again at the following Yule. Her planet is the moon which also never dies, but merely shows a different face as she passes through her three phases of waxing, fullness, and waning. These three faces are symbolized by the colors white, red, and black. White for the youthful maiden goddess, red for the fullness of motherhood as in her menstrual blood, and black for the mysterious realm of the crone which presages death and rebirth.

Many well-known faery tales and nursery rhymes have kept the memory of the Triple Goddesses alive through thousands of years of pagan persecution. The colors red, white, and black are deeply rooted in Irish mythology and are intimately associated with the Triple Goddess. One of the most obvious is the story of Snow White who has black hair, red lips, white skin, and lives deep within nature with seven others—the same number as were planets known at the time. These colors were also the colors of the Hounds of the Underworld in Irish mythology, and the colors of the priestesses who guard the cauldron of the Caillech (the crone), and who, in later tales, stand guard over the mythical Holy Grail.

The first Great Mother goddess worshiped in old Ireland was Dana (pronounced Dawn-na). The strongest and most potent conquerors of Ireland in the myth cycles were the Tuatha De Danann, or "the people of of the goddess Dana." For reasons unknown, Dana was later renamed Brigid who even today in Witta is worshiped as the supreme Mother Goddess.

Brigid (pronounced Breed) is the unequivocal Irish Great Mother who shares her triplicity with Danu (a form of Dana) and Badb, the crone. Brigid was also a goddess of sovereignty who birthed all things into being including her god consorts. She was also worshiped as the goddess of creativity, warrior power, smithing, crafting, poetry, music, writing, children, and pregnancy. More than any other Irish deity, she survives all other Celtic folk heroes and deities mostly intact. Her much beloved shrine at Kildare was taken over by a Christian monument honoring Saint Bridgit whose fabricated life story reflected many of the same skills of the Irish Goddess—creative inspiration, midwifery, and fearlessness. But where the Irish Goddess represented the Great Mother at her peak, even the Triple Goddess in all her aspects, the saint chose to remain a virgin.

The principal male deity of Witta is the Great Horned God. He is sometimes referred to by the Greek name Cernunnos, and he is probably the most persistent image worshiped as a god throughout all of Western paganism. Unfortunately his original Irish name is lost in the distant past. He is a god of the woodlands who is sometimes called the Lord of the Greenwood, a god of music and dance, of sex and fertility, and of mischief making. Like his Greek counterpart Pan, he is drawn as a half man, half cloven-footed animal with two large horns. As with Brigid, shrines to him existed all over Ireland. But the early clergy realized that they could not have another male deity competing with their God so they diabolized the Horned God by equating him with their Satan. The early Christians perpetuated the belief that Satan was a cloven-footed beast with horns in a direct attempt at drawing people away from worship of the Horned God.

The God of Light and Sun, Lugh, who is honored at the Lugh-nasadh sabbat, is another of the major Irish deities. He was a male counterpart to Brigid for he was also honored as a god of many crafts and creative endeavors. He is the god of the harvests and of growth, of fire and light. Where the Horned God is the fertility god of spring, Lugh is the harvest lord of autumn, and Lughnasadh is the first of the three harvest sabbats. Lugh was allowed to pass freely from the Land of the Dead to the Land of Living. As proof of his otherworldly exploits he brought back a boat which was steered by the thoughts of the captain, a sword named Fragarach which could cut through any substance and knew truth from falsehood, and a horse which could be ridden on either land or sea. The Book of Leinster recounts most of Lugh's heroic tales.

Another male god nearly as well known and widely worshiped as Lugh is Dagda, the "good god." Originally he was the son of Brigid, but the later myths which underwent patriarchalization made him the father of her and of the entire feminine triplicity. So far did the rewrite of his life story go in denying the feminine life force that he was even given possession of the great cauldron of death and rebirth which belongs in the hands of the crone. Dagda also gained possession of the great golden harp of Ireland, still symbolic of the country today.

In the early myths of Ireland the status and interaction of the deities reflected the lifestyle of the people, in that the status of women was equal to that of men. Celtic women were trained as warriors and fought alongside the men, a practice which lasted until the sixth century. Older mothers were the central focus of the clans even when clans eventually became headed by men. Property was passed through the female line, and it was once believed that only women could teach men battle skills and only men could teach them to women.

The myth of the goddess Aine illustrates that women were sovereign beings. When Aine was raped by Aillil Olum, a king of Munster, she slew him. A cult of women warriors dedicated to the memory of Aine was established in early Ireland, and they were much feared by the invaders. Aine has also found her way into modern Irish folk practice. She is said to appear on Aine's Hill in Kilkenny on Saint John's Eve to lead the religious procession as a warrioress of the new religion.

Crone images have always been important in paganism, representing the strongest, most vibrant, and most destructive of all deity energies. The Caillech, also known as Macha, is the Irish Goddess in her crone aspect. Many Wittans mistakenly use Cerridwen for this aspect, but that is the crone name from Wales and Scotland. The Caillech lives in Tir-na-nog, the land of the dead in the west, and presides over the cauldron of death and rebirth. She is in her full flower at Samhain, and it was from this crone image that the modern Halloween witch was born.

Badb is another name for the Irish crone, and is probably the oldest of the Irish crone names. Literally her name means "one who boils," as in the boiling of a cauldron. The image of a hag hovering over a churning cauldron full of grotesque ingredients was popularized in Shakespeare's *Macbeth*.

Another curious deity of sorts which is native to Ireland is the Shiela-na-gig. Nothing is known of her except that she was the carved image found on Irish doorways and stone carvings presumably for protection. She is a crude rendering of a goddess holding wide her vulva in a triangular pattern. Many of these carvings were later used by nuns to adorn the doors of Irish convents. When discovered by horrified clergy they were broken off and destroyed. A hundred years ago an archaeologist found a pile of them buried near the ruins of an old Irish church.

For several centuries after the coming of Christianity to Ireland, women's religions might have functioned side by side, but separately, from the largely male-involved new religion. Celtic folktales of "faery" or pagan women who married Christian men have led feminist scholars to believe this separation existed in the early years of the Church. One such example of this is the cult of the goddess Kele-De. Her all-female followers were exempt from patriarchal law, free to take lovers as they chose, and to own property not confiscated by the Church. However, seeing that the Church needed women as well as men to uphold its tenets, the Church set out on the first of its persecution campaigns effectively using fear and threats to force all people, male and female, to conform to the standards and rules of the new religion.

One ancient worship site remains as a testament to this religious separation practice. On the small island of Innishmurray, a few miles off the coast of County Sligo, is an abandoned monastery dating to the sixth century. Aside from the usual religious relics one expects to find at such a place there is a "women's church" and a "women's cemetery," and nearby these sites are the famous Five Speckled Stones which are richly inscribed with pagan symbols.

To eradicate the feminine deities the pagan goddesses were demonized and witch hunts became standard practice. Witches and midwives (synonymous with "witch" in that it means "wise woman") were destroyed for practicing herbal medicine which the clergy said interfered with the will of their God.

The Old Religion in Ireland was preserved mostly by women, though there was a good number of men who also gathered on Irish hillsides and in dark groves to carry on the traditions of their people.

THE DRUIDS

When one thinks of the ancient Celts one immediately thinks of the Druids, the secret society of priests and bards second only to the high kings of Ireland in power and importance. Who were the Druids? How did they get their power? And how do they fit in with Witta?

The Druids were the priestly class of old Ireland whose power flourished for over four hundred years from the second century B.C.E. to the second century C.E. Their increasing insistence on the dominance of males in religious life forged a link between the age of Witta and the coming of the completely patriarchal Christianity. They divided themselves into orders, called fil, based upon their particular talents in music, art, poetry, storytelling, and magick.

The Druids began to patriarchalize Witta by subtly altering some of the basic beliefs. Instead of a dead soul being reabsorbed into the Great Mother and entering Tir-na-nog, the Druids insisted that the discarnate soul moved almost immediately into the body of a newborn child without ever leaving the earth plane. They taught that mystical knowledge, particularly in healing arts, was a gift to be revealed to and manipulated by only a chosen few. Instead of interceding with nature on human behalf, the Druids looked increasingly to spirits for aid, and accordingly they developed rituals to compel their assistance. The

Druids held deity to be their personal possession and eventually created the popular belief that they were the ordained intercessories between the gods and goddesses and humankind.

Throughout Celtic lands their power, both personal and magickal, increased until they became indispensable to the high king at Tara and the kings of the four provinces. They were especially adept at divination, a necessary art in those years of uneasy rule, regional wars, and the constant threat of invasion.

One of their least complicated divination methods was to take twigs from the thirteen sacred trees and toss them into a small circle. Where these twigs fell in relation to the others provided insight into the questions asked by the diviner. Each tree was related to one of the moons of the year which were named by the Druids. These moon names gave each stick its own divinatory meaning.

- ❧ Alder: self-reliance, friends and family, betrayal
- ❧ Ash: female mysteries, women
- ❧ Birch: beginnings, firsts, unlimited potential, renewal
- ❧ Elder: completeness, fulfillment, union
- ❧ Hawthorn: blockages, negative influences, stagnation, sorrow
- ❧ Hazel: the unknowable, the unrevealed, secrets, death
- ❧ Holly: polarity, security, trust
- ❧ Ivy: overcoming difficulties, struggle, eventual success
- ❧ Oak: strength, men, war, fire, air, rulership, the sun
- ❧ Reed: the home, truths revealed
- ❧ Rowan: travels, water, earth, money, animals
- ❧ Vine: happiness, peace
- ❧ Willow: balances, the moon, night

Many of the Druidic divinations have been lost to history and some, such as reading the patterns of blood spatters from victims of ritual sacrifice, we do not want to repeat.

There are many stories of Druidic barbarism, some exaggerated and some very real. The reputation of Druids as headhunters is not a fabrication. Greek historians traveling through Celtic lands witnessed this practice firsthand and found it abhorrent. Presumably this derived from a need to prove one's prowess in war, a solidly patriarchal concept. However, it is more conceivable that in the beginning this custom originated from a practice of necromancy, that of using a human head as a mystic oracle. Ritual killing in Druidism was not done for the purpose of sacrificing a life to a deity to obtain favor, but for the purpose of divining the future. Usually the victim was a volunteer who would be accorded a hero's funeral for his martyrdom.

Another divination method used was that of contacting discarnate humans, such as powerful Druids who had died or slain war heroes and heroines. These contacts were initiated in a ritual circle with a specific place set aside outside of the protection of the circle for the entity to manifest and be contained. This practice was very similar to the one used today in high magick to summon angels and demons.

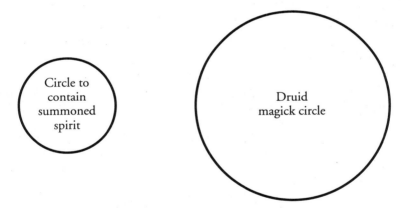

Though the practice of human sacrifice was not documented among the Irish Druids as it was elsewhere in the Celtic world, there is no doubt it took place in Ireland when Druidism became an all-powerful institution. The Book of Leinster alludes to a "bloody crescent," a stone believed to have been used as a dais for human sacrifice. In return for sacrifice the Druids asked not for crops, but for knowledge of the future; although one highly regarded ethnologist once claimed that milk and corn (any of several cereal plants, such as wheat, rye, oats, or barley) were the gifts asked for in exchange for sacrifice—the sacrifice of children no less. But since Druidism waned in the second century one can only conclude that this was a deliberate attempt at sensationalism rather than anything resembling scholarly enlightenment.

Needless to say, modern Druidic practitioners are as appalled by the thought of taking a life as are other pagans. Once again it is clear that human thought and reason evolved along with human religious practice. But the fact remained that the island nation of Ireland was always in danger of invasion, and many invasions succeeded, therefore divination was an important art among the Druids and much of their magick concerned sacrificial prophecies.

To their belts the Druids attached a pouch which contained their "totem," or source of their divine power—a black snake. Snakes, because of their annual shedding of skin, have always been sacred to the Goddess. Just as the snake shows a different face but is always the same being, the Goddess in her triple form does the same. To kill a snake, even accidentally, in old Ireland would have been to bring the worst of luck upon oneself.

Yet for all the alterations to the Old Religion of Ireland made by the Druids they still remained pagan, that is they were a nature religion. They further developed and codified the Celtic Tree calendar and ogham alphabet which was by legend a gift to them from the god Ogham, though in fact both predate them. They utilized the four elements in magick more than had ever been done before in Celtic lands, and used stone sculptures called dolmens in their circles as altars. Ruins of these dolmens can still be seen wherever Druidism flourished.

A dolmen
(Druidic altar)

The Druids were assisted by female Druidesses who often functioned as prophetesses. These women were sometimes called Dryads, their name given to them by the Irish tree spirits. However these priestesses were not accorded the honor, prestige, or privileges of the male Druids. For instance male Druids were exempt from military service and taxes and were generally supported by the community during their twenty year education period. The Dryads were largely taught by other women whenever leisure time could be found, and had only short training periods with male Druids during which time they had to be self-supporting.

Entered into the myth cycles was the story of a famous Druidess named Birog who enabled the warrior Cian to take revenge on the god Balor. Cian was taught how to shapeshift, an art traditionally attributed to the island's wise women and, disguised as a female, he had his revenge for the trickery and thievery of Balor.

Astrology in western Europe came into its own in the hands of the Druids, and the movement of the heavens was looked to for guidance in and understanding of human situations. From this the Druids developed an entire concept of the macrocosm which they held in greatest secret. This cosmogonic teaching literally died with their power and only small fragments of it remain. However, what can be gleaned from these splinters of information shows the cosmology to have much in common with the teachings of the Hebrew Kaballah in that it decreed spheres of existence for all beings which generally could not be entered into by other beings. It further placed the gods and goddesses on an outer plane where they were inaccessible to all but a few adepts. This was a dramatic deviation from the Wittan belief that gods and goddesses are always attainable because a great part of deity is within ourselves.

Because the Druids took possession of all learning they were respected by many, even the very learned and feared Julius Caesar. As they monopolized both the knowledge of the common people and the modern scientific discoveries of the age, they were able to manipulate everyday events and ordinary phenomena to appear as magickal manifestations which further impressed and awed the people and the kings.

Megaliths such as the famous Stonehenge indicate a highly advanced knowledge of astronomy and mathematics among the ancient Celts, and many sources have credited the Druids with their construction. However, it seems clear that organized structures such as Stonehenge predate the peak of Druidic power by several centuries. The most famous standing stone site in Ireland is at Newgrange, near the site of Tara in County Meath. It also predates the centuries of Druidic power, but is intimately linked with their practices, especially as it is so close to the seat of the high kings who greatly valued the Druids' work.

Modern astronomers have taken a close look at these megaliths and have found that they are designed to point out the rising and setting place of the sun on the dates of the solar equinoxes and solstices which correspond to four of the Irish sabbats—Yule (Winter Solstice), Ostara (Spring Equinox), Midsummer (Summer Solstice), and Mabon (Autumn Equinox). Further mathematical study has shown that several points of the stone can be used to chart the movements of the major planets.

The Druids gave their final service to the Celts by leading them against the Roman invaders. In this they were more successful in Ireland than in other Celtic areas. Ultimately the Druids were stripped of their power by the Gallic uprising, and then by the coming of the Christian missionaries.

Druidism broke away from traditional Witta in so many ways that today Druidism has been revived as a valid tradition of paganism separate from Witta. Their ancient secrets are being rediscovered and revealed by interested pagans the world over. Isaac Bonowitz, who heads the Reformed Druid movement, has written many books on the subject of Druids past and present.

TARA

Tara, a hill in County Meath, was the seat of the Ard-Ri, the high king of Ireland, for many centuries. Modern archaeologists claim that there is no evidence that there was ever more than an ancient castle on the Tara site, but Irish mythology and the writings of the early monks tell a different story.

Tara was a vast fortress where the power of Ireland sat from approximately 400 B.C.E. until the fourth century when its function as a central authority was brought down by papal power. It had its own grazing land, arsenal, oak grove, living quarters, court, and worship sites. By Tara's high king, Ireland was divided into four quarters or provinces just like a magick circle is marked off into quarters. These ancient quarter names remain as regional designations in Ireland even today. To the north was Ulaid or Ulster (which is now British owned Northern Ireland), to the east was Laigin or Leinster, to the south was Mumhain or Munster, and to the west lay Connachta or Connacht. At the center lay Meath. Meath is derived from the old Irish word midhe (pronounced mee) meaning "center." Like a magick circle these places represented the four elements plus the element of spirit.

Recent research into early Irish life has led scholars to believe that the high kings wielded much more centralized power than was once supposed. Studies of later myths, which preserve the rationale of the "divine king," underscore the true meaning of royal divinity which is all but lost to the modern world. The high king acts as an earthly consort to the Goddess, and was a partner in a sacred marriage whose union was thought to ensure that the people and the land of Ireland would be fruitful. Such a concept also makes sense in terms of the old Celtic and Brythonic practice of regicide, or king-killing. A king, since he represented the God, had to periodically die, as did the God during the solar year. In keeping with the ancient belief of "blood" sacrifice, a king was killed in years which were a multiple of seven, a number thought to represent the God and manifest power. His blood had to be spilled directly onto the land in a gesture of fertilization. Later, the spilling of blood became symbolic, occasionally taking the form of spilled wine.

Most everyone knows through folk stories or research that the traditional number for a coven is thirteen. The high king took on twelve advisors, usually Druids, to form a High Court of Ireland—a coven of thirteen. Laws and judgments handed down by this court were final.

The new hierarchy of the island allowed that each province be governed by another king known as the Ri-ruirech, or occasionally by a queen, directly subordinate to the high king at Tara. Each clan, which now had moved from being matrifocal to patrifocal, was headed by the most powerful warrior among them, and he was directly responsible to the king's judges. These judges, called brehons, dispensed justice and resolved disputes within each province in keeping with the laws of the high court at Tara.

It is interesting to note that in much of the later folklore the kings and queens of the provinces acted much in accord with the old gods and elements which traditionally govern the four directions. Queen Madb, a warrioress queen who embodied the destructive power of the crone, was from Connacht in the west—the Land of the Dead. And Cormac, who challenged the high king's power, hailed from Ulster in the north from where also came many of the faery race invaders.

It is recorded that at Tara was a great banquet hall which could hold thousands of people quite easily at its great tables. The high kings hosted lavish dinners for warriors and warrioresses sworn to protect their island, and gathered the Druids and witches of Ireland at Tara for celebration of the eight sabbats. It was law that no Bealtaine bonfire in all of Ireland could be lit until the high king had lit his. From high on Tara Hill the sign would be seen and on hills around the island bonfires would light up the night skies.

One reason that Tara was chosen for the seat of the high kings, aside from the obvious height advantage it afforded, was that much of the mythology took place at this central location. The god Lugh purportedly took up residence here, and it was from here that he handed down his judgment of murder upon the sons of Tureen. Here it was said that Midhir the Proud, king of the Tuatha De Danann and a son of the god Dagda, appeared to the warrior King Eochy. Here is said to be buried the head and right hand of the mythical warrior Cuchulain. And here was where judges presided over divinations done to choose new rulers of the clans.

Each high king's antics, wars, follies, and judgments created new chapters in Irish mythology. Many of these tales were based in fact. But the high kings weren't nearly as well-ensconced in their control of the island as they would like to have believed. They did have all respect and sovereign power, and their laws were never challenged, but they could not always control the actions of people in the far reaches of their kingdom. As a result, many regional wars plagued Ireland until the ninth century. At that time patriarchalization had been long completed and King Brian Boru was on the throne. Brian usurped the rulership of the corrupt O'Neill dynasty and finally was able to unite the Irish people under one banner ending the centuries of conflict which began with the Druids' and the monks' attempts at stratifying an otherwise egalitarian society.

Tara held out as a center of pagan worship and study even after its political power was dismantled in the fourth century, though the site was not formally abandoned until 1022.

SAINT PATRICK

The arrival in Antrim of a young Caledonian slave named Succat would hardly seem worthy of historical note. But that slave boy became Saint Patrick, patron saint of Ireland, and the person who single-handedly opened the island to mass Christianization. He began by converting his fellow slaves who later aided his escape to England. In an angelic vision he saw the people of Ireland calling out to him, and he was told to go to back to them and be their spiritual guide.

Christian missionaries were not unknown in Ireland before Patrick, but most had had little success. Patrick knew that to gain any credibility with the Irish people he must first convert the high king, Lagohaire. Though he never managed that feat, he did get together enough of an army to gain access to Tara on Easter Sunday of 453 C.E.

Much of the legends which have grown up around him are apocryphal at best and clearly show the systematic attempt at purging power of the Goddess from the Irish mind. It is said that during a period of famine he made a herd of pigs appear. Pigs were sacred to the Goddess and only consumed on ritual occasions. And it is no accident that one of the most persistent legends about Saint Patrick is that he "drove the snakes out of Ireland." This is a metaphor for the destruction of the power of the Druids who used a small black snake as their power familiars. He is also credited with making the trefoil figure of the shamrock the symbol of Ireland by likening it to the Christian Holy Trinity. In truth the shamrock was already a sacred plant to the Irish because of its association with the Triple Goddess.

Patrick worked furiously building monasteries over the sacred sites of the Wittans. Sacred wells and standing stones were enclosed in churchyards, and shrines to the Irish deities were dismantled or Christianized. He instituted the office of "bishop" and dispersed one to each clan willing or not. Yet for all this feverish effort one of Patrick's greatest contributions to Witta was the preservation of some of the earliest known pagan legends. In an effort to preserve the native culture and history, Patrick had Brogan, his chief scribe, record some of the oral tradition of the island. His reasons for this remain unclear, for later he burned many of the known original Celtic works of literature and religion.

Patrick and those who would follow him were aware of the Druidic veneration for trees, and of the high regard in which plant life was held by the Irish people in general. Yet it was not the mistaken notion that these people worshiped trees which became an issue with these missionaries, but the idea they worshiped stones. No doubt this impression was created by the stone megaliths and dolmens erected from antiquity throughout the British Isles. Neither the Wittans nor the Druids worshiped stones, though many papal and saintly denunciations for the practice abounded.

Patrick began undermining Druidic power by convincing his new converts that the Druids got their power directly from Satan. Because of the black snakes possessed by them, and because snakes were associated with the Christian Devil, this leap was an easy one to make, and it was a rationale which would later be used to decimate the native Latin Americans who in fact worshiped a serpent deity.

The Christian influence on Ireland was temporarily shattered by wars with the invading Scandinavians who were somewhat sympathetic to the Irish pagan cause. The Church took an "ignore them and they'll go away" attitude and never lifted a finger against the invaders. The Vikings were not dispatched until 1014 when King Brian Boru routed them at the Battle of Clontarf.

In keeping with Celtic custom, the failure of the Church to protect the island caused Christianity to lose some of its followers who could not trust leaders who were not proven warriors.

The Church decided it could no longer tolerate Irish women's separate worshiping of their Goddess, so in 1155 King Henry II obtained a papal bull authorizing his possession of the island. The Old Religion now began to be dismantled by force.

❧ 2 ❧

RELIGIOUS BELIEFS AND MAGICKAL PRACTICES

Belief in magick as part of religious practice was an accepted part of everyday Celtic Irish life. Magick was not thought of as an operation of supernatural forces, indeed logically nothing supernatural can exist and these people knew it. Magick was, and still should be, as natural as breathing. Whether one believes the universe was created by a sentient deity, or that it exploded into existence of its own accord, the facts are that certain natural laws operate from which no deviation can occur. Therefore every force and energy—including the energy of magick—must operate within those laws and it is perfectly "natural."

Practitioners of the craft view magick as the manipulation of forces and energies not yet understood by science. For example, an internal combustion engine would have been an awesome manifestation of magick several hundred years ago, but for those who understand the scientific principles on which it runs, it is not "magickal" at all.

Witta, like its sister pagan religions, has few hard and fast rules. But there are two laws which it acknowledges. The first is commonly called the Wiccan or Wittan Rede: *As ye harm none, do what ye will.* Memorize this rede and call it to mind each time you begin a power ritual or magickal working. This law prohibits a witch from doing anything that might harm any other living being, and most significantly prohibits us from violating any living being's free will. This law also applies to the self. You have an obligation to keep yourself from harm.

If one chooses to do anything magickally which might cause harm, one should remember the second law known as the Threefold Law. Witches believe that any energy sent out, either good or bad, will be revisited on the sender three times over. This is a good karmic law to keep in mind if you doubt that your spells are entirely harm free.

Some witches will add a line to their incantations such as "as it harms none," or "as all will it freely," or something similar to insure that they are not violating the rede. Love magick is especially vulnerable to this law. Many witches wish to work a love charm to draw a specific person to them. Nothing could be more against the Wittan Rede, or more dangerous. If you want to draw love into your life, make a charm or construct a ritual which draws "the right person for me now," or "the person who seeks me as I seek him/her." Don't ever risk manipulating another person through magick, the consequences are too great.

Old Wittan religious and magickal practices were noted for stark simplicity. Reverence for the deities was the primary concern, and intercession and magick on human behalf came secondary. Standing under a night sky and raising one's arms heavenward was all that was needed, and spells and worship were done extemporaneously with the words and the energy coming directly from the heart.

THE ELEMENTS

Earth, air, fire, and water have long been regarded by pagans as the basic building blocks with which all things are created. Each element is associated with a direction and these are fairly consistent throughout Western paganism. In Witta, earth is associated with the north, air with the east, fire with the south, and water with the west.

Furthermore, each element had certain magickal associations with which they had an affinity. For instance it gives your magick an extra boost to work love magick with water because water shares an affinity for love. However, this would not have stopped a Wittan from using fire magick if that was what was readily available.

Each direction also had an association with one of the four seasons, therefore so did its element. In Witta, west and water are winter, north and earth are autumn, east and air are spring, and south and fire are summer. In Wicca, winter—the time of death and renewal—is associated with the north. Witta uses the west for this association because Tir-na-nog, the land of the dead, is said to be in the west. In winter Tir-na-nog is believed to be at its closest to the land of the living.

Some traditions also talk of various objects as being "ruled" by a particular element. In Witta we talk of items being "associated" with, or as having an "affinity" with an element. A stone has an affinity with earth, it is not ruled by it.

Below is a list of some of the magick long thought to be associated with each element. You may use this as a guide to begin spell crafting, but once again, your own gut instincts are your best guide as to what practice corresponds to which element.

❧ Earth: fertility, pregnancy, prosperity, grounding, stabilizing, money, planting and growth, home, herds and pets, strength, cattle, burying of objects, burrowing animals, stones, tubers, non-hibernating animals, image magick, drumming. (Note: Though all plants are somewhat associated with earth, for magickal purposes each has its own association with an individual element.)

❧ Fire: transformation, protection, cleansing, exorcism, purification, petitions to deities, burning, honoring a spirit, scrying, guidance, divination, banishing, lizards and other reptiles, the God, candle magick.

❧ Water: spells relating to children or childbirth, transformation, purification, cauldron, healing, manifesting, gaining psychic intuition, fish, death and rebirth, regression work, dream work, new beginnings, the Goddess.

❧ Air: increase in intellect, writing, study, birds, astral travel, banishing, communication, spells relating to the elderly, flying insects, astral projection, wind instruments, power raising, cord magick.

❧ A fifth element is spirit, usually called by its Vedic Indian name "Akasha." Spirit is in and of all the elements, and it transcends them. In Native American traditions spirit is honored in the direction of "above." Wittans knew of and honored spirit, not so much as a fifth element, but as the unifying force which animates all the other elements.

MAGICKAL TOOLS

The traditional tools of Western pagan religions were influenced largely by ceremonial magick, a highly codified ritualistic practice based on the structure of Jewish and Gnostic Christian mystic texts known as the Kaballah. Ceremonial magicians used lavish ritual adornments of the body, and had a distinct set of ritual tools (called "weapons") to represent each of the four elements. Lavish colored robes, a written body of secret knowledge, and specific head gear and jewelry were standard paraphernalia of ceremonial magick. Pagans, who have always valued a more simplistic and gentle approach to magick, have rejected much of this pomp and circumstance. However, the idea of specific ritual tools took hold and has become a standard part of both Wicca and Witta.

The melding of ideas between these divergent paths occurred in the late fifteenth century when Spain initiated its sacrilegious Inquisition aimed at ferreting out non-Christians and "Devil worshiping witches." After 1492 many of Spain's pagans, Jews, Moors, Gnostics, and other non-traditional believers fled the Iberian Peninsula under fear of death. A great many of them found their way to the west of Ireland, the end of the known world in 1492, where the laws against them were not so harsh and were often lazily enforced. Many Kaballists and pagans alike believe a great body of knowledge was shared between these two refugee groups. One tradition of Wicca, the Alexandrian (named for founder Alexander Saunders), combines practices from both paths.

Galway, a city of about 30,000 people in the west of Ireland, has one of the most cosmopolitan populations in the world. This is a direct result of the Spanish refugees who came there and stayed. Many believe that western Ireland saw the birth of the modern forms of Western paganism, and in this atmosphere of relative tolerance, Irish witches shared information with others and adopted ceremonial concepts into their own rituals.

Witta did not overly concern itself with the appeasing and representing of the elements. Wittans knew the elements were there, and were acutely aware of their symbology. They used these tools when they could, or when they chose to, but did not find them prerequisite for magickal or ritual working. Modern Witta has adopted some of these ceremonial tools, and it is perfectly fine to use them if they feel comfortable to you. I use some of them myself. But if one wants to harken back to the very old Wittan ways, simplicity is the key.

Modern witchcraft generally uses four tools to represent the four elements: a knife, sword, or wand for air or fire; a cup for water; salt, stone, soil, or a wooden pentacle for earth; and a cauldron for either water or spirit.

Different traditions also might add to this list a besom or broomstick and special wands for various workings.

From ceremonial magick Wicca took the idea of elaborate decorations and/or carving on the tools. This is unnecessary, but many Wittans also do this as a method of personalizing and placing their own vibrations firmly onto the tool. But the tools will absorb your vibrations best through contact with you and through use in your circle. Purists feel that the unadorned tools of nature are best when seeking to use natural forces on their behalf.

Old Witta has some variations on all these themes, and very old Witta even eliminates some of them altogether. Below is a list of correspondences used in Witta:

ELEMENT	COLOR	SEASON	DIRECTION	TOOL
Air	Yellow	Spring	East	Knife or Wand
Water	Blue	Winter	West	Cup or Cauldron
Earth	Green	Autumn	North	Salt or Stone
Fire	Red	Summer	South	Candle

All ritual tools should be cleansed and blessed before use. This is especially important if the history of the item is not known. Sit down with your tool and visualize it being filled with your own energies which are driving out all previous ones. See it filling with your own essence as the old energies are harmlessly absorbed into the ground.

After you have done this you should pass it through the smoke of a purifying incense. Smoke is an important part of Wittan practice. Try making an incense from lavender, jasmine, and rosemary. Any other combinations of herbs can be used but it is traditional to use multiples of three. So if you create your own purifying incense, use either three, six, or nine ingredients.

Pass your tool through the smoke and say something like this:

> *May this* (name tool) *be an instrument for my spiritual growth, an extension of my personal energies, used for only good in worship, in ritual, and in magick. May the Goddess and God bless my work with fruition and my life with their peace. In accordance with the free will of all ... So Mote It Be!*

Knife or Sword

The ritual black-handled knife known as an athame (ath-ah-may) and the sword of Scottish Wita were not used in Witta until introduced by ceremonial magick. Some women's covens shun them altogether as tools of slaughter created by the patriarchy, even though the athame is never used for cutting of any kind, but for directing energy. Most certainly these tools were not a part of old Wittan worship.

Stories of heroes and knights usually involved a powerful blade. The Arthurian legend of the great sword Excalibur makes much use of this imagery. Arthur becomes king only when he has removed a magick sword from its embedment in a large stone. This fertility image of masculine knife and feminine earth stone is enacted in Witta in the Great Rite (fully described in Chapter 7). This legend further makes clear the belief that kings had to get their authority from women.

Non-Wittan witches usually use the athame to direct power, particularly in the ritual of drawing down the moon (see Chapter 6).

In modern Witta the athame symbolizes the element air. If an air representation was used in old Witta at all, it was more likely to have been incense made from native herbs rather than a blade of any kind. And incense is still the most popular choice for an air representative in the modern Irish tradition.

Wand

The wand as a tool to store and direct magick has been around since the first human lifted a tree limb to use as a practical aid. In Wicca wands usually represent the element of fire and the direction south. In Witta they are used to represent the element of air and the direction of east. As projectors of energy, wands are often used to cast circles and direct energy. Often invocations to the God and Goddess are made with an uplifted wand.

In the Celtic Tree calendar thirteen wands are cut from special sacred trees to correspond to the thirteen lunar months of the year. The Druids used a different wand for each type of magickal working.

In keeping with the practical nature of Witta, it is likely that the first wands were the walking staves which were needed to traverse the rugged and rocky island. The walking staff popularly called a shillelagh (shah-lay-lee) is linked with Irish culture. The staff is named for Shillelagh Forest in County Wicklow. They were once made of solid oak, but the ones found today are beautifully crafted of varnished blackthorn. They can be found for sale all over Ireland, through Irish mail order houses, and in America at Irish import shops.

The shape of the wand or staff is a masculine symbol often linked with male fertility. Air is a masculine element (the other is fire).

Making your own wand is very simple. Cut an appropriate length from a chosen tree and strip it of all small limbs and leaves. Be sure to ask the tree's permission to take the branch and then leave a token of thanks at its base. The wand may be used in this rough stage or you can pick off the bark and use sandpaper to smooth the length of the wand, tapering slightly as you reach the tip. I find this tapered look helps me to remember that a wand is for helping to direct a witch's personal power. You can then carve personal symbols onto the wand with a knife or a woodburning tool, or you can use the ogham alphabet (discussed in Chapter 6) to write names or words of power. When you have formed the wand into the desired shape, it is a good idea to seal it with either a coat of polyurethane or a commercial wood stain available at hardware stores.

A staff is simply a longer, stronger wand and can be made in the same way. Consider staining a staff dark to resemble a traditional blackthorn shillelagh.

If you would rather not have a wand at all, you might use for your air element another symbol of Ireland—a pipe made of Irish clay.

Cup or Cauldron

The cup (or chalice) is the most strongly archetypal of all feminine images. A ritual receptacle of some type used to represent the womb of the Goddess was used in Witta as soon as the ancient Celts began their famous metallurgical works. In very old Witta this might have been the only ritual tool which was used. Cups of silver or colored glass now are used to represent the element of water and the west direction.

In the Arthurian myths, King Arthur expends much energy in his search for the Holy Grail. The grail is a goddess symbol, a small cauldron. The need to find the grail may have been a carry-over of an earlier belief that a king needed a queen to legitimize his rule. Note the multitude of ancient engravings where a king is depicted with his feet on the lap of a queen. It was this belief which drove King Arthur to search for Queen Guinevere after she left him. Camelot was in chaos not because she was a "bad girl" who left her man, but because without her Arthur had no claim to rulership. In Irish mythology this belief is reflected in the tale of King Eremon, whose succession could be passed on only through the female line of his family whose banner held a representation of a silver chalice.

In 1868 archaeologists discovered a chalice at Ardagh which dates to the seventh century. The Ardagh Chalice is a beautiful representation of Celtic-pagan metalcraft. The body of the large cup is cast of silver and bronze and is decorated with gold filigree. It is ornamented with blue and red glass studs and native crystals which are joined to form sun wheels or Brigid's cross patterns all around the chalice's rim and body indicating that it was probably dedicated to her worship.

Cauldrons date from the Iron Age and are intimately associated with the Goddess. It is believed that the first ones used in goddess worship were fashioned in India as early as 7000 B.C.E., and were brought across the continent to Ireland many centuries later. Their symbolism is twofold: abundance and rebirth. The cauldron's depths represent the womb of the Great Mother and within it all life is said to begin, end, and be born again. So strong is the old Irish belief in Tir-na-nog with its cauldron guarding crone, that a cauldron has probably been used more actively in Witta than in any other pagan tradition.

The negative patriarchal view of cauldrons dates from the Middle Ages when the Roman Church stamped out the last visible vestiges of the Old Religion in the British Isles claiming that in their profane rituals hags boiled the blood of Christian children in cauldrons.

Unlike athames, herbs, or colored candles, the cauldron was a necessity to daily living and could not be removed easily from people or, apparently, from their primal memories.

The ancient Irish believed that human folly, not the whim of the deities, would cause the crone of the cauldron to turn the world into a wasteland. Badb, the Goddess of Fate whose name means "one who boils," would churn the cauldron of destruction when all virtue was gone among humans. These end-of-the-world prophecies share startling parallels with the effects of a nuclear holocaust, and are rooted in the Indian myths which surrounded the crone goddess Kali. Many scholars believe all the folktales of Europe spread from the Indian myths when prehistoric people migrated from the Indian subcontinent.

In Irish mythology it is believed that when all human virtue is gone the cauldron will boil over causing the world to explode in fire. Then the wasteland of nothingness will visit the earth beginning with a three-year winter.

Cauldrons of all sizes can be found by searching out antique shops or smithing forges. Around Halloween plastic ones can be found in drugstores. A traditional cauldron has three legs—representative of the Triple Goddess. While three-legged cauldrons are traditional, four-legged ones are probably easier to find and have just as much symbolism. The four legs represent the four elements, the pillar on which the magick can manifest. Four legs also create a sturdier base which may be necessary for the larger, heavier cauldrons.

Another cauldron symbol is the horn. The horn, a phallic symbol, is associated with the Great Horned God and other male fertility deities. When filled with water or wine the horn becomes whole and complete—a symbol of the union of male and female in which creation can take place. Many people interested in Celtic rituals use hollow horns as chalices.

Salt or Stone

Various objects have been used in paganism to represent the element of earth and the direction north, and this has been the one area where ceremonial magick has had the least influence on Witta. Ceremonial magick uses a pentacle, a circular wood or metal disc with a pentagram on one side, and a Solomon's seal (a six-pointed star) on the other. Modern Wittans opt for something simpler like a clay bowl of salt, a handful of fresh black earth, or a simple earth-embedded stone.

Salt is often used in combination with water to bless a newly cast ritual circle. Earth elements have a grounding effect, that is they neutralize or absorb, and are perceived as stable and sturdy. They are used for protection and strength, and to ground away excess energy after working a magick spell.

After any spell or ritual in which energy is raised the excess should always be grounded to prevent it from causing you to feel frazzled or from "haunting" you. The best way to do this is to place your hands palms down on the earth (a bowl of soil is sufficient) and feel the excess energy draining out of you.

Earth is one of the feminine elements (the other is water). Inside the womb of the earth grows new life, and the Goddess often is called Mother Earth. Plants and vegetables which grow underground are associated with fertility in Irish herb lore.

Candles

Candles are used in Witta to represent the element of fire and the direction of south. Wicca more commonly uses the wand, and the Gardnerian tradition uses a knife. Candles used to represent fire on a Wittan altar are usually red or orange, though white is perfectly acceptable. Votive candles in clear glass holders are easier and safer to work with than long tapers, especially if you are working outdoors.

Fire is the principal element of transformation, and fire magick is as old as humankind. Candles are used to scry, to light the circle, to represent deities or directions, and as a catalyst for magick.

Besom

The besom is the witches' broomstick, and though it is not a tool of Witta in the classic sense, it was often utilized in magickal practice. The besom is a basic phallic symbol and was used by female witches in fertility rites. Often women rode them over fields to encourage growth, and it is from this that the idea of the Halloween witch riding around on broomstick may have materialized.

The sweeping end was usually made of the broom herb, a feminine herb. Thus the broom was complete as a representation of male and female union. Using the besom to sweep away negativity from a circle or household area was common practice, one still observed by many Wittans. Specially constructed besoms were used by midwives to clean the homes of expectant mothers, and to sweep the threshold just before and after a woman gave birth to expel negative influence from the dwelling.

Like the cauldron the besom was a necessary everyday household object and could not be held up as a sign of witchcraft in the clerical courts. This fact elevated their prominence as magickal tools, often taking the place of wands. From this association they then quickly became objects of magickal protection. They were often placed near the hearth of the home to protect this perpetual opening. Many Wittans still believe a besom at the fireplace will prevent evil from entering.

Other Wittans have placed inverted besoms against their locked doors at night to prevent burglars from entering. Others lay it lengthwise behind a door. Undoubtedly anyone entering would trip on it and therefore be scared away. Other locations where besoms were placed for protection were under a bed or next to a baby's cradle.

Placing the broom you jumped at your handfasting (pagan marriage) under your bed is not only protective, but is said to perk up waning sexual appetites. For those who wish to be married, a strong act of sympathetic magick is to jump a broom each morning upon arising and each night before going to bed from the new to the full moon.

Ashes from a fireplace which are to be used in a spell or charm should be swept up by a magick besom and not an everyday cleaning broom which might negate the beneficial energies of the ashes.

Two crossed brooms will prevent negativity from entering your home, especially if they are crossed in front of a fireplace. And if negativity is really a problem just take your besom and imagine yourself sweeping it out the door.

Pentagram

The pentagram is the five-pointed star which is a universal symbol of Western paganism. It is used as a protective amulet, and was one of the earliest renderings used to represent deity. The pentagram as a pagan symbol is always shown with its apex pointing up. Together the five points represent the four elements which are tied together, or controlled by, the element of spirit on the top.

There are some who would have people believe that the pentagram is a symbol of evil because Satanists have adopted and perverted this sacred symbol for use in their own rituals. The inverted pentagram represents matter over spirit. The fact that they invert this for their own purposes does not make the pagan pentagram a "Devil symbol"—just a misappropriated one.

Like other Western pagans Wittans use the pentagram both in magick and as a personal symbol of their faith. Encircled pentagrams are worn on necklaces or drawn on altars. They are painted on sacred sites and carved onto ritual tools, but not carved on trees, as to do so would harm a living plant.

In magick the symbol of the pentagram is used to invoke or banish. By "drawing" the pentagram before you with a finger or ritual tool you can utilize the imagery of spirit and matter to aid a spell. Basically if you want to gain or invoke something, bring something out of the unseen world into manifestation, you draw your pentagram beginning with the top. Likewise, if you wish to banish or decrease something, eliminate it from the world of matter, you begin drawing at the bottom.

Some traditions have a complex set of pentagrams to be drawn beginning from various points depending on the elemental "ruler" of your magickal goal. No doubt they work well for those traditions, but this is not a part of Witta. These two pentagrams are all you need for any magickal operation.

(start here)

The Banishing Pentagram

(start here)

The Invoking Pentagram

Book of Shadows

A Book of Shadows, an idea which dates only from the late Middle Ages, is a black bound collection of the way one individual witch or coven works. In it are texts of rituals, spells, and recipes. Traditionally these books were written in a secret alphabet in case they fell into the hands of witch hunters. These books were often necessary to preserve witch lore from being lost to the next generation during the persecutions. Now many such books have been published, old and new, and are for sale in some of the most mainstream bookstores.

All new witches are encouraged to keep such a book for themselves to chart their growth in the Wittan religion and to record rituals and spells which have been particularly meaningful or successful. It should be thought of as a witches' diary, and as such, its privacy should be respected. The book doesn't have to be an expensive black bound one. Mine is in a loose leaf notebook. I prefer this method so I can change the format at will, or add and delete pages as needed.

The name of the book is thought to have two derivations. One is that the book had to be hidden in the shadows, just like witches themselves, to avoid detection by clerical witch hunters. Others say it indicates that spells and rituals which are not enacted are without form and therefore merely shadows.

The Book of Shadows is really a working guide rather than a magickal "tool." While it should be protected because it is of value to you, there are no ritual blessings for it. But you may create a blessing for it if you like by passing it through the smoke of a purifying incense and saying something like this:

> *May this Book of Shadows be more than a recording of my past work, but also a guide to my future by showing me where I have erred and what I have yet to learn. May it aid me in growing spiritually and magickally in accordance with all free will.*

Bells, Balls, and Ballyhoo

Sonorous bells, large crystal balls, white-handled knives, jewel-studded zodiac symbols, solid gold wands, statuettes, and other occult paraphernalia are being purchased everyday—to someone's great glee. All have been used in various magickal practices, but none are necessary, though there will always be someone around to insist that they are.

No matter which pagan tradition one chooses to work within, everyone brings into the craft items not traditionally used in that path, but which the user feels are necessary for personal workings. This is fine; it shows you are thinking for yourself. If you think you must own an amethyst encrusted gold wand, and you feel drawn to its energies, then you should use it. However, be warned that many witches enjoy riding the crest of the latest occult fad just as they are drawn to latest fashions and slang. Those people often find themselves surrounded by lots of useless objects which eventually end up at a garage sale.

Once again I will say what new witches often hate hearing. Find out all you can about magick and ritual and then decide for yourself what you wish to use. Those practiced in the craft will agree with me that this is the only sane approach. It is certainly saner than rushing out to throw away hundreds of dollars on items with which you may later find you feel no affinity.

If one wishes to emulate the old Wittan ways this paraphernalia will do nothing but clutter the home and the mind. Keep things simple and natural and the old ways will just happen for you, and you will no doubt feel it too.

Altar

An altar is a place where deity is honored, a resting place for the powers of the macrocosm to exist in the microcosm. It is a place to set out and arrange items of power, or items which honor the deities. It is a place where magick spells can be laid out, and where the power of the elements can reside.

Altars create an easy and accessible workplace. Anything can become an altar, even a special spot of ground. Use a flat stone, a table, a portable cloth, a box—whatever you need to place your working tools and spells upon inside your circle. It is traditional to orient your altar to one of the cardinal directions—which one is up to you. Then arrange your magickal tools, or any other items you have chosen to bring to your circle, on the altar each in their proper direction.

In very old Witta an altar might have been no more than a designated spot on a beautiful piece of ground where gifts such as flowers and food were left for the deities. Later small tables or flat stones were used as altars and were viewed as a more permanent fixture in a home or community. At each sabbat they were decorated with the bounty of the season just as they are today. Some Wittans leave a permanent altar in their homes year round, and others only bring one out for rituals.

An altar can be large and elaborate and can hold items such as Tarot cards, statuettes, or stone collections—whatever you feel ought to be there. On the other hand, an altar can be set very simply in keeping with the old Wittan ways. Those who choose this can merely set out a small offering to the God and Goddess—a bouquet of spring flowers or a newly picked red apple, for instance.

Circle

From ancient times this symbol of eternity and completeness has been utilized for protection and containment. In virtually all pagan traditions, as well as in ceremonial magick, the boundaries of a circle are used to protect the magician or witch and contain his or her power.

A circle is cast by directing energy which is commonly visualized as an intense blue-white light. Often the circle is physically outlined with stones, herbs, or candles. But it is the witch's own energy which creates it anew each time it is needed.

The first use of the circle is protection. Many entities, both human discarnates and others, are attracted by the energy of magick. A circle keeps them out during ritual. When the ritual is over and the energy is grounded, the uninvited entities disperse.

Some traditions create three separate and complete circles before they do a ritual. In the very old Irish tradition witches were to do their magick in the abred, the innermost of three circles. This was later conceptualized by the Druids who envisioned three veils of existence for all things much in the same way that the Hebrew Kaballah divides them. That is, existence was divided into three areas: an earth center which the first circle represented, an astral or ethereal center which humans could enter with practice, and a godhead where the unknowable force of the deities lived.

This later conception went against all the original Wittan tradition stood for by separating the deities from the people and placing them in a world which was to be entered by none but a chosen few. In Witta it is believed that the deities are accessible and knowable and a part of them lives within each of us.

The other use of a circle is for containment. A witch wants to arouse and store raised energy until it is ready to be sent to its goal. The "force field" of the circle holds it in until it is directed outward.

Some new witches often will not see the need for a circle of protection for simple spells and will try to fumble through a ritual without one. This is a serious mistake! As you improve in your visualization and energy-raising skills your higher vibrations will attract an increasing number of entities which will come to feed upon your energy. This draining of your power will diminish the efficacy of your spells at best, and could cause you psychic harm at worst. Also a circle will help you feel the energy you raise as it will remain close to you and not be scattered. Working with smaller circles at first will also aid you to feel when you have accomplished your task.

Until a ritual is finished and the energy has been grounded, a circle is not to be broken once cast, though some allow that cutting an opening in the energy field with an athame will allow one to pass safely in and out. Others are of the mind that no break in the circle is "safe." It is best not to go in and out of the circle unless absolutely necessary.

For reasons unknown, animals and small children can move freely in and out of a circle without ever disturbing the energy or risking harm to themselves and others. This may be attributed to the fact that children, like animals, have not learned to divide their thinking into the supposed real and unreal. Children naturally see psychic phenomena and are comfortable with it until society teaches them otherwise. Their minds see a magick circle as an everyday occurrence, part of the natural order of the world, and they can therefore move freely through it without disturbing its energies.

To cast your own circle select a tool to help you, or choose instead to use the forefinger of your dominant hand (the one you write with). Stand quietly for a moment in what will be the center of your circle, making sure first that all the things you will need for your ritual or spell are present. When you are ready raise your arms skyward and feel yourself filling with energy. Walk to the edge of your circle and point your finger or tool at the ground. It can touch the ground if you wish, but it is not necessary.

It is traditional in Wicca to start this process at the north, but in Witta it is traditional to begin in the west. As the west is the home of the crone and her cauldron where all life begins, ends, and begins again, it is an appropriate place to create this sacred space.

Visualize energy coming from the end of your finger or magickal tool and creating a wall of intense blue-white light. For people psychically sensitive enough to actually see the subtle body of a magick circle this is the color they report it to be. Continue around clockwise until you are back at your starting point. Visualize the energy surrounding you and know that you are protected.

This method of casting a circle is older than anyone knows and it and similar methods are still being used by pagans today. It may very well have been the exact same method used in ancient Ireland.

Color

The old Wittans knew the value of color in sympathetic magick—the magickal principle that like attracts like. For instance, if you were to create a spell for the growth of your houseplants you would wish to incorporate the color green because of its likeness to your intended goal which is the flourishing of green houseplants. As with the elements, color was less important than intent in Wittan magick. If color was readily available to add to a spell or ritual then it was added. If not, then it was not missed.

Color associations in magick are taken from nature and from the nature of the animals and other beings which inhabit the earth. Color can be added to a spell or ritual through stones, plants, colored water, paper, drawings, colored candles, colored robes, jewelry, or any other way your imagination devises. Colored cloth can be used to tie up special herbs, and colored candles can clearly make your magickal intent known to your subconscious.

Below is a discussion of some colors and their Wittan associations. Keep in mind that these may differ slightly from the associations used in other traditions.

Red is the color of fire and passion and is used to arouse sexuality or restore vigor to the lethargic. Red is the color of heat and is highly projective (it appears to come forth rather than recede), therefore it is often used to represent the God. But red can be overly stimulating to the nerves. Studies have shown that people who have been in red colored rooms often overestimate the time spent in them. Use red when trying to summon inner strength and courage, or when facing legal difficulties. Avoid decorating heavily with red unless your goal is argument and flaring tempers.

Orange is softer than red. It is a color of warmth to which humans are attracted, and it is also a mild stimulant. Therefore it can be used in spells to attract something into your life or to get a stagnant situation moving along. Sometimes it is used in place of red to represent the God. Orange also stimulates the appetite. Notice how many fast food restaurants use orange in their decorating schemes.

Yellow stimulates the conscious mind and increases intellect, concentration, and self-confidence. Several years ago some educators did studies on the effects of color on learning disabled students and found that when placed in a yellow room their concentration and learning capabilities improved markedly. Yellow is also the color of creativity.

Green is the color of Mother Earth and it has a calming, soothing effect. For two centuries actors have collected themselves and prepared to perform while sequestered in a "Green Room." Green is the color of prosperity, fertility, and growth. Money spells often utilize the color green. In Ireland green is the color worn by faery folk and was considered their private domain much as purple was the exclusive color of royalty, and it was once considered bad luck to wear green lest you offend the faery folk. If one wishes to contact faeries during magick, use green, but don't wear it.

Blue is another calming color as it reflects images of water and sky. Blue is used in healing spells and spells to induce sleep and inner peace. Studies have shown that people underestimate the time spent in blue rooms. Blue has been said to heal headaches and is occasionally used in dream magick.

Violet is used in healing. It is associated with coolness, mystery, and meditative states. Violet has the shortest vibration of the entire visible spectrum and therefore is perceived as a very tranquil color. Use violet when trying to stop a quarrel.

Pink, a blending of white and red, is used in love charms, and in spells for peace at home.

Silver is the color of the moon and moon magick. Silver metal has been used to fashion goddess jewelry for thousands of years. Any spells associated with the Goddess or the moon can be boosted by the use of silver. Its color is cool and receptive, use it in fertility spells or to enhance psychic powers. Silver is also the color of the subconscious, use it liberally during divinations.

Gold is the opposite of silver, it is hot and projective. Gold is the color of the sun and sun-oriented spells can benefit from the color gold. The ancient Celts fashioned gold into intricate designs and jewelry. Use gold in protection and money spells. Gold is the color of the conscious mind.

A good way to practice feeling your personal power is to visualize gold and silver swirling balls of energy in the palms of your hand. Hold your hands before you. In your projective hand, the one which is dominant, visualize a gold ball of personal energy swirling clockwise. In the other hand picture a silver ball of personal energy swirling counterclockwise. Make the power ebb and flow. You are in control. When you are done with this exercise ground the energy back into yourself.

White is the color of peace, protection, purification, and spirituality. When you can't decide on an appropriate color to use choose white and you cannot go wrong. In some traditions the Goddess is represented by a white candle.

Black is not a color of evil as popular superstition would have us believe. Black is the absence of all color and is therefore used to absorb negativity and aid in banishing spells, that is, spells to rid one's dwelling of a negative influence or presence. It can be used when you want a spell to keep your home neutral in a dispute, and can assist you in absorbing a serious illness (with a physician's aid, of course).

Ritual Dress

Ritual dress no doubt came into prominence with ceremonial magick. Long before patriarchy, many believe Wittans once went skyclad (naked). This was especially practical as Wittans were largely solitary in their practice, that is, they usually worked alone rather than within a coven. The idea of ritual nudity is to present yourself to the deities as pure and unadorned, as themselves incarnate. With patriarchal society came the sad and disturbing fetishizing of human bodies. Now most covens, and even some solitaries, choose instead to wear robes for their rituals.

The idea of having some special type of clothing for these special times is also a very old one. Stepping into clothing used only for magickal and ritual purposes sends a signal to your deep mind that you are about to shift consciousness from the mundane world to the magickal world, also called the astral world or the spiritual world.

I work nude when alone, and in a black robe when with a group. Do what is most comfortable to you, making sure not to make anyone else uncomfortable in the process. And regardless of what you decide to wear please try to go barefoot. This contact with Mother Earth—even if your earth is just your apartment floor—is almost essential for Wittan ritual worship.

Music and Dance

Music and dance have had honored roles in pagan practice since humankind recognized deity.

Whether soothing or invigorating, music can bring about an immediate shift in consciousness. It can evoke strong emotion and powerful sentiment. It is no accident that for centuries men have marched off to war with the stirring strains of valiant marches ringing in their ears. Though Plato wrote about the effects of music many centuries ago, modern psychology is just now starting to explore the full range of consequence it has on the human psyche.

The harp is probably the most potent and ancient symbol of Ireland. Its likeness adorns Irish coins and coats of arms, and it was placed against a field of green on the country's old flag. Much Irish energy has gone into the study of and composition of pieces for the harp. The harp was believed to have been invented in Sumer around 3000 B.C.E., and was thought to have been brought into Ireland with the first Celts. In Irish mythology the great golden harp of Ireland was owned by the god Dagda who could bring forth music from it at will, or bid the faery folk to play. The harp was fought over continuously in the myths, and was finally captured by the high king at Tara, and hung on the wall in the great hall. Sir Thomas Moore commemorates this in his famous poem *The Harp That Once Through Tara's Halls.*

So beloved was the harp in Ireland that its popularity saw no decline until the middle nineteenth century. Today it is enjoying a revival both in Ireland and in the United States.

Two other instruments deeply associated with Irish culture are more readily available than the harp, and much easier to learn to use. One is the bodhran (baow-rahn), a goat skin drum which is still used in Celtic music and is of ancient origin. The other is the more contemporary pennywhistle. Pennywhistles are tin, cylindrical flutes first manufactured in England in the late eighteenth century, though their wooden forebears are ancient. They were, and still are, very inexpensive. They sound like fifes and have been hugely popular in Ireland, especially since they became produced in tin form. The Chieftains, one of the world's most well-known Irish bands, use the pennywhistle in many of their numbers. It makes a lonely sound when playing airs, and is at its showiest performing quick reels and jigs. It is quite easy to learn to play even for someone with little or no musical background.

The fiddle is another more contemporary instrument heard in Celtic music, but learning to play it takes years of practice. A fiddle is a nickname for a violin. They never were two separate instruments. The nickname came about because people who played folk music instead of "classics" were said to be "fiddling" with the instruments.

However, anyone who has ever listened carefully to the intricacies of Celtic fiddle music knows that the player is doing much more than "fiddling" around.

The bagpipe, usually associated with the music of the Highland Scots, is another instrument often heard in Ireland. The instrument was indigenous to northern Africa and was probably not brought to the Celts until around the twelfth century. A variation of bagpipes, called the Uilleann (ell-ee-un) pipes, is used more often in the Irish music which is heard now than is the Highland bagpipe. Once again this is an instrument that takes a lot of study, and a lot of wind power. Purchasing bagpipes can be quite a hefty investment. Be aware that teachers of both the bagpipes and Uilleann pipes require that a potential student first master the inexpensive pennywhistle.

The Roche Collection of Irish Music, Volumes I, II, and III is a comprehensive collection of 566 Irish melodies complied by musicologist Frank Roche during the first three decades of this century. This collection is easy to read and most of the tunes can be played with some proficiency by even a novice musician.

If you're not musically inclined, try using recordings of Irish music to help you raise power, shift your consciousness in a circle, or just to relax and put you in an Irish kind of mood. Appendix III gives sources for obtaining recordings of traditional Irish music.

Dance is visually expressive. It can enact an event or display a desire. It can mimic a need or represent an idea. Dance stirs the blood and heart, and has been used in circles for millennia to help raise power. Cultures all over the world have a body of folk dances which often stem from their earlier religious practices.

I encourage all Wittans to become involved with ceilidh dancing. These Irish folk dances are easy to learn, and are the forerunners of the American square dances. In the movements of the folk dances of Ireland one can often see remnants of a time when they were used as sympathetic magick to attract a magickal solution to a need. Fertility of crops, animals, and humans was the primary goal of these dances. The Irish version of the morris dance, the name for the Bealtaine maypole dances in England, retains virtually all of its fertility symbolism.

In the Irish morris reel four couples stand facing each other in what American square dancing calls a "squared set." Here we have a couple for each season, and eight people, one for each sabbat of the year. The couples dance in a circle with their partners to represent the God and Goddess moving throughout the year. The female dancers unite their hands in the center to form a sun wheel and circle around, picking up their partners when they pass them again. Then the males do the same thing. The couples now take turns passing under the upraised arms of other couples, an obvious mimicry of the Great Rite, a fertility ritual celebrated at Wittan spring sabbats.

If you are a solitary and wish to use Irish dance steps in your rituals try a simple jig-step to help raise power. Place one foot in front of the other and do a step-kick raising the foreleg, still slightly bent at the knee, straight out in front of you. (Those who are familiar with country-western dances will know this step-kick movement from the Texas cotton-eyed joe line-dance.) Bring the foot back quickly to its starting position and, on your toes, shift your weight from foot to foot four times. Repeat with the other foot.

Groups have more leeway to improvise. Though the usual number in a dance set is eight people, or four couples, many of the traditional dance sequences can be modified to include more or less.

Groups can try weaving in and out in what American square dancing calls the grand right and left. This is the basic step used to weave the ribbons of a Bealtaine maypole and involves every other person going in the opposite direction. The woman's position is on her partner's right. Have partners face each other and join right hands. Walk forward, passing each other, and extend your left hand to the new partner you are now facing. Repeat until you have returned to your own partner.

The dancers pass hand-over-hand, "pulling" themselves past each other until they are back facing their own partner.

Another basic Irish set dance step is called the sevens and is used for sliding back and forth. To slide to the right make a slight jump into the air and place your right foot, toes pointed down, in front of the left. Quickly move your right foot to the side and move your left foot behind it. This makes one count. Do this six more times in quick succession. To come back, wait four counts, moving your left foot in front of you for two counts, and then your right foot before you make your slight jump and reverse the process.

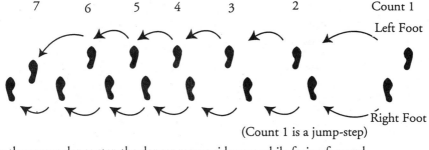

(Count 1 is a jump-step)

In the sevens dance step the dancer moves sideways while facing forward.

The sevens can have people going in different directions either individually or in couples. One rule of Irish dancing is that when you slide past someone, if you are moving to the right, you go behind anyone moving to the left, and if you are moving to the left, you go in front of anyone moving to the right. The simple idiomatic phrase "I'll be right back" can help you remember this.

Couples or individuals may also pass under each other's raised arms when doing dances linked with fertility. These are common movements in the old morris dances which celebrate Bealtaine.

Another formation mimics a sun wheel or Brigid's Cross, both equilateral crosses. This movement uses either four or eight people, or if your group is larger you can take turns. For a usual dance set of eight have the women come into the center and join right hands. Move clockwise until you have made a complete circle, turn, join left hands, and go the other way picking up your partner as you go by. Then have the men go to the center and do the same thing.

Sun wheel formation with women in the center, right hands joined, moving clockwise.

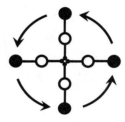

Sun wheel formation with women reversing their circle and moving counterclockwise. Left hands are joined in the center and their male partners are picked up by the hand when they are passed, and all eight people (a goddess and god for each seasonal sabbat) continue around the circle.

SHIFTS IN CONSCIOUSNESS

Acquiring an altered state of consciousness has taken on an aura of mystery in our modern world, yet we all do it everyday. You change your focus of consciousness every night when you go to sleep. If you were attached to an EEG (brain scanner) machine as you read this page, the cycles per second readout would show that you are in an alpha state, a light hypnotic trance just below the level of normal wakefulness. Likewise, watching television induces an altered state of consciousness.

Pagans know that being able to tap into unseen worlds and places is essential to living the magickal life, of being one with nature and your deities. To do so is not a mysterious trip into unknown realms which can only be attained by some great adept. Anyone who would tell you otherwise does not know what he or she is talking about.

Not all shifts in consciousness require a formal meditative procedure. When you concentrate your efforts and energy on a spell you have shifted your consciousness. When you prepare for a ritual your deep mind, often conditioned by your preparations, will automatically slip down into a slower cycle per second state. At that relaxed level your subconscious is more in tune with your conscious mind and the two are able to act in accord to help you focus on your magickal goal. With practice in meditation and sustained concentration your altered states can become longer and deeper, and at these deeper states (the theta and delta levels) you can do more advanced work such as astral projection and regression work. These are events which happen nightly as you sleep and are very natural. The only difference here is that you are seeking to gain some conscious control of them. The key is learning to concentrate for increasing periods of time on one thing.

Astral projection has been defined as the art of sending one's consciousness at will to a location away from the physical body. Some people believe you have a subtle, or astral, body which actually leaves your physical being during this practice. I am of the school of thought that believes *you* go nowhere. It is your deep mind which projects its consciousness into other places or realms very much as it does when you are dreaming. In fact, "lucid dreaming" is one of the best terms for astral projection that I know. But don't be confused by the word "dream." Projections are very real. Don't think that because they take place only in your mind that they are not. After all, it is within your mind where magick takes place.

Not everyone is as adept at consciously controlled astral projection as they would like to be. It takes much effort, more than most people are willing to give. But with lots of practice, and a little luck, you can "go" anywhere astrally and witness virtually anything, even transcending time and space.

The Druids were said to be skilled in the art of "becoming invisible." Their method included a dead raven, a crossroads, and baneful herbs. Many now believe that being "invisible" was a metaphor for astral projection where one can go about seeing but not being seen.

In rural Ireland astral projection is commonly called being "oot and aboot," and seems to be accepted there more easily as a natural occurrence than in the rest of the West. The inert physical body tends to get cold during projection as it does in sleep so the old Wittans used to practice this art while lying near their hearth fires. That and the sensation of flying one has when projecting is partially responsible for the idea that witches fly about on broomsticks (besoms were usually kept by the hearth too).

Wittans once used dangerous herbal concoctions to induce projection states. Today "flying ointments" are still made by Wittans to facilitate this state, but without the baneful ingredients. One witch I know burns jasmine incense to promote astral travel. If you wish to use an ointment try some of the following combinations:

Mugwort
Lavender
Jasmine oil

Dittany of Crete
$1/2$ cup boiled lettuce juice (allow to boil for 30 minutes)
Lavender oil

Sage
Mugwort
Lilac oil

Poplar bark and $1/2$ of the water it was boiled in
Mugwort
Jasmine oil

Mix the herbs or oils in a base of one cup of petroleum jelly, lard, or vegetable shortening. Or if you want a less messy ointment try mixing these herbs and oils into a half-cup of unscented body lotion. You must then find a warm place to relax, such as near a fire, since using the ointment requires complete nudity. Smear the ointment over your entire body and then make a pallet where you won't create a stain while you are astral projecting. A large beach towel will do. You can avoid smearing your hair if you anoint it sparingly with one of the flying oils such as lilac, lavender, or jasmine.

For those interested in other flying formulas, including the baneful ones, I refer you to Scott Cunningham's *The Complete Book of Incense, Oils & Brews* (Llewellyn Publications).

Another practice of the Wittans was regression, or the trance viewing of oneself in a previous incarnation. While some people make involved karmic cases (i.e., you get back what you give to others) for viewing past lives to solve present problems, Wittans didn't view karma in that way. The Wittans understood time to be what physicists have just recently proven—all time is now. Linear time is a delusion of the human mind. Since all time is now all your incarnations are happening simultaneously and karma is merely a metaphor for the influence for good or bad which one aspect of yourself has upon another. Wittans also acknowledge the oneness of spirit which connects all living things. We are all birthed from the Great Mother and we will all return to her, therefore to the Wittan mind all souls were merely aspects of her. Therefore, on some level all lives, past and future, are perceived as a common experience. So when a Wittan went into a trance to view a past life, it was done from the standpoint of one human being helping another. Rather than experiencing something which was thought to be personally theirs, they believed themselves to be viewing another human who was already learning a lesson or solving a same problem they were facing, their only connection to each other being the oneness of all spirits. They used these shared experiences to help themselves grow spiritually and to avoid future problems.

Oils or teas were often used to facilitate past life visions. One of the most popular was lilac oil placed on the temples, palms, third eye (just above and between the eyes), between the breasts, on the solar plexus, just below the navel, and on the soles of the feet. These roughly correspond to the chakra points, or centers of energy, used in Indian and Hindu rituals, and might have come to Ireland across the continent from India with the ancient Celts.

Try drinking any one of these herbal teas before attempting a regression. As always when ingesting anything new, test it first to make sure that you are not allergic. To make the teas place a half-teaspoon of each herb in a cup of boiled water and let it steep for about five minutes.

Valerian
Peppermint
Hyssop

Catnip
Mugwort
Ginger

Valerian
Orange peel
Mugwort

LIFE CYCLES

Wiccaning, coming of age, handfasting, and passing over rituals are events marking the life cycle of a Wittan. Formal recognition of milestones in one's life has been of central importance to human beings for many thousands of years. In graves over 40,000 years old the remains of flowers and tools have been found indicating that some sort of passing rituals existed even then.

Wiccaning

Wiccaning, or Wittaning in the Irish tradition, is the formal presentation of a new life to the deities. This can be done alone with your child, or in celebration with a coven. In a circle at a sabbat or esbat, present your child to the deities, stating your intention to raise him or her within the craft, and dedicate him or her to the Goddess and God. It is traditional to sprinkle the child with salt water as this is done. The child is given a craft name to be used until he or she has come of age.

Some covens have elaborate rituals to welcome a new life, and many have been published. This is a joyous occasion. Find the right words, the right night, and feast and celebrate. Lavish some extra attention on your baby. But always remember that this new life is an individual who will have to make his or her own choices in life, and that includes choices about a spiritual path. Acknowledge that your child might choose a different tradition when he or she is older just as you chose yours. As you present your baby to the old gods remember to not make any statements attempting to bind the child's free will.

Coming of Age

The coming of age celebration marks a child's passage into adulthood. As a boy turns thirteen or as a girl has her first menstrual period, he or she is considered old enough to be a spiritual adult capable of deciding if the Wittan path is the one he or she wants to tread upon through life. At this time he or she again is taken into circle and re-presented to the deities. This time it is the child, and not the parent or parents, who makes a formal dedication to the craft. On this night he or she is permitted to fully participate in the circle rituals with the other adults.

It is traditional for the parent or parents to present the newly adult Wittan with a wand or walking staff. This is his or her first ritual tool. He or she will have to obtain other tools according to his or her own needs and desires. But if others wish to give gifts, ritual jewelry is a fine idea, as is a book in which to record his or her own Book of Shadows. A set of untouched Tarot cards or divination stones is also a good gift.

It has been a long-standing pagan tradition to adopt a new name when one is initiated (either by self or others) into the craft. Adopting a new name at a coming of age rite (or an initiation) is an important step in Wittan spiritual growth; it reflects the outward adoption of a new way of life.

In Ireland the practice of taking on craft names began long ago. Often these were the names of the deities one felt a personal affinity with, or often petitioned or invoked. Some people adopt the new name as their legal name, and others keep it a close guarded secret to be used only in private or within a trusted coven. However you decide to use your new name you should choose one that you feel best represents yourself. This might be a place name, a common given name, a planetary name, or an ethnic name. Or it may be the name of a god, goddess, or entity whose characteristics you wish to add to your own.

Those involved in Witta usually choose names of Gaelic origin. Deity names are always appropriate, and so are place names. Shannon, a great river in Ireland, has always been a favorite name of Irish females, as has Colleen (Cailin), meaning a lovely young girl. Mary (Maire or Mare), Kathleen (Caitlin), Deirdre, Colum, Clare, Kevin, Michael, Patrick (Padriac), and Bonnie are also popular Irish given names. You can adopt the name of a beloved Irish grandparent, or choose a Gaelic name which reflects an interest or talent such as the Irish names for musician, herder, or weaver. The Irish myth cycles are rich with stories of heroes and heroines whose names are readily adopted by Wittans.

The following is a very brief list of name ideas. It is perfectly all right to adopt a name now and change it later when the right one comes along. Don't limit yourself. Try a variety of names. When you stumble across the right one for you, you will know it immediately. The name might even find you. For the sake of brevity, deity names have been omitted from this list. Names of Irish deities can be found in Appendix I in the back of this book.

- ❧ Abhainn (Aw-vin): river

- ❧ Amhranai (Awv-ray-nee): singer

- ❧ Bioma Gealac (Bwoma Gooh-lac): moonbeam

- ❧ Brian: Brian Boru, an eleventh-century high king of Ireland

- ❧ Ceol (Kel): music

- ❧ Ceoltoir (Kel-toorr): musician

- ❧ Cuchulain (Coo-cul-lan): mythical hero whom neither mortals, demons, nor faeries could destroy

- ❧ Dealgnaid (Dal-nee): queen of the Partholans

- ❧ Deirdre (Deer-dra): prophetess who was captured by the hero Conor; popularly known as "Deirdre of the Sorrows," her story is one of the Three Sorrows of the Irish myths

- ❧ Eochy (Y'oh-kee): a high king of Ireland

- ❧ Etain (Ai-dawn): blonde queen of the Tuatha De Danann; wife of Midhir; fine horsewoman

- ❧ Falia: a faery subrace of the Tuatha De Danann

- ❧ Fluirseac (Fw'loor-shak): bountiful

- ❧ Gealac (Gooh-lac): moon

- ❧ Madb (Mayv): legendary high queen of Ireland

- ❧ Midhir (My-ter or Myah-ter): king of the Tuatha De Danann; husband of Etain

- ❧ Muria: a faery subrace of the Tuatha De Danann
- ❧ Rinceoir (Rreen-kir): dancer
- ❧ Sera (Shee-rah): father-chief of the first faery race of Ireland; Partholan's right arm
- ❧ Tara (Tair-ah): the hill in County Meath where the high kings of Ireland sat
- ❧ Tuan (Toon): king of the Nemed faery invaders of Ireland; king of Irish deer

Handfasting

Handfasting is pagan marriage, but unlike the patriarchal marriage which binds partners for life, handfasting is contracted for a period of nine years, or less depending on the participants' request. Nine was chosen because it was three times three, a number which represents completion. If civil legality is important to you handfasting can be presided over by a high priest or priestess, several of whom possess a legal license to perform marriage. If you are more concerned with the old ways than being wed in the eyes of patriarchal law, handfasting can be done within one's coven or in the complete privacy of the couple's own circle. In earlier days the ceremony was conducted by the elder woman of the village or covenstead. A couple would pledge to be each others' incarnate goddess or god for the agreed upon period of time.

The wedding ring as a symbol has taken a lot of abuse in patriarchal times. It has been used as goods of value for the "purchase" of females, and it has been viewed as a circle of legal enslavement. In Witta, however, the wedding ring represents the wheel of the year, endless and ever-turning, and it represents the magick circle into which deity is invited. The pagan concept of marriage is that of the union of the Goddess and God incarnate, and rings symbolized that sacredness. Don't be afraid to wear a wedding ring if you really want one. Remember that it is just another pagan symbol which was distorted by those who sought to destroy the old ways.

In Ireland it was an old custom for young women to borrow the bride's ring, and for young men to borrow the groom's to enable them to get a glimpse of their own future spouse. They would take a portion of wedding cake, pass it through the ring three times, and then gaze into a candlelit mirror. In modern times we acknowledge this ritual by placing wedding cake under our pillows in order to dream of our future mates.

Many handfasting ceremonies symbolically unite the couple by draping them with a handwoven garland of flowers and leaves. The pagan custom of "jumping the broom" at the end of the ritual was part of an old fertility custom much as throwing rice is today.

After the expiration of the nine-year period the couple has the option to reaffirm their commitment to each other or to part ways. Pagan marriages tend to be very strong because couples aren't bound by laws which seek to force them to stay together no matter how miserable they are. No document is signed pledging each other all their fidelity and all their worldly goods. Knowing that one has the option to leave the union when the agreed upon time is up makes each partner more willing to take that extra effort to make the marriage work rather than taking for granted that it will always be there. Each partner is seen as an equal, indeed as one half of deity. Each couple is able to decide for themselves how they choose to live, if they will be faithful or have an "open" relationship, and if and how they will raise children. When a couple chooses not to renew their vows they are not ostracized from the pagan community, nor is one partner forced to live in poverty. There is no stigma or shame attached to them, and the word "divorce" is unknown. Unfortunately United States' law with its desire to force conformity, despite its insistence that we have freedom of religion, has made all but lifelong handfastings almost unavailable.

Witta acknowledges free will, and when a couple handfasts they are encouraged to choose a partner who shares their freely chosen goals, both physical and spiritual. This comes from an old Aryan-Indian belief that marriages of the spirit, or sacred marriages, are the only ones which last. Within Witta every couple might have their own way of living, and unlike living in the larger world, no prejudicial views of them are held.

Witta, like other forms of paganism, offers several other alternatives to the traditional patriarchal marriage. Witta will recognize two females or two males who wish to be handfasted, and will even recognize the sacredness of group marriage. The only important criteria is that of love, personal commitment for the duration of the agreement, and a desire to build a life together for each partner's mutual benefit.

Passing Over

Passing over rituals commemorate a loved one who has gone to Tir-na-nog. In circle, either alone or with others, light a candle in memory of the one passed over. Speak whatever farewells or blessings you wish. This is a time to say good-bye. Some pagan books publish elaborate rituals for the passing over observance, and many of them tend to be desperately solemn. It is all right and healthy to grieve, but remember that according to the tenets of Witta you will be reunited again with the loved one for we are all one spirit. After the ritual is over do not put out the candle, but place it near a window to guide the loved soul on their way to Tir-na-nog. (Word of caution: Never leave a burning candle unattended!)

Anthropologists have noted that color symbolism is part of all funeral customs worldwide, though the color chosen by each differs. Witta shares with the Chinese and Koreans the belief that white is a proper mourning color as opposed to the black used in most of the West. White is the color of the earth in winter when all life appears to have ceased. The second most common color used in Wittan passing over rituals is blue, the color of water in the west where lies Tir-na-nog.

The custom of the wake, a ritual where community and family sit up with the dead body until burial, is still very popular among the Irish. This custom is a cross between the Wittan belief of death as a transition as demonstrated in the storytelling and party atmosphere which surround the wake, and the patriarchal cult of death denial as seen in customs that view the body and pretend it is merely "asleep." Candles are traditionally placed at the head and foot of the corpse to light the soul's footsteps and aid his or her vision when passing on to the Land of the Dead.

Keening (caoine in Irish) is an important part of the mourning ritual. This grieving wail is similar to the one made by the bean sídhe (banshee), the spirit whose voice is heard when a death is imminent. It was believed that the keening which is done by humans—usually women—was in imitation of the bean sídhe and done to frighten away any malevolent spirits which might be trying to hinder the dead soul's journey to Tir-na-nog, and prevent him or her from enjoying his or her own wake.

After the burial, it is believed that Death himself, often called Ankou from the Breton word for death, comes for the deceased soul in his black cart. When a death occurs in rural Ireland the cart can be heard creaking over the rutted roads. One turn-of-the-century family in Roscommon reported to mythologist W.Y. Evans-Wentz of hearing the cart regularly on the road in front of their house, but when they looked out they could see nothing.

THE AFTERLIFE

Death in paganism is never seen as an ending, but as a transition. Witta shares that view.

According to Irish mythology the Land of the Dead is in the west with the setting sun. This belief is shared by several other pagan cultures including the Cherokee Indians of North America. In Ireland all dead souls went west to Tir-na-nog, also called "the land of the ever young." Another name for it was "the land of women." The ancient Irish believed that all souls had to re-enter the Great Mother's womb from which they were born in order to enter Tir-na-nog. A later variation on this theme was that all souls had to re-enter the womb of the grandmother of their own matricentric clan. Therefore all souls inhabiting Tir-na-nog were mothers. Here souls were thought of as being placed into another womb image, the great cauldron of the Caillech, the crone of the Irish pantheon. All ended life entered this cauldron, and from this cauldron all life would be reborn.

It is a known fact that the universe is expanding. Physicists theorize that eventually the tide will turn and everything will contract back into one central energy source. Then the process will begin again and the universe will be reborn and expand once more. In essence they share a world view with Wittans. Both believe we will all be reabsorbed in time by the Great Mother, and then rebirthed by her.

As previously stated, in Witta reincarnation is a metaphor for the singularity of existence. But here, as within all religious doctrine, there are as many beliefs as there are people, and Witta will not attempt to coerce you to accept any one idea about afterlife. The view presented here is taken from the old myths themselves and represents one very ancient belief. You are free to develop your own thoughts and theories. But reincarnation, however one chooses to understand it, is a basic tenet of all paganism. In fact it is probably one of humanity's oldest beliefs.

The Wittans would cling to their religious beliefs to conquer the fear of death. Whether they succeeded any better or worse than we do now is a matter of pure speculation.

SELF-DEDICATION

Witta was a way of life shared by families. Teaching Wittan ways was by word of mouth, and little or nothing was written down. Children were educated through socialization much as patriarchal religion uses families for the same purpose today. The stories of the old gods, goddesses, heroes, and heroines were told around the hearthside, or as people worked in the fields or around cook fires. Those with recognized abilities in one particular area were sent to a skilled teacher in that field, when one was available, to be further instructed. This was especially true in the field of medicinal herbalism. Even in modern Ireland many rural villages still have a "wise woman" to whom they go for herbal remedies and charms.

As Witta was largely a solitary religion the idea of a formal initiation was unknown. People grew up in their faith, were presented to the deities at their Wittaning, and made their own pledge to follow this path at their coming of age. Many modern Wittans keep that concept in mind and shun formal, hierarchical initiation rituals even within covens. Within Witta it has always been acceptable to dedicate oneself to the path by way of self-initiation, even though recent years have seen movements towards stratification and strict initiatory acceptance within Witta. The bondage-style initiations performed by many modern covens would have been abhorrent to the old Wittans who cherished personal freedom in a way modern democracies only give lip service to.

In Western paganism it is traditional that initiation or self-dedication be made after a year and a day of study. I would suggest that this is a minimum amount of time for someone to study the Wittan path before officially dedicating him or herself to it. Make sure it is the path you really want to be on first.

For solitary Wittans who want a meaningful self-initiation, here is a brief ceremony to adapt for yourself. Each person has his or her own concept of how best to serve deity and walk on a positive Wittan pathway. Use your own words and call upon your own favorite aspects of the Irish deities when dedicating yourself.

Begin with a well-cast circle, preferably one with an unobstructed sight of the full moon. Have with you on the ground or altar a chalice of water, a bowl of salt, and a wand, staff, or shillelagh. You can wear robes or be nude, whatever feels most comfortable. Do make some effort to change from your everyday clothing. You are making a statement of life-changing proportion here, and it is traditional to wear garments which show this both to the deities you honor and to your subconscious wherein all such changes occur.

If you choose to work with elementals or friendly spirits call them in your normal manner. Then raise your staff to the moon and invite your deities' presence. It might go something like this:

> *Oh blessed Lady Brigid, Great Mother of heaven and earth from whom I was born. I ask your presence here as I, your child, who has stumbled upon the Wittan path once more, present myself to be dedicated to your service in this earthly incarnation. As did my ancestors long ago, I too acknowledge you as the Great Mother Goddess, giver of all life.*

Add salt to the water in your chalice and sprinkle it on your feet.

Bless my feet as I walk along your ancient pathway.

Place the salt water on your heart.

Bless my heart which humbly turns to you in love, and is given to you freely.

Carefully place the salt water near your eyes.

Bless my eyes that they might be opened to the wonders of your world. That I might see the unseen and know all "truths" through them.

Place the salt water on the crown of your head and then kneel.

Great Mother Brigid, bless my mind that it will always be open to you, and guard it that it not conceive to do harm to any fellow living creatures. May I always remember and follow the Wittan Rede. I know that if through your path I bring harm to any living creature I will experience the same three times over. As all living things are one, as I harm others, I also harm myself.

Stand erect and raise your wand or staff to the moon.

Ancient Brigid, warrioress, protectress, instructress, inspirer, and Great Mother. I present myself to you as your child, (state new name), *and ask that you accept my dedication to you. So Mote it Be. Blessed Be!*

I suggest that you spend much time in private meditation before breaking the circle. Bond with your deities and consider what your new life means to you.

CAKES AND ALE

The concept that what one consumes will be made manifest is another Wittan belief whose roots are buried in antiquity. Ancient warriors used to consume parts of their dead so that they could be reborn into the clan. Native Americans would eat the heart of a brave animal they felled to take on its characteristics and to keep it propagating. Even in the Irish myth cycles we see the faery queen Etain consumed by Etar and reappearing as a mortal child. The pagan celebratory feast of cakes and ale which is observed at esbats is also a fertility rite of this type.

This magick belief is now practiced in Witta by the "Kitchen Witch." Eating foods charged with magical incantations or food which is molded into the shape of the desired goal is a common folk magick practice both in and out of Ireland. This practice is said to be most efficacious when working towards fertility or prosperity goals because of the earth and water imagery of most foods.

Cakes and ale is the traditional ending to an esbat circle. Cake, representing earth and matter, and ale or wine, representing spirit and transcendancy, are blessed, dedicated to the deities, and consumed. The union of matter and spirit is the equivalent of the union of the Goddess and God and functions primarily as a fertility rite. But the practice is far older than human knowledge of the male role in reproduction. Cakes and ale once represented the essence of deity in both corporal and non-corporal form. God-eating rituals were prominent in old pagan cultures around the globe, and they still survive today, particularly among Polynesian pagans. These ancient beliefs are still at work in the Christian communion service and Jewish blessings for wine and bread.

Expensive types of ale need not be used in your rites. In fact, wine is often chosen to represent the water aspect. Wine comes in a variety of strengths and flavors and it should be easy to find ones which suit every palate. Fruit juices or apple cider are also acceptable substitutes.

Be imaginative when creating your cakes. You can bake cookies cut into moon-shaped crescents, and you can frost them white or blue, or add silver sprinkles. You can cut thin sheet cakes in the same manner and decorate them. Bread is an acceptable substitute for cake. Home baked bread with blackberry jam, blackberries being sacred to

Brigid, would also be an appropriate alternative.

Here are two recipes that you might like to try at your next celebration. One is a recipe for simple sugar cookies which can be cut into shapes and decorated. This particular recipe has been used for baking holiday cookies in our family for three generations. The other recipe is traditional Irish soda bread, a sort of "poor man's loaf," which can be purchased on almost any corner in Ireland. There are many recipes for the bread, all of them almost identical, but this is the one I like.

Holiday Sugar Cookies

> 2 cups all-purpose flour
> 1/4 teaspoon ground nutmeg
> 1/8 teaspoon ground allspice
> 1 1/4 teaspoon baking powder
> 1/4 teaspoon salt
> 1 1/2 teaspoon vanilla
> 1 beaten egg
> 1/3 cup vegetable oil
> 1/4 cup milk

Mix all the dry ingredients and the oil thoroughly together in a large bowl. Beat all other ingredients together until they appear light and fluffy, then put them in the bowl with the other mixture and stir them together.

Put the mixture in the refrigerator for at least two hours—overnight is better.

Divide the mixture into four sections to make it easier to handle. One section at a time, roll the dough out onto a generously floured cutting board until it is about 1/8 of an inch thick. Cut with a cookie cutter and place the cut-outs onto an ungreased cookie sheet.

Bake at 400° for 7-8 minutes. The cookies will be stiff and show signs of starting to change to a golden color. Do not bake until brown or they will become hard and brittle. Makes about 2 1/2 dozen.

Irish Soda Bread

    3 cups all-purpose flour
    3 cups whole-wheat flour
    1 1/4 teaspoon cream of tartar
    1 1/4 teaspoon baking soda
    1/2 teaspoon salt
    1 teaspoon sugar (raw sugar is better)
    2 cups sour milk (sour milk with a teaspoon of vinegar or orange
      juice, or set out at room temperature for 3 days)

Mix all ingredients together, except the milk, making sure they are well-blended. Add the milk a quarter-cup at a time, blending it in well each time. The dough should be tacky but not crumbly and should be holding together well. If not, add another tablespoon of milk. Knead the dough well for at least 15 minutes.

Work the dough into a ball and place it in the center of a greased and lightly floured baking sheet (any cookie sheet will work fine) and flatten slightly. Take a sharp knife and cut three straight deep slash marks across the top. If you like you can brush a little melted butter on top, but cream is used traditionally.

Bake at 375° for 45-50 minutes, then turn the loaf over and bake another 5-7 minutes or until it has a hollow sound when tapped with the blunt edge of a knife.

Soda bread is traditionally served with butter, but you can serve it with jams or as an accompaniment to other foods.

Try variations on the recipe by adding a cup of nuts or raisins.

WORKING IN A COVEN

Often we wish for and need connection and companionship with others who share our views. Sabbats are an excellent time for Wittans to gather in covens to feast and worship together. In old Ireland, sabbats remained community affairs long after the new religion wiped out the memory of the holiday's meaning.

If you choose to work within a coven let me offer from experience some guidelines for structuring yourselves in a way which benefits not only you and your fellow covenors, but also honors the pagan tradition and the Wittan path.

First of all, don't rely on so-called high priests and priestesses to carry the load. Everyone who will be participating in the rituals should have a hand in their construction. Never believe that any one person is any more qualified than any other to perform that task. In spiritual matters we are all seekers and none of us are masters, and we all have something to share. And everyone should have an additional task aside from a role in the creating of the rituals. Some can bring food for the feasts, others can bring beverages, and others can bring oils, candles, or seasonal decorations.

If you wish to have designated leaders, form your coven not in a hierarchy, but in a consensus. That is, rotate the leadership roles. Everyone will get a chance at some time to lead the rituals, and at that time he or she can add personal touches to the ceremonies. If an individual prefers to call out to Dana rather than Brigid, then let him or her. A consensus is not a democracy. In fact, a democracy can lead to a tyranny of the majority. In a consensus EVERYONE'S WAY gets to be THE WAY at some point.

Do not coerce others into dressing as you do, or choosing to use the same ritual tools you use. Do not indulge in gossip of any kind about your fellow covenors. A good guide for this is that if you find yourself saying something you would not want to say to that person's face then shut up! Be responsible to others and for yourself, and never break your word to your coven. Do not force someone to do anything with which they feel uncomfortable or afraid. You are trying to build a group based on ultimate trust. People who are afraid or distrustful of your motives will be useless in magick workings or in the raising of power.

Some people find bondage and other forms of forced initiation or ritual intimidating. Respect this. Rather than using bondage and blindfolds to initiate (which is not a Wittan tradition) use the more ancient "birthing" ritual. Line up your coven with their legs spread apart and have the new covenor crawl between them. This is a very ancient ceremony used by covens everywhere to adopt individuals into their clan.

Adoption in the Old Religion carried no stigma of "not quite belong-ing" as it has since the pathological need for guaranteed paternity was foisted upon us. All over the world pagan cultures have stories about a foundling who was adopted by a chief or a matriarch of the clan or tribe and later inherited his or her throne. A birthing ritual makes someone truly a part of you and is a much more significant and loving way to accept a new coven member than by binding him or her in ropes.

Respect your circle and its meaning. Remember that when cast, a circle is sacred space, and that also means "safe" space. Everyone should be free to be him or herself and speak his or her mind without fear of ridicule. You have created a space into which you have invited deity. It is no place for quarrels or pettiness, or any form of ego and self-aggrandizement. If those are the perks you seek from religion, then paganism is not for you.

Playing circle games—and making sure they are non-threatening games—after a ritual is a fun way to form bonds. Tell riddles, sing, and play other party games which you adapt to have a Wittan meaning. *Do not* indulge in sexual games which put others ill at ease or offend the personal moral codes of any of your members. Remember that they have a right to live their life by their own standards just as you do. Leave your personal codes at home if they are in conflict with the group as a whole, or seek out another coven that thinks more like you do. The coven *must* be a comfortable spot for everyone where all can come to worship, work, and socialize in an accepting and loving envi-ronment. If you can't produce that then there is really no purpose in having a coven.

If you find you have troubles in circle with everyone talking and nobody listening, or if you have a couple of people you need to draw out of their shells, adopt the "talking stick" method from the Native Americans. Have a stick or candle or some other object which is passed from person to person within the circle. Only the person holding the object will be allowed to speak.

Remember that all people have special gifts, talents, and inherent value. Each will have something uniquely his or her own to contribute to the group. A good coven will respect each person's strengths and weaknesses and try to balance out the group.

If you do not know of any other Wittans in your area place ads in some of the pagan journals and see if you get a response. Or try making a talisman of vervain, dill, and sandalwood tied up in an orange cloth. This is a very old "witch finder" charm of unknown origin.

LIVING THE MAGICKAL LIFE

Being a Wittan is more than just following a set of religious beliefs, it is a way of life, a magickal life. Wittan religious ritual is less important than is daily comportment which reflects the deeper values of the faith and honors the deities. Our Wittan ancestors did not have to be reminded that the earth is our home and that we are not her masters, but merely her caretakers.

Care for the environment. Earth is our Mother, she is the Goddess herself and she is to be cherished and respected, for she is the only home we have. The patriarchal religions denigrate the earth as they venerate heaven, thereby making it perfectly acceptable to trash our planet. Take back the right to love our Mother Earth. Plant trees or other foliage whenever and wherever you can, and get involved in environmental issues. Give what you can to organizations who share your goals. Recycle everything you can, and buy recycled products when they are available. Write to your political representatives and let them know how you feel about these issues.

Grow your own magickal or medicinal herbs when possible. If you don't have a yard for a garden then try a window box, or even just one lone pot in a sunny corner of your apartment. Just having herbal scents filling your home can trigger changes in your consciousness and remind you often of the special life you have chosen.

Show care and concern for all living creatures. Put up a bird feeder or wild animal feeder. Join in efforts to preserve wildlife refuges. Give to animal causes which share your world views. If you have room and time for a pet, adopt one from a local shelter. Pets give us so much, and they can be an added boon to any magick you do in their presence.

Consider becoming a vegetarian. If you don't want to make that commitment then resolve to give up a certain percentage of meat meals each week. This is not just for the purpose of saving an animal life, but it aids the environment as a whole. Rain forests are being destroyed at an alarming rate (up to 1000 acres a day) to make way for grazing lands, and cows are the world's largest producers of methane gas.

Never forget that all life is intimately connected with every other life. Every time a fellow creature suffers from persecution or want it is just as if it is being done directly to everyone else. If this sounds familiar it is because this wisdom is taught daily in the patriarchal religions though it is rarely practiced. Get outraged over human rights violations—get involved.

Act honorably. You don't have to be a walking model of perfection, but stick to your convictions and don't be swayed by situational ethics. Take responsibility for yourself and your actions. Remember that you have a right to live happily and peacefully, and so does everyone else.

❧ 3 ❧

SPELLS

Witta, as it was several thousand years ago, was a very "home-spun" religion, a faith of those who lived close to the earth and could feel the gentle pulse of her yearly ebb and flow. They knew Mother Earth sustained them, and they looked to her and her natural resources to solve their problems. When a spell was needed someone, or a small group, went out and took care of it with the aid of whatever was at hand; the gathering of seven or eight complex tools was definitely not done.

Generally Wittans were solitary witches, or else they did their spell work and worship within their close-knit family groups. Modern Witta, like modern Wicca and other neo-pagan faiths, has become more involved and complex, just like modern life itself. Whether you choose to simplify your spells and rituals or to use a more elaborate approach is a matter of personal choice, and both are quite correct. One form is merely older than the other, and despite popular thought, older does not always mean better.

Living simply and close to nature meant that the spells used by the Celts of Ireland were also simple in their form and content. Witches have long said that spells need not be elaborate to be efficacious, and I believe that when these early Irish people had a magickal need they immediately did not rush to gather up their vast collections of magickal paraphernalia. Instead they would walk out onto the land and seek out the tools nature provided.

An abundance of books, good and bad, are available on pagan rituals and spells. Most are generic in nature and are meant to be used as a guide to the reader and not as dogma to be slavishly followed. Because of this proliferation I shall avoid any effort to repeat what is already available and try to confine this chapter to what can be reconstructed of the most ancient of Irish worship and magick.

Space considerations do not permit this book to be a comprehensive primer on basic magick. The spells which are included are presented as samples only, representative of spells which have roots in Ireland. The bibliography lists several excellent sources of information on basic pagan rituals and magick for those who wish to explore it further.

Four things are necessary to work acts of magick. The first thing is need. You must truly need that which you are working for. Second is deep emotional desire. Third is the knowledge to work the spell, which is easily obtained in spell books and herbal books readily available in occult bookstores or by mail order. The final element you need is the most important, and is often the one to which most witches pay too little attention. It is the ability to visualize your goal. Visualization is simply the ability to "see" magickal results with your creative mind. In as much detail as possible you must "see" the desired outcome of your magick. With practice you will be able to build up elaborate pictures of your need and hold them in your mind, filling them with your energy, for long periods of time. This is where the magick takes place, not within a sword or cup.

In preparing to do a magick rite it is suggested that you mentally prepare yourself with some time of quiet and meditation. Some Wittans like to take a purifying bath beforehand, or stroll through a woods. Making a ritual of setting out the objects with which you will be working is an excellent way to cue your deep mind that changes are about to occur. With practice you will feel your consciousness slipping into a magickal state whenever you begin preparing to work a spell. This works rather like a post-hypnotic suggestion and is the very purpose of ritual.

A final discussion before the spells are presented, one about negative magick. Because witches believe that whatever energy we send out will return to us threefold, it is an extremely bad idea to even contemplate using magick to harm or manipulate anyone. Many intelligent grimoires seek to eradicate even the faintest chance of this happening by including words such as, "in accordance with the Threefold Law," or "for the good of all," or "and in harming none," in their spell work. Keep the Wittan Rede in mind as you seek to work magick.

As we have already seen, it is highly improbable that the ancient people of Ireland had extended covens or elaborate tools in their circles. The shillelagh, a practical instrument, took the place of the wand and was used to direct energy much as a wand or athame is used today. Chalices and cups were crude objects, and though these ancient people were highly aware of the symbology inherent in them, they were more likely to go to a natural source, such as a lough (lake), river, or seaside if they wished to work with the element of water. While the Irish were one of the first groups to extensively craft metal, the average Irish person did not own these cherished items.

Probably the most popular method of folk magick in old Ireland, as elsewhere, was candle magick. Fire, which lit the darkest night and provided heat, warmth, and the primary source of energy, was held in awe until quite recently in human history. Long after human beings figured out how to make a fire the creation of it was still considered a magickal act, and fires were closely guarded night and day to keep them from burning out. As an element of transformation the power of fire made itself known. Fire could consume, cook, destroy, and create. And candles, precious as they were, were often utilized in magick. Even today candle magick remains extremely popular, not only because of these associations which remain in our primal memory, but because it is very efficacious and relatively easy to do.

They also used the native stones and herbs provided by nature, and again, many modern books cover a variety of ways in which to use them. Many of the methods are quite ancient and share a startling commonality with the practices of pagan people worldwide. In old Ireland the people were less concerned with the color and cut of a stone than with the associations which a stone had for them personally. While some stones, such as bloodstone, were used for any magick involving blood such as healing or childbirth, any stone could be used for magick because it was of the earth and therefore of the Great Mother.

The magick of old Ireland probably fell into one of these five categories: healing, fertility, protection, love, or divination. Interestingly enough, human needs have changed very little over the centuries, and these are the same areas of magickal concern which still take up most of the space in today's magickal "cookbooks."

WHEN TO WORK MAGICK

People were much more concerned with achieving quick results than they were in figuring out the best time to do their spells, or which element was best suited to aid in the working. This timing concern is probably a concept grafted onto paganism from ceremonial magick. And though calling on one particular element which has an affinity for the problem can give the working an added boost, choosing to use the resources at hand has never been known to negate or ruin any spell. Remember that magick takes place in the human psyche, and convincing it of a change is what makes the change manifest in the concrete world. Just how that deep mind is contacted and manipulated is up to the witch.

Though many people concern themselves with determining the best times for certain spells, magick is best used when you have a deep need for it because then you are emotionally involved and that helps raise the needed energy. By tradition, magick is not worked at sabbats because magick is work (sometimes very hard work) and work is prohibited at festivals. But if you are in desperate need, Witta makes an exception to this rule.

If you care about astrology in relation to your spell work, remember that generally spells for things one wants to gain or increase are best done during the waxing phase of the moon. These generally include spells to aid crop growth, to bring about health, to gain wealth, to win love, and for all types of fertility. Spells designed to eliminate or decrease something are best performed on the waning phase. These usually include things like banishing a negative energy, ridding oneself of a bad habit, or destroying an illness or crop blight. Other astrological influences can be consulted when spell work is to be done. Many rural people still prefer to do spells for their crops when the moon is in the sign of Cancer, the sign of growth and fertility.

The use of astrology in planning the most propitious times for spell work, healings and non-festival rituals in ancient Ireland has been hotly debated. Many modern day Wittans rely doggedly on their ephemerides, and others, while not so enslaved to astrology, still find themselves worrying that doing a spell for increase on a waning moon will somehow be lacking. Many others claim that the ancients were too ignorant of the detailed workings of the heavens to be concerned with these matters, citing the common belief in a flat earth as factual evidence of their opinion.

Certainly the fact that the earth was round was not the universal secret it is made out to be for today's school children. While some cultures were still fleeing and hiding from the terror of a solar eclipse, the Chinese had mapped much of the heavens and their movements. Even in Iron Age Britain and Ireland megaliths such as Stonehenge, on Cornwall's Salisbury Plain, pointed out the movements of the planets as early as 3000 B.C.E. Similar monuments scattered throughout Britain and Ireland are a testament to the fact that many of those early people knew a great deal more about our universe than we generally credit them with. Remember that the ancient Wittans lived close to the earth and nature, and were much more in tune with its subtle rhythms than we are today.

If possible, spells were worked at the most astrologically efficacious times. But keep in mind that magick works best on the basis of need. If you have a need that can wait until the heavens are in perfect alignment, that is fine. But if not, it is best to go ahead with your spell work knowing that it will be every bit as effective because of your emotional investment. Think of astrology not as making or breaking a spell, but as giving it a little boost when it can. An Irish mother with a sick child certainly couldn't wait until the moon was where she wanted it to be before she could work magick for healing. She would gather whatever symbols she had at hand to help her contact her deity, probably the Great Mother Brigid, and petition her aid magically for her child with something as simple as a single candle.

Aside from moon phases, many pagans wish to take into consideration the days of the week when working magick. Again, this is a fine way to get a little boost of added energy, but it is not essential.

How the seven days of the week became associated with the seven known planets of ancient times is shrouded in mystery. But throughout most of Western paganism and in all branches of high magick, the same planets are associated with each day. Witta further attributes each day to a goddess or god aspect. These deities share energy characteristics with their day's ruling planet, and they can be petitioned for aid in conjunction with spells worked on that day. The herb sacred to each deity is also provided.

Day	Irish Day Name	Planet	Deity	Herb
Sunday	De Domhnaigh	Sun	Lugh	Oak/Acorn
Monday	De Luain	Moon	Brigid	Blackberry
Tuesday	De Mairt	Mars	Luchtain	Saffron
Wednesday	De De Ceadaoin	Mercury	Airmid	Clover
Thursday	De Ardaoin	Jupiter	Manann	Irish Moss
Friday	De h'Aoine	Venus	Fand	Primrose
Saturday	De Sathairn	Saturn	Beltene	Mistletoe

Note that on Saturday the God of Death, Beltene, is given as the deity associated with the planetary influences of Saturn. Some followers of Witta may prefer to substitute a crone name, such as Badb, for Beltene because of Saturn's associations not only with death, but with rebirth which is the province of the crone. The choice is yours to make, and both are correct. The principal herb sacred to the Irish crone is the apple because of its life-giving fruit which covers and hides the death-giving seeds inside.

Spells for specific goals, if they can wait a few days, can be worked on the day their planetary influence is its greatest. You can also call upon the deity of the day (or any other deity you feel will best aid your cause) to add their blessings to your spell. The following is an example of a simple petition to Lugh for prosperity. Add this after the rest of your spell has been done.

> *Hear me, Lugh the Shining One, and bless me in my hour of need on this day when the sun rains its energies all around me. Look favorably upon me as I seek to gain the money I need to pay my mortgage. Imbue me with your vibrant energy that my need may soon manifest.*

Feel Lugh's energies fill you and the materials set out for your spell. Use acorns on your altar to help further connect you with Lugh, or use them in place of other herbs in your spell.

Thank you, Lugh, and Blessed Be!

The sun's energy is concerned with matters of wealth and prosperity, protection, movement and dance, power, male mysteries, property, law, self-defense, spiritual attainment, purification, and exorcism.

The moon is concerned with fertility, childbirth, death, growth, dreams, divination, the Triple Goddess, astral projection, normal waking consciousness, heat and light, female mysteries, self-confidence, spiritual attainment, and psychism.

The energies of Mars concern war, medicine, dreams, sleep, passion, coolness and dark, sex, courage, lust, banishing, physical protection, hardship, physical exertion, disagreements, and vanquishing an enemy's power over you.

The energies of Mercury are used for matters of healing, communication, blessing faeries (Wednesday is said to be their day of rest), writing, wisdom, reading, books, stopping gossip, vocal music, and intellectual matters.

Jupiter's energies concern themselves with employment, prosperity, good fortune, fair judgments, friendship, investments, ambition, growth concerning wealth and prestige, and success.

Venus pertains to love, peace, home life, music, children, fidelity, acts of kindness and generosity, art, poetry, family, romance, and beauty.

Saturn is associated with spells for past life recall, self-undoing, lies, mental and emotional distress, recovering losses, long life, the elderly, completion, spirit communication, meditation, accepting or changing bad situations, and protection from psychic attack.

MAGICKAL NUMBERS

The number three has had special meaning in almost all traditions of paganism around the world. This is a natural extension of the almost universal belief in the three faces of the Goddess, or Triple Goddess. Because she is represented by the three faces of the moon, and these three phases together complete an entire monthly cycle, three became the number of completion. Three, and any multiple of three, was sacred to the Goddess.

Three times three, or nine, has long been held in Witta (and even in ceremonial magick) as the mystical number assigned to the moon. In fact nine was used so heavily in Ireland, and later in the Nordic regions, that one scholar described it as "the northern counterpart to the sacred (number) seven" of Asia and the Middle East. Groups of things in nine abound in the Irish myths. Queen Madb rode to battle with nine chariots, the hero Cuchulain wielded nine weapons, and Finn MacCool had nine faery servants. Because it is the number of the moon, nine, as three times three, is also the number of the Goddess.

Some grimoires require that a spell be done in multiples of three before it is considered finished, and it is traditional to pass an object to be ritually consecrated through fire, water, incense or earth three times. Some protection rituals require three circles to be drawn around the person or place to be guarded, and many healing spells involved the making of three walks around a tree, fire, or the person who is ill.

And finally, three represents the manifestation of all life—the creative life force itself and its male and female principles. This union is usually represented by an inverted triangle.

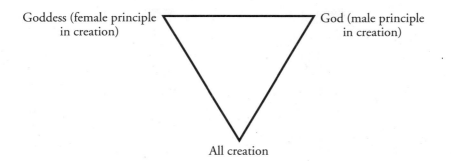

Goddess (female principle in creation)

God (male principle in creation)

All creation

Many of the healing superstitions of Ireland require banishing an illness by doing something in sets of three. One such carry-over of this belief is seen in an Irish folk method of healing a wound in which three is invoked three times in three different forms. One must first invoke the three daughters of Fliethas (a faery king/queen), then command the "poisons" to come out by teeth of dog, thorn of rose, and hide of whip. Then one must finish the incantation in the name of the Father, the Son and the Holy Ghost. No doubt that this last was once a plea to the Triple Goddess.

When weaving magick be aware of how numbers are used, particularly the number three. Three, or multiples of three, are the traditional number of herbs to add to a charm. Adding or doing anything in multiples of three will strengthen any spell.

Also of importance in Witta is the number thirty-three which, of course, is a written as a double three. Many Irish legends contain references to thirty-three year periods, most notably those banished from Tara had to be gone for thirty-three years.

Thirteen, as evidenced in groups of twelve plus one, are also prevalent in the Irish myths. Thirteen, of course, is the traditional number of members for a coven to have in most of Western paganism. The high kings of Ireland would assemble twelve Druid advisors, and the god Crom Cruiach had twelve sacred standing stones. All of them made up a coven of thirteen.

There seems to be a cloud of mystery about why thirteen was the number chosen for covens. One possible explanation goes back to the sacredness of the number three. Twelve is three times four. So it might have followed that early covens wanted three people to represent each of the four elements, and then an acting priest or priestess to direct and coordinate their rituals. Three times four plus one is thirteen.

Five is the number of families or groups. It is said that faeries count themselves in fives. The ogham alphabet is written in groups of fives. And the giant god, Finn MacCool, could only count by fives for he knew no other numbers, nor did he seem to think them important.

Five was viewed as a number of death and resurrection. Grouping things by fives was thought to send death looking elsewhere for victims since his number, or mark, was already upon whatever was grouped in fives. This number also facilitated rebirth and many burial cairns were thought to have been put together with stones in multiples of five.

Seventeen was an extremely unlucky number. Sixteen generations was as far as kinship was recognized in ancient Ireland. The matrifocal kin groups at the seventeenth generation had to divide and reform under new matriarchs, or later, under new clan chieftains. Many Irish believed the seventeenth generation to be cursed, possibly because these families were weakened temporarily by their separation. As patriarchy gave rise to clan warfare no doubt these smaller kin groups were prey to the larger, stronger clans. Just when this counting of generations began is uncertain, nor is it known why the sixteenth generation was targeted. It may have been because by then it was generally felt that the clans had grown too large and unwieldy to be effective as extended family units.

Other important Wittan numbers are four, the number of the elements; eight, a number of good fortune which also represents the eight sabbats; two, the number of polarity; and, seven, the number of the God and of power manifest.

EMPOWERING

To work any act of magick one must charge or empower the objects they are using. Any magickal tools you are currently using will already be attuned to your needs and energies. But you will need to attune with and empower any herbs, stones, twigs, or other objects you intend to use as a catalyst for your magick.

This is done by holding the objects in your power hand—the one you write with or use the most—and feeling your energy and your need flow into them. Say, for example, that you are mixing together several herbs that will later be placed in a pouch which you will carry. You will stir those herbs together with that power hand feeling your energy meld with theirs, and all the while visualizing your magickal goal. This will take some time, but you should be able to feel it happening.

Many new witches want to cut right to the actual spell working and skimp on the emotional investments such as empowering and visualization. Don't! It is this investment of your personal energy which makes the spell work just like gasoline makes a car engine work. Without gasoline you can go through all the motions of turning on your car and nothing will happen. The same is true of a spell worked without empowering emotions.

While it is true that magick takes place in the mind where your thoughts act upon the astral plane to form things which will manifest, most witches use herbs, stones, etc., which are known to share an affinity for the desired goal. The magick is not in the objects themselves, they merely act as a catalyst which helps you focus, direct, and receive energy.

Note: The words empower, charge, and enchant are interchangeable and will all be used in this chapter to mean the same thing.

HERB MAGICK

Appendix III in this book lists several reputable companies that sell herbs, either the whole plant, cuttings, ground and dried herbs, or the seeds. If you have trouble finding any of the herbs you need locally, try these resources. Please patronize your local occult shops and health food stores before trying mail order. These establishments need your support, and they are good places to make contact with other pagans.

Herbs have been used for magick for countless centuries and were very popular in Ireland because the Druids used them liberally in ritual. Herbs were also utilized by the common folk. All villages had a wise woman, an elderly witch who had made a lifework of the study of healing and magickal plants. She was so much an institution which refused to die that the medieval church decreed that to cure anyone by herbal methods was evidence of one's being in league with the Devil.

Not only was the medicinal effect of many of the plants evident by human reaction to them, but it was also believed that herbs, like other life throughout nature, possessed certain energies which could also be magickally beneficial if tapped. Several excellent books on magickal herbalism exist and I highly recommend that at least one be included in your personal library. My favorite is Scott Cunningham's *Encyclopedia of Magical Herbs* (Llewellyn Publications) which includes interesting herb lore from around the world.

I offer a word of caution here about ingesting herbal concoctions. Herbalism is an art related to the science of botany, and it takes many years of study to master its nuances. In-depth knowledge is required to sort through the familial relationships and chemical make-up of plants. For instance, chamomile, a common herb used as a stomach soother, is a first cousin of ragweed. If you are prone to hay fever then you should not drink chamomile. Do not take any herbal brew internally without first knowing exactly how the plants will react and interact within you. Furthermore, many people have a host of unknown allergies which manifest dangerously when provoked. Always use herbs cautiously and conservatively until you are sure of your reaction to them.

Herbs were used as brews, incenses, ointments, and talismans depending on the property of the herb, whether or not it was toxic, and the desired outcome. In Ireland the most popular magickal and medicinal herbs were:

❧ Alder, a Druidic sacred tree, was used to carve magickal flutes. Druids and other Celtic bards made a study of the magickal correlations of musical tones whose energies produced magickal results. Incense made from alder bark was used to raise spiritual vibrations, much in the same way that frankincense was used in India and the far east.

❧ Apples are sacred to goddesses virtually everywhere. When sliced crosswise a five-pointed star, the sacred symbol of Western paganism, appears. The health benefits of the fruit are well-known as is the fact that the seeds contain deadly cyanide. Apples were used as a catalyst in all manner of spells, especially spells for love and protection.

❧ Ash was used by the Druids in both incense and tea forms to induce psychic states of consciousness.

❧ Beans, sacred to the many goddesses of western Europe, were dried and placed in a rattle for exorcisms and protection rites. They were also gathered and charged to be used like divination stones.

❧ Birch, sacred to the goddess Dana, was used in love potions. It was also used in rituals of purification, and in spells to protect children.

❧ Blackberry, sacred to the goddess Brigid, was used for healing, wealth, strength, sexual potency, and in spells for creative endeavors. Using blackberries in protection spells helped invoke Brigid's own protective shield. Blackberry pies and blackberry wine are an Irish tradition at the feast of Lughnasadh.

❧ Comfrey was used in healing rituals probably because it was often used medicinally for treating skin ailments and fungus. Drinking comfrey tea will induce relaxation.

❧ Elder was held to allow one to see faeries who jealously guard the wood as their personal property. Children placed in cradles of elder wood risked being stolen by faeries. Elder flowers and leaves were used for home blessings.

❧ Gorse, which grows wild in much of Europe, was used for protection spells. In Wales it was reputedly used to keep mischievous faeries from entering a dwelling. Witta uses it as a general protective herb.

❧ Heather was an herb sacred to the Druids. A delicate wine made from heather is still made in Ireland and Scotland and drunk on sabbats and other festivals. Use heather in purification rites, and in rituals to honor the crone.

❧ Holly was one of the most sacred of the Druidic holy trees. Druids revered the tree as a blending of the Goddess and God, and the tree was the only one sacred to both male and female Irish deities. Holly has been used in protective spells, especially those to guard children. A brew of holly rubbed on the belly of a pregnant woman was said to prevent miscarriage. The Holly King in Ireland is the king of the waning year (Midsummer to Yule).

❧ Mistletoe, though quite toxic, was highly prized by the Druids, and was used for every conceivable magickal goal, especially for divination and in spells to boost sagging male sexual prowess. So revered was this herb that the Druids reserved special solid gold sickles to cut it with. Mistletoe was cut at Midsummer, and was considered especially potent if found on a sacred oak tree. If you have children or pets it is best to avoid having mistletoe around as the poisonous berries can look very enticing.

❧ Oak trees were sacred to the gods of Ireland, especially to the sun god, Lugh, and to the Great Horned God. Oak leaves, bark, and acorns were used for healing, male fertility rites, protection, divination, and in spells for prosperity. Oak was the most sacred of all the Druidic holy trees. The Oak King in Ireland is the king of the waxing year (Yule to Midsummer).

❧ Potatoes, Ireland's staple crop, were used magickally in spells for healing and fertility, and were also carved into various forms for image magick much as the mandrake root is today. Because they grew underground potatoes were sacred to the Goddess and used in female fertility rites. Potatoes have a grounding effect. If you feel frazzled and stressed out cuddle a potato.

❧ Rowan, called "witchwood," was utilized in rites to increase one's psychic powers, and for divination. Some accounts claim it was carried to afford protection and to enhance personal power.

❧ Saffron, a costly herb, was used by the ancient Celts to adorn themselves for battle, and to draw into themselves personal power and healing. The Druids were credited with using saffron extensively for ritual purposes, especially as a tea to induce trance states.

❧ Turnips are another staple crop of Ireland and share the magickal properties of potatoes. The turnip is also a symbol of protection, and the first Samhain jack-o'-lanterns in Ireland were carved from turnips.

❧ Vervain, once said to be consumed for poetic inspiration, was used in purification rites, healing rituals, and love charms.

❧ Willow was used for healing, love charms, and protection (even burial mounds had willow placed in them). It is the wood of choice for wands. Willow is also used medicinally, particularly in treating women's unique health problems, and for decreasing inflammations and reducing fever. Fertility spells can also make use of willow.

There are several ways to use herbs magickally. They can be empowered and placed in a tub of water where you can sit and soak up their energies. They can be carried in a pouch or pocket, or they can be burned as an incense. Their power can also be released by burying them in the ground, throwing them into bodies of water, placing them about a dwelling, or blowing them into the wind. A number of herbal spells will be given in this chapter.

HEALING MAGICK

Before medical science knew enough to aid the healing process, magick, herbal remedies, and petitions to the deities were all people had to work with, and miraculous cures often occurred. However, many diseases simply needed a miracle called an antibiotic. There are several rules to follow when working for healing. Number one is *do not avoid seeking the aid of a medical practitioner you trust.* Magick and medicine are more closely related than most people realize, and one should use both in support of the other. After all, it was through many a magickal cure that medical answers were discovered. For centuries people in Ireland and elsewhere routinely prescribed willow bark tea for fevers and inflammations. It was from willow bark in the 1890s that the property commonly known as aspirin was isolated. The second rule is *do not work magick on behalf of anyone without his or her permission.* To do so is considered a violation of free will in conflict with the Wittan Rede.

In healing magick, as in most pre-Christian Irish cures, the Goddess in her guise as Mother Earth was often called upon to purge the sickness. This contact was made by using natural resources associated with earth and water, the two feminine elements. A sick person might have been asked to lie in a shallow pool of water and visualize the illness being washed from him or her, especially if near a flowing river where the illness could float away downstream. Another method was to encase the person in earth and do similar visualizations. In central

Africa, pagans utilize a cure which requires the patient to be buried up to the neck for a week. Though no visualization or ritual accompanies this act, the vast majority of the patients quickly recover; a fact which has baffled and upset missionaries for centuries.

Winds in Ireland were used to aid in healing for centuries. Patients were taken to a hill where brisk winds could blow away the sickness.

The oak tree, sacred to the Druids and to the ancient gods of the Celts, was said to have great healing power. To heal yourself find a large, friendly oak and concentrate on blending your energy with that of the tree. Ask if you might use its strength on your behalf. If you intuitively feel you have been given the tree's permission, put your arms around it, and let the tree draw the illness out of you and down into the earth.

Willow is another tree sacred to the ancient Celts and can be utilized in a similar manner, though the willow was viewed as a feminine tree whereas the oak was masculine. Hug a willow to cure reproductive problems, menstrual cramps, or emotional upheavals.

It is traditional to leave a gift for the tree afterwards, and many modern grimoires suggest a coin or precious stone. My suggestion is to leave food for the birds which build their homes in the tree's branches. Think of the tree as a mother. A coin is appreciated, but food with which to feed her young is really special.

Healing Waters Spell

This Irish healing charm comes in liquid form. Take equal parts of the herbs lavender, violet, and rosemary, empower them, and then boil them in a pot with about a quart of water over medium heat. When the water is richly colored and the herbs are scenting your kitchen, drain the water off into a jar. A plain coffee filter works great for this. Then take the jar and place it in the sunlight for an entire day to absorb the radiant energies of the sun (you can do this on a Wednesday if you wish to add the healing energies of Mercury to the spell). Occasionally look out at the jar and add your own energy to it.

Just before sundown fetch the jar and hold it firmly between your hands just below your navel. In India the navel chakra is associated with personal desire and will, and spell lore from all over Europe occasionally shows vestiges of this belief which no doubt traveled west thousands of years ago. Feel your desire to be well filling the jar, and with your mind's eye see it glowing as brightly as the sun itself. Chant these words over and over until you feel you have filled the jar with as much energy as it will hold.

By the herb and by the sun,
Wellness and I are now as one.
Strengthening energies now are merged,
Baneful energies now be purged.

The mixture is to be used to anoint spots where illness lurks, or on your belly if you are unsure where the source of your discomfort lies. Or you could even pour the contents of the jar into your bath water. Repeat the lines above as you anoint yourself or bathe.

Honegar

A great general tonic used throughout western Europe was called honegar. During the waxing moon in Ireland, advocates of folk medicine still make and use this mixture.

Pour one and a half pounds of raw honey and one and a half pounds of apple cider vinegar into a large pan (preferably one that is non-metal). There are a variety of vinegars available, but to attain a Wittan flavor use apple cider vinegar because of the apple's association with healing magick.

With a wooden spoon, constantly stir the mixture over medium heat. At first you will feel the heaviness of the honey settling on the bottom. As you keep stirring and the mixture warms you will gradually feel the honey blending with the vinegar. After 10-15 minutes you should no longer feel this sense of heaviness.

Remove the honegar from the stove top and let cool. Pour into jars with tight lids.

This recipe should make enough to dose two people for thirty days.

Before using, make an invoking pentagram on the jar while visualizing the honegar's restorative and preventative power. To administer, take two to three tablespoons daily. As many people find taking this straight distasteful, the honegar can be placed in an herbal tea or a glass of cold water to help cut the taste.

WIND MAGICK

Many ancient myths accompany wind, and this is probably one of the few areas in which a Wittan would have been really concerned about the geographical direction in which a spell took place.

West winds were powerful sources of magickal energy, and were used for spells involving the need to have something banished or for a complete life change, because in the pagan mind, rebirth would naturally follow any death. Very serious illnesses were treated with a west wind, as were pleas to the crone for wisdom, knowledge, or the sparing of someone's life.

In contrast, the east wind was one which indicated birth, light, intelligence, and creativity. This was where the sun rose each morning, and therefore the east was thought of as the source of all light. The creative aspect of the east and its light is still known today in the terms "bright idea," "see the light," and by the cartoon drawings of a light bulb over the heads of characters suddenly struck with inspiration. East winds were used in rituals for personal strength and creative endeavors. East winds were used to treat mental illness and slowness, and to initiate and cleanse the bards of poetry. If you have a creative block you need to overcome, go sit in an east wind.

A north wind, the traditional death wind in most of neo-paganism, is the wind of autumn which in Witta blows cold and strong, but does not blow death. To the ancient Wittans the north wind was one of mystery and of approaching winter. It was in the north, the place where the sun never traveled, that one could go to seek inner guidance. This wind is to be petitioned in times of deepest distress or confusion, and it is the wind most sought for divination rituals.

The wind of the south, in keeping with its polarity of the north, was a wind of warmth and summer. In later times it became associated with various sun gods such as Lugh. In general it was the most favorable wind for spell working of any kind, and was used for healing spells unless the person was on the verge of death, in which case the petitioner probably sought the power of the crone in the west wind. Because of the south's obvious affinity with the sun, protection, purification, and prosperity rituals were done in a south wind whenever possible.

FERTILITY MAGICK

The guaranteed proliferation of crops, animals, and people was a major concern to the old Wittans. Most of the sabbat rituals were (and still are) acts of sympathetic magick to promote fertility of the land and herds. Without irrigation, pesticides, or knowledge of soil mineralogy, raising the food supply for a community was a scary responsibility, especially if nature should turn hostile. Likewise a barren couple had nowhere to turn but to magick for their difficulties for no medical knowledge of the fine workings of the human reproductive system existed. In fact, of the 50,000 years of human history, the male role in reproduction has only been known for the last 8000, and the exact way in which both systems work together is a twentieth-century discovery.

Since the earth was where the Mother Goddess showed her fertile abundance, most fertility spells are related to the earth element, and occasionally to water.

The discovery of a stone with a natural hole in it was considered a powerful amulet for fertility. It was a stone of the earth whose form had been carved by water, both elements of the Goddess. Many of the ancient standing stone sites in Ireland and Britain contain very large holey stones through which women passed themselves in fertility rituals. Irish women would pass through these nine times clockwise while murmuring prayers to Brigid. Near one of these large holey stones one usually finds at least one large, projective standing stone which was used as a potent phallic symbol. The best known of these types of stone groups is the Men-an-Tol in Celtic Cornwall to where many pilgrimages were made by barren Celtic women.

Small children were gathered to crawl on their hands and knees under the spread legs of a woman who wanted to conceive. The sympathetic magick image of this act is quite apparent. In some Native American and African cultures similar rituals still exist and the entire tribe contributes their energy and visualization powers to the working.

Green, the color of abundant nature, was also called into action. Green candles, talismans, and clothing (if you are not afraid of offending faeries who jealously guard their exclusive right to green clothes) were used by infertile women to enact sympathetic fertility spells.

Pine trees, prevalent in the magick of western Europe, were also used as talismans and arbiters of fertility. Structure-wise they are phallic symbols, and yet they represent the eternal Great Mother because they are evergreen. Pine needles can be magickally charged and carried, or the tree can be hugged, drawing the fertile power of the united God and Goddess into oneself.

In Ireland it was customary to tie up a small clump of hair from living rabbits, goats, and the tail of a horse. Rabbits and goats were viewed as animals of great fertile powers. The horse tail is something of a mystery, but may have some association with the Celtic horse goddess, Epona, the bringer of dreams. Tie the hairs together with a green or white thread and carry them with you.

Rice and wheat promote fertility, and for centuries many cultures have practiced showering newly married couples with these grains. Try burying a small bag of rice, wheat, and mugwort while visualizing your pregnancy. Or invest your energy in some seeds which you plant near your home. As the seeds grow, hopefully, so will you.

Caves, viewed as wombs of Mother Earth, were also used in fertility rites. Sometimes couples made love out under a full moon—representative of the mother aspect of the Goddess—to absorb those beneficial fertility energies.

Fertility Spell

You will need to have enough fertility herbs to work this spell in multiples of three. Some of these herbs include rice, wheat, mugwort, bistort, pine needles, oats, saffron, willow leaves, jasmine, moonwort, oak leaves, green grass, and primrose. Gather up either three, six, or nine of these and carry them in your bare hands to a place outside where you will be alone and where you can dig a small hole to bury them. Try to pick a place where you believe they will be undisturbed for a long period of time.

When you find the spot, stop and collect your thoughts. Begin concentrating on your fertility. If you are female distend your stomach in an imitation of pregnancy and let yourself believe it is real.

Kneel, and with your non-dominant hand dig a small hole about six inches deep. Hold the herbs up to your mouth and breathe on them as you visualize yourself (or your mate) pregnant with a healthy baby. Breath, like blood, was thought by ancient people to be the essence of life; so in effect you are "breathing life" into the fertility herbs, and consequently into your womb.

When you feel you have accomplished that task, place the herbs in the hole and cover them saying:

> *Blessed herbs of Mother Earth, return to the earth to be the perfect catalyst for my fertility. In the name of Brigid, the Mother Goddess, I say ... So Mote It Be!*

With the forefinger of your power hand, draw an invoking pentagram on the earth where the herbs are buried. Don't forget to follow up this spell with the necessary physical requirements!

Bealtaine Fertility Talisman

Bealtaine is a sabbat which celebrates the fertility of people, animals, and crops, and is a perfect time to start a fertility talisman. Since no magickal work should be done on a sabbat (a time of rest), do this the night after.

You will need a small section of green or white cloth, a needle and thread, a piece of silver (a coin will do), some ashes from the Bealtaine bonfire, and any fertility herbs you choose to use. Make sure that the items you are using are in multiples of three.

Take the white cloth and sew a small square, leaving one end open. Turn the pouch inside out for a neater, finished look.

With two pieces of fabric held together, sew up only three sides.

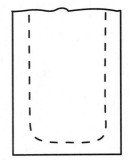

Turn the pouch inside out to present a more finished look. Place herbs and other items in the open side, then sew the open side closed.

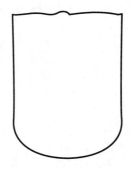

As you sew visualize your goal of pregnancy and a healthy child. You might even want to slip in a picture of a baby (cut from a catalog, for example) to help you make a better connection with the talisman.

Then take the items you have collected and empower them. When you are ready, place them in the pouch one by one while still focusing upon your goal.

With the needle and thread sew up the top of the pouch. You should then carry this with you during the day and place it under your bed at night until you achieve your goal.

PREGNANCY AND CHILDBIRTH SPELLS

Even today women are acutely aware that the mere fact of pregnancy does not assure that a baby will live to be born, or that it will be born healthy and whole. Quite naturally spells were created to aid the unborn child's growth and his or her eventual safe emergence into the world.

In Ireland, bloodstones were carried by pregnant women to guard against miscarriage. Then the stones were placed inside the covers of the birthing bed to help prevent hemorrhaging and breech births.

Holly water, made from boiling holly berries, was used to anoint the stomach during pregnancy to prevent miscarriage. Later, holly sprigs would be hung over the cradle to help ward off "crib death."

If you are fearful of miscarriage get lots of rest, see a doctor, and keep visualizing the joyful, perfect outcome of your pregnancy.

Childbirth was another fearful time as many new mothers died in childbirth at alarming rates. As mentioned above, the worst fear was hemorrhaging. Washing the sheets of the birthing bed in saffron was thought to help prevent this. Blackberries, sacred to Brigid, the supreme Great Mother, were given to the mother-to-be in the form of blackberry tea. This was thought to help ease the pains of childbirth and to prevent hemorrhaging.

LOVE MAGICK

As I mentioned before, love magick is especially susceptible to infractions of the Wittan Rede simply because when one is faced with the pain of unrequited love it is hard not to use every means at one's disposal to change that fact. Please don't! It is best simply to use magick to draw—not force—love into your life. By not naming the person in your spells, you will not violate anyone else's free will, and the spells will work a lot faster by being less encumbered.

The oldest form of love spells are charms, talismans, or ointments which are worn on the person to attract love.

The apple, sacred to the Goddess, is a love herb of long standing. One Irish folk practice which survives to this day says that if a young woman eats an apple while sitting before a mirror on May Eve she will see the face of her future husband.

Apples have been hung and dried as magick cords to draw love, and their toxic seeds buried deep in the earth to ground any negative influence which prevents love from entering one's life. Visualizing yourself having love while eating an apple is another way to make an apple's love energies work for you.

Tying up a small pouch with willow, rose, and apple is another old charm for attracting love. Traditionally the pouch is white, but try pink for peaceful love, yellow for intellectual love, or red for passionate love.

Rose or vanilla oils and ointments rubbed onto the skin also have been said to be an effective love charm, though I would avoid the use of vanilla if you are not partial to sweet, confectionary scents.

Burning a love-related herb, such as vervain, in a fireplace, or burning an empowered willow log is also thought to work. Vervain hung over a doorway will entice your love to walk through it to you. Other love-related herbs are orris root, lavender, dogwood, vanilla, apples and apple blossoms, rose, violet, myrtle, gardenia, apricots, and yarrow.

Musk was once considered to be a potent love scent which would attract passionate romance when worn on the skin. But musk comes from animals, usually from deer, and should not be used. A few companies however do market synthetic types of "musk."

Another Irish love potion is a hair rinse made from orris root, parsley, and lavender. Boil the herbs for about thirty minutes in two cups of water then drain them. A coffee filter is best for this. The rinse actually smells like a soft perfume. Be sure to empower your herbs and visualize.

Remember that with any spell you must put your energy and visualization into it to get anything out of it. No matter how tempting it may be, try not to visualize the face of any one particular person, though it is perfectly all right to dwell on the qualities of a person you admire.

Dogwood Flowers Love Spell

Dogwood flowers are another love catalyst. Take nine flowers from a dogwood tree, and on a piece of paper draw a representation of the perfect mate for you. Focus on inner rather than outer characteristics.

To set up the spell, find a place in your home which is not likely to be disturbed for a long time. A dresser drawer is a good place if nowhere else can be found. But it is best to leave it in sight where you will be reminded to feed it energy from time to time.

Set the drawing in the center of the work area and begin to empower your spell by feeling your psychic connection with your mate-to-be. Now, one by one, place the flowers around the picture moving clockwise. With each flower you lay, say this charm:

> *Love flower one, the spell's begun.*
> *Love flower two, I search for you.*
> *Love flower three, be drawn to me.*
> *Love flower four, come through my door.*
> *Love flower five, to you I strive.*
> *Love flower six, you are who I pick.*
> *Love flower seven, our love like bread leaven.*
> *Love flower eight, come be my mate.*
> *Love flower nine, our love is fine.*
> *Back to one, the spell is done.*
> *Nine flowers of love here do lay,*
> *Bringing now new love my way.*

Leave the flowers and drawing out until the flowers are completely withered, then bury them in the earth or toss them in a body of flowing water such as a river. Keep the drawing with you until the spell has manifested.

Mandrake Mate Spell

Get a mandrake root, an herbal root which naturally resembles a human form, and, with a sharp knife, carve an image of the love you seek. While you fill out the physical form be sure to concentrate on the qualities of the person you desire without stepping over the line and actually visualizing a specific person.

When you have finished, prick the end of your ring finger (third finger of the left hand) and allow a small drop of blood to fall onto the mandrake.

Place the mandrake under your bed. Every night before you go to sleep remove it from under the bed and and hold it while focusing on your love goal. Say these words with all the meaning you can muster.

> *Mandrake root, my mate so right,*
> *Send out my call for love tonight.*
> *May all I have invested in you*
> *Send me soon my love come true.*

DIVINATION

The Druids drank saffron tea before attempting divination as the herb was reputed to open the psychic centers. If you find you have trouble getting accurate divinations, you might try this. Another remedy is making an incense of wormwood, myrtle, and mugwort. Toss the dried herbs on hot charcoal blocks to release their power.

Elaborate aids such as the Tarot (which has its roots in the ancient Middle East) were virtually unknown in Celtic Ireland. Divination, the act of seeking information about the future, was done with the natural materials at hand.

One of the most common methods of divination is scrying. Scrying is the act of gazing at something while concentrating on your question until the deep mind produces a prophetic vision. Some books on witchcraft give complex formulas for creating an object to scry into, and others suggest the classic crystal ball. But in old Ireland scrying was most commonly done in a fire, candle, shiny stone, or in a pond with the sun or moon's light reflecting off the surface.

The technique is not complicated, but it usually takes practice to become successful. Simply relax, clear your mind of all but your question, and gaze at and into the surface you are using. Don't stare, but soften your focus and simply gaze. With practice, visions will come more quickly, and can come as either completely played out dramas, or as simple symbol pictures which only you can interpret. Above all, trust yourself to interpret your own symbols for they are a projection of your own subconscious and therefore only you can fully know the symbology of its darkest realms.

Tossing stones was another method very popular among the ancient Celts. An individual would gather stones which either by their color or shape had certain archetypal meaning. The stones were then placed in a pouch which were carried around so that their energy would meld with that of the carrier. While mentally focusing upon the question, the petitioner tossed the stones at a circle drawn on the ground. Stones falling in the circle had the most direct influence on the petitioner, and those outside had less. Which stones fell where, and how closely they fell to others, was interpreted for meaning.

The Druids' practices of divination were closely guarded secrets, often performed only in times of national crises at the request of the high king of Ireland. Exactly what went on is shrouded in two thousand years of mystery and rumor. Some believe the Druids fed a chosen seer small doses of poisonous herbs until a vision was induced. The seer would not live through the ritual, but was honored with a hero's burial. Others contend that they used group ritual trances to contact benevolent spirits who would provide answers. It is possible both or neither of these methods was used, but books on Druidic divination practice make fascinating reading for those interested in Celtic paganism.

Wittans often looked to nature not only for answers to problems, but for information, confirmation, or warnings about choices already made. They would venture into nature in much the same manner as a Native American vision quest, and seek signs, either positive or negative, about the path their lives were taking. Traditional times for these ventures were at the Spring and Fall Equinoxes, on May Eve (Bealtaine), or at the new moon.

Many books on Native American spirituality have tried to make comprehensive lists of birds, animals, and natural phenomena and what they might mean to a seeker. But the best guide to the meaning of something you see is what it means to you alone.

Some people become very belligerent when they are asked to trust their own feelings about symbolism, but to have an accurate divination that is all one can do. Take the symbol of a dog, for example.

Say two people out walking see a dog. One person who has had long associations with dogs as loving and loyal family pets interprets the sighting of a dog as a positive sign, possibly with overtones of fidelity to whatever his or her concerns are. The other person is afraid of dogs. He or she has never owned one, or maybe had been bitten by one or even encountered a rabid dog at some point. In any case, the second person sees the dog as a negative sign, perhaps even as a portent of impending illness or accident.

Use another person's symbology list only as a raw guide, and only then when you are in doubt. Let your own higher mind tell you what any sighting or vision means for you. After all, you are seeking answers for yourself, not for somebody else.

Projection Magick

Another important Wittan practice centered around projecting oneself into the consciousness of an animal, tree, plant, or stone. The purpose was to experience life through the senses of that animal or object, to learn lessons from the experience, and to glean any useful information those beings or objects might have to share. This was a very practical exercise in old Ireland. For instance, if you projected yourself into a deer, and that deer had witnessed the massing together of an army to move against you, this was something you would need to know. And if you projected your consciousness into a stone and learned the virtue of patience, the experience would be well worth the effort.

This is a somewhat advanced magickal technique, and to do this you must be fairly adept at projecting your consciousness outside of your body (astral projection) and directing its movements. You must send yourself to an animal, tree, stone, or other part of nature and feel yourself meld and move with it, rather like an astral piggyback ride. You must also ask permission of that animal or object first. To invade it uninvited is a violation of the Wittan Rede.

There are many methods of achieving astral projection. One of the easiest is to lie or sit still, relaxing as fully as possible, until you can no longer feel the sensation of being part of your physical body. All the while focus on only one thing such as a symbol or a name. Counting backwards from one hundred over and over helps relax and blank your mind. After an extended period of this, your brain will rebel and your consciousness, bored with the inactivity, automatically will go elsewhere.

Conscious control of astral projection takes effort and practice. If you feel you can gain and grow from astral experiences, then you should begin to work with them as soon as possible.

MIRROR MAGICK

There are several methods for obtaining your own magick mirror. The simplest way is to buy one. Find a round one that is about eight inches in diameter. That is a rough figure. Your mirror can be smaller or larger, but you don't want it to be too large or you will have trouble controlling what is reflecting on its surface. Cleanse the mirror by boiling a teaspoonful of mugwort in two cups of water. Wipe the mirror with the water and a clean cloth or paper towel. Mugwort is the herb usually recommended for cleaning any magickal object. As you wipe, let as much of your energy as possible flow into the mirror.

On the night of the full moon take your mirror outside and let the moon shine onto its surface. If you can't get outside then go to a window. The only thing needed here is for the moon itself to reflect off the surface. The moon is the planet of psychism and is the perfect way to charge and bless your magick mirror.

When you feel your mirror has absorbed enough energy hold it up and consecrate it by saying something like this:

> *Mother Moon, thank you for sharing your*
> *energies with this magick tool of mine. I*
> *bless it in your name, Mother Brigid, that*
> *it will be used as an instrument of positive*
> *magick only. May it open my second sight*
> *for the mutual good. So Mote It Be!*

It is suggested that you keep your mirror in a dark place when not in use, and never let the rays of the sun reflect off it or it will "burn off" the moon energies and you will have to recharge it. Some witches like to periodically recharge their mirrors anyway, just for an added boost of lunar energy.

To make a mirror specifically for scrying take a circle of plain glass and paint several coats of black flat paint on the back. Cleanse and consecrate it in the same way as you would a regular mirror.

Your mirror can be used for spirit contact by scrying into it (instructions are provided in Chapter 5). It can be used to reflect away negativity by placing it near a burning candle of protection. You can use it for divination by gazing into it when only the light of the full moon or a single candle is reflected off its surface. You can practice divination by focusing on a question as you look into its depths, or satisfy yourself that a distant loved one is well by concentrating on the individual as you will yourself to see him or her as he or she is at that moment.

PROTECTION MAGICK

In the not too distant past it was common to believe that negative influences dogged people who were having a bad time with their health, crops, or personal life. Often these influences were thought to come from evil spirits, and at other times from the baneful magick of a jealous neighbor. Negative energy is certainly very real, and the extent to which it can do harm is dependent upon the energy with which it was sent to you, intentionally or unintentionally. It was believed to be more prudent to take preventative measures to stop negativity before it reached you than to have to fight it off once it was there. Many grimoires, new and old, devote much space to a variety of magickal protection rites.

The most common form of protection is the circle, that magickal energy barrier. The symbol of a circle as a veil of protection comes from deepest antiquity. To protect yourself or your home, visualize a protective circle building an impenetrable "force field" around yourself or your dwelling. If possible light candles at the directional quarters as you raise the energy. This latter ritual once served the practical purpose of scaring wild animals away from a settlement.

Placing a knife inside a chalice each night is another way to prevent negativity, in either astral or physical form, from entering your home. This works best if a man places the knife in the chalice while it is being held by a woman. As the knife is placed inside say these words.

> *Knife so sharp with cutting blade,*
> *Guard this dwelling from thief and shade.*
> *Chalice open, yawning wide,*
> *Let no being enter where we abide.*
> *Knife well-honed, and chalice deep,*
> *Guard this dwelling while we sleep.*

Burning candles before reflective surfaces such as glass, water, or a mirror can be used to send the negativity back from whence it came. But to some this act violates the idea of the Wittan Rede. If this image bothers you, think of the negative energy being deflected harmlessly out into the heavens far away from you.

Spell to Reflect Negativity

You will need your magick mirror, a wide-mouthed glass jar, ashes, vinegar, a knife or other carving tool, and an apple.

After sundown, set the glass before the mirror. Inside it place some ashes and then fill the jar about two thirds of the way with vinegar.

Take the apple and with the carving tool draw a representation of the negativity which is following you. Make this as clear and unmistakable as you can. While you are carving, infuse the apple with the essence of the negativity.

Raise the apple above the glass and say:

> *Evil send must come to rest,*
> *Reflect it back to who knows it best.*
> *Energy spent for evil and bane,*
> *Go back now from whence you came.*
> *Far away I send you this hour,*
> *May all your attempts to harm turn sour.*

Place the apple in the jar. The chemical reaction you get will be worth watching. In essence you have created the same acidic condition present in a battery. The apple should dance and fizzle as the negativity around you is collected and sent away. For best results, this spell should be repeated for three consecutive nights.

Witch Bottles

Bottles of earth are sometimes kept in Irish cottages because of an ancient belief that evil spirits had to count all grains of earth within a dwelling before they could take up residence there.

No one knows where the idea of the witch bottle originated. The many cultures which clamor to claim it are testament to its effectiveness.

This bottle is a container—usually a glass jar—filled with various items which symbolize protection to the maker. Broken glass, rosemary, salt, ashes, vinegar, pins, alcohol, garlic, basil, dill, oak twigs, broom, needles, nails, urine, saliva, and blood have all been used in witch bottles. I have made a number of these and have found them excellent deflectors of negativity. I personally prefer to top mine off with urine. The thought of doing this rather disgusting thing to your unknown enemies provides the kind of belly laugh which gives a boost to your deep mind from where the protection energy actually emanates.

As you place each item in the bottle imagine how that item will attack and destroy negativity. Picture the needles puncturing it, the herbs diffusing it, the blood grounding it, and the glass cutting it.

When you have filled your jar with all the things you wish to include, seal it and bury it outside your front door while visualizing the bottle stopping the negativity which has been dogging you. After you bury the bottle draw a banishing pentagram in the earth over it.

FIRE MAGICK

Fire was probably the most commonly used element for spell working simply because it was always available. Wood, magickally charged and burned in a fireplace, was used for magickal purposes, and divinations were performed by gazing into the fire and watching for visions.

The bonfires of the sabbats are also symbols of magickal transformation from one season to another. Throwing empowered herbs on any sabbat fire was thought to produce quick results as the old gods (and possibly some sympathetic ancestral spirits) were nearby joining in the festivities.

The smooring (smothering) of peat fires has been given magickal associations in Ireland clear up to the present day. Fire was magick in and of itself, a gift of the deities. It was once believed that to extinguish a fire was to risk death—not a hard to reach conclusion when until recently it was the only form of heat and energy we had. Having no native coal, the Irish would cut peat from the peat bogs to burn as fuel. Peat is still the major source of household energy in much of rural Ireland. When the fire was smoored, or banked, for the night it was traditional for mothers to use the smoke to offer up prayers for the protection of their children.

When using fire or candle magick (see following page) confine yourself to one magickal goal per fire or candlestick. To do more scatters your energies and will do you little good.

CANDLE MAGICK

Candle spells were simple affairs requiring nothing more than the witch and a candle. Occasionally the candle would be anointed with an herb or oil whose energies were known to be friendly to the goal. Sometimes candles were colored according to magickal need (e.g., green for fertility, white for protection, etc.), but most often whatever candle was inexpensive and on hand was used.

The basic method for doing this type of spell is to sit before a candle and gaze into the flame while concentrating on your magickal goal. Know that as the candle is consumed, your desire is being taken into the world of spirit to be returned manifest in the world of form. Spells can be dressed up with all sorts of charges and ritual dances and other energy builders, but those are not strictly necessary.

Candles also can be used to banish something from your life. With a knife or another carving tool draw upon the candle that which you seek to lose such as a bad habit, extra weight, or too many bills. Then burn the empowered candle with the clear visualization that as the flames consume the physical representation of your problem, that it is also being consumed in the astral and will come to be ... or rather, not to be.

Candles make good scrying instruments as well. As you scry into the candle flames chant these words:

> *Candle, candle burning bright,*
> *In the darkness of the night.*
> *Bring to me my second sight,*
> *Past and future in your light.*

FIREPLACE MAGICK

No matter how well old Irish cottages were closed up against the winter or other elements, there was one opening which by necessity had to remain open—the fireplace flue. The fireplace has long been regarded as the magickal portal of a home. It was through this opening that witches were said to fly away on their broomsticks, and in modern mythology it is the opening through which Santa Claus comes and goes. The word hearth contains the word "heart," and indeed it was the center of home life. In it food was cooked, clothes washed, and by its light families gathered to visit and tell stories. Due to its vital importance, Wittans devised magickal ways to protect the fireplace.

One of the easiest ways to protect the fireplace was by tossing a handful of protective herbs onto the already smoldering fire, or to add a log of protective wood. Common herbs of protection include oak leaves, cloves, holly, rosemary, frankincense, cinnamon, and nettles. Oranges are also protective and their skins burn fragrantly.

Setting a witch's besom near the fireplace or crossing the andirons were also ways of blocking the entrance of negativity. Keeping a cauldron boiling on the hearth was another. Some fireplaces were decorated with three circles above the opening, often interlinked like rings. This ancient practice probably harkens back to a very old belief that the Triple Goddess protected any home wherein a fire was kindled. The sun god Lugh could also be called upon to protect the hearth by hanging a pouch containing the first harvest's first picked grain on the mantle. This also had the added bonus of being a fertility charm.

Other herbs and grains were often hung to dry near the hearth, the heat and dryness curing and preserving the plants until they were ready to be used. These herbs could be enchanted and hung up as an additional talisman to protect the fireplace.

Scrying by hearth light is a relaxing pastime, and gazing softly into a roaring fire is an age old practice. As you relax your gaze, visions should appear in the flames. Various bits of folklore say one can predict the future by the manner in which the coals, peat, or wood burns. Whether they sputter, or pop, or glow red, or flame high all answer questions about the future.

The fireplace can be as magickal as your imagination will allow. Here you are working directly with the transformative element of fire, and how you choose to utilize it is up to you and your inner self.

CORD AND KNOT MAGICK

Cord and knot magick are very familiar in Ireland. Druids were said to tie cords around their waists in various colors dependent upon their craft specialty, with the number of knots in it dependent upon their rank. Cords as an archetype have long been thought to "tie up" and "hold" power, and the abundant cord lore of the island is still heard today. It is common to make sure no knots are to be found in the household of a pregnant woman until after she has given birth for fear that the sympathetic magick of the knots will tie the umbilical cord around the infant's neck. Circles were often drawn with a cord to measure its radius, and high priests and priestesses were bound together with them for fertility rituals. Handfastings used garlands as cords to symbolize the union of marriage, and cords have been used to symbolically tie up negativity, and to bind an object to its owner.

Knotted cords are used to store moon energies so that the energies can be utilized in magick when the moon phase is not best for the spell being worked. As with other magickal tools, the more you are involved in the crafting of them, the better they are attuned to you, and therefore the better they will serve you.

To make a cord for storing moon energy find three links of natural material (wool is best) and during the proper moon phase braid them together to form a cord approximately three feet long. Different traditions have different colors they associate with each cord. In ancient Ireland people would have used whatever material was at hand, in more modern times (and please remember that "modern" here is a relative term) it is traditional to use the colors of the Triple Goddess. Use white for the waxing moon, or her virgin aspect. Use red for the full moon, the Great Mother aspect. And choose the traditional black of the crone for the waning moon.

To capture the moon energy you need a clear night where you can see the moon clearly and can stand beneath her with no visual obstructions. Cast a circle and begin drawing moon energy into your cord by presenting it to the moon. Call on the name of the proper aspect of the Triple Goddess of Ireland if you wish (Danu, Brigid, Badb), and feel the energy flowing into the cord. Then, while still holding the cord before the moon, begin tying nine knots in the cord. Nine is the traditional number of the moon which dates back far into ancient history. In tying each knot know that a part of that moon phase's energy is held within. When you make your ninth knot it will be the knot which ties the cord in a full circle.

The energy is there to stay, but if you feel it necessary you can lay the cord out beneath the proper moon phase to recharge it. Keep the cords in individual pouches away from all other magickal objects and definitely out of any sunlight.

The cords can then be utilized in future spell work. For example, if you need to quickly banish a negative influence and don't want to work your spell while the moon is waxing, use your waning moon cord to lend banishing energy to your magick. You can hold it, wear it around your neck, encircle a candle or stone with it, or use it to charge herbs.

Other magickal energy can be stored in a cord. If you have an economic windfall and know you might be in need of another one in the future, use a cord to capture the energy of the prosperity so that it can be tapped in future money spells. Cords can be picked out for their color in relation to the work you wish to do either by a guide book or, better still, your own intuition. The number of knots and length of the cord should likewise be chosen by your own gut feeling. In the case of money, most witches would choose a green cord, the color of fertility and crops. They would devise a ritual in which the money or check or some representation of the windfall comes in contact with the cord, transferring its energy to the cord. Knots are usually chosen in multiples of three, the traditional Wittan and Wiccan number of completion.

Cords can also help you lose things as well as attain them. If you wish, for example, to rid yourself of a bad habit such as nail biting, tie up the energy in the cord. Infuse each knot you tie with the bad habit. You might even want to tie a bit of broken nail into one of them. Set the cord aside for a week or so to let the energy of the habit become well set into the cord. While the cord is setting you should be consciously remembering the habit you are trying to break and thinking about ways to help yourself do this.

When you are ready to banish the problem for good, take the cord and untie each knot, releasing the negative energy of the habit. Visualize the unwanted energy flowing into the ground out of harm's way.

Be creative with your cord magick. You have at hand one of Ireland's most ancient and respected magickal formulas. The energy is there for you to use.

HAIR MAGICK

Witta uses as many natural resources and natural objects as possible for magick, and one of the most utilized was human or animal hair. The folklore of the world is rife with stories of power tied up in locks of hair.

Have you ever sat brushing your hair, or that of a pet, on a cold night and felt the static electricity rise in intensity with each swipe of the brush? Stroking, combing or brushing hair raises energy, and concentrating on just what to do with that energy gives you an opportunity each day to send energy towards some goal.

As you are brushing your hair, or your pets, imagine the energy concentrating in a huge swirling cone above you. As you do this also visualize your magickal intention. When you are ready to stop, project the energy outward either with the brush, your hand, or your mind.

STONE MAGICK

Stone magick was popular for things other than divinations. Stones were carried as amulets based on their color and shape. Round stones were for wishes, and square ones were protective. Red stones healed and green stones brought fertility or prosperity. Some were said to bestow magickal powers. The famous Blarney Stone is a carry-over of this belief, as kissing it in the prescribed ritual manner is said to produce the gift of "blarney" or glib speech.

EARTH TO WATER SPELL

One simple spell (for gaining or banishing) which still exists both in Ireland and in other European cultures is an earth to water spell. Find a secluded spot near a river. A river is best, but an ocean, lake, or even a shallow creek will work. Sit on the earth, take off your shoes, make as much contact between yourself and the earth as possible. Try to choose a spot of rich, fertile earth with as few stones as possible. In your power hand (your dominant one) gather up a handful of earth. Get the feel of it between your fingers, feel the life and energy within it. Pour your difficulty into the clump of earth, tell it what you need or what you wish banished from your life. Be sure to visualize clearly. When you feel the earth has absorbed your energy, cast it into the water knowing that your troubles are gone, or that your desire will be realized.

If one is lucky enough to live near the sea one could draw desires or ills into the sand and let the surf carry them out to manifestation.

SPELLS FOR SAFE TRAVEL

If you wish to perform a spell to insure your safe return from a trip, pick up three small stones at random and place them in your pocket. Tell the stones that you will return them to their home when you return. The stones will protect you until you come back and return them to their original resting spots. Be sure to thank them for their aid.

A similar spell consists of taking the three herbs (or just one if that's all you can find) most closely associated with safe travel—mugwort, Irish moss, and hazel—and tying them into a small white or gold pouch.

Empower the pouch and place it in your car if you will be driving, or in your luggage. This charm will protect you until you arrive home. At that time you should return the herbs to the earth, thank them for their aid, and then burn the pouch.

SPELL TO GAIN THE WISDOM OF THE CRONE

The crone aspect of the Goddess is associated with winter, a time of repose and death. If you want to tap into the vast energies of wisdom she possesses, collect some snow, enough to make a cup of tea, and boil the snow while visualizing the vast crone energy of winter. You may drink the water plain, or add some herbs to make an herbal tea. Associated with the crone are apple, heather, dittany of Crete, catnip, wintergreen, boneset, hazel, valerian, peppermint, and willow.

If you live in an area where you are not likely to ever get snow, try empowering some of these herbs with the energies of a waning moon (the darker the moon, the better) and making a tea of them.

SPELL FOR PEACE IN THE HOME

Peace in the home can be shattered by argument, addictions, negative energies from outside, or just from the stress of daily living. Try this spell to help bring peace and contentment to your home. It is best to do this spell on three consecutive Fridays.

You will need a pink or white taper candle, some matches, and a glass of water. You will also need one of the herbs which has an affinity for peace such as huckleberry root, vervain, lavender, burdock, chamomile, or linden.

Empower your herbs and candle. Boil the herbs in a cup of water. Strain, and place the water in a small glass cup.

Concentrate on your home as a peaceful and happy place. Then light the candle. Carry it into every room of your home while visualizing peace lighting every inch of the place. Say this chant as you go:

> *Candle shine and candle glow,*
> *Spreading peace where e'er you go.*

Return to your starting point and pick up the cup with the herb water. Walk through every room in your house and, with your fingertips, toss small particles of the water around you. Say this chant as you go:

> *Water of blessing, water of peace,*
> *Strife and arguments must now cease.*

Return to your starting point and spend a few moments in quiet visualizations and meditations.

Remember that all spells have to be backed up with actions in the physical world. In this case family counseling, stress management classes, or medical intervention for an addiction may be needed.

HOUSE BLESSING

When you move into a new home, or to give boost to the energies of your old one, you might want to try a Celtic house blessing. The original form of this spell required driving livestock through one door and out another, but I think we can dispense with that aspect of the spell.

Place some salt in a chalice of water. You might also want to add elder flowers and huckleberry root. With your power hand, sprinkle this mixture around the house. As you do, say the following:

This house is blessed by water,
This house is blessed by earth,
May the air here always be sweet,
And a fire glow in our hearth.

SPELL FOR MENTAL POWERS

On a day when the wind is blowing from the east, go outside with a handful of ground rosemary. Starting in the west blow some of the herbs into the wind while concentrating on increasing your intelligence and your mental powers. Turn next to the north and repeat. Then do this in the east and the south.

When the herbs are spent turn into the east wind and say:

East wind, blow to me the powers of intel-
lect. Stimulate my brain that it may have
the strength to accomplish all that is asked
of it. So Mote It Be!

ANTI-GOSSIP SPELL

This is a spell a friend and I did several years ago when an organization we were trying to establish was being threatened by vicious lies and backstabbing. The spell was successful within a month and we have had no trouble with gossip from the guilty parties since.

This spell is very simple. Go out to where there is a spot of earth where you can dig a small hole, one which will not be disturbed for some time. Take three small cloves and empower them with your need to have gossip halted. It is especially good if you know the source of the gossip and can visualize that person's mouth being silenced—do not, however, visualize that person being harmed in any way.

Bury the herbs in the earth and visualize the earth diffusing and grounding the gossip. Walk away without looking back.

Remember that if you want an anti-gossip spell to work you must not give into the temptation to gossip yourself. Ignoring gossip seems to be the one social skill that children are never taught, or if they are, they learn differently by their parents' actions. It is unbefitting for a Wittan to gossip. Gossip, like bigotry, is one of the most potent weapons humans have with which to hurt each other. Therefore gossip causes harm, and to indulge in it violates the Wittan Rede.

SPELL FOR PROPHETIC DREAMS

Make a small pouch out of white fabric or a lace material. This pouch will be a pillow which you will place underneath your usual pillow to induce prophetic dreams. Fill the pillow with herbs which are known to aid prophecy. Use them in multiples of three. Some of these herbs are mugwort, jasmine, willow, oak leaves, holly berries, mistletoe, yarrow, broom, orris root, ivy, shamrock, rose, and heliotrope.

Empower them with your need and sew them up. Place the pillow under your own pillow. Every night before you go to sleep tell yourself that you will dream true. Kiss the herb pillow and then go to sleep.

Note: Keeping a dream diary can be very helpful. If you record your dreams the absolute second that you awaken you will find that within a few weeks you will be remembering an incredible number of dreams. Over time you will be able to notice the prophetic patterns.

ALL-PURPOSE MONEY SPELL

Money is associated with the element earth, and this money spell is a very earthy one. It utilizes the potato, that old staple of the Irish diet.

You will need a raw potato, a knife, nine toothpicks, and any three money herbs. Some of these are pine needles, dill seed, barley, hay, turnips, sugar beets, nuts, peas, oak leaves, rice, oats, shamrocks, cowslip, and wheat. Turnips are another staple crop of Ireland and can be used in place of the potato in this spell.

Empower all your items and then cut the potato in half. Hollow out a small place in the halves where you can place any three of your money herbs. When you have done that, use the nine toothpicks to put the potato back together again.

Go to a place where you can dig a small hole, one which will not be disturbed for a long time. It is best to find the blackest, richest earth you can find in the area where you live.

Visualize your need for money. It will help if you have a specific goal for the money, such as paying a pressing bill. Bury the potato in the earth. As you place the dirt back over the potato let your hands work the dirt. Feel the richness of the land, know you are a part of it and that the needed money is on its way.

With your non-dominant hand draw an invoking pentagram over the place where the potato is buried. You use this hand because it is your receptive hand and is used to draw things—such as money—to you.

THE CONE OF POWER

If you have done much reading about witchcraft you have no doubt heard of the cone of power. This vortex of magickal energy is raised and contained within a ritual circle by one or more witches working for the same goal. The idea of a cone of energy overhead gave rise to the popular patriarchal image of the Halloween witch wearing a pointed hat.

The idea of the cone is that the power can be raised to a peak, held within the confines of the magick circle, and then released and sent to do its assigned job. The people of the United Kingdom had great respect for the power raised within a circle. In one well-known folktale, the pagans of the islands raised the cone of power, bringing on the massive storm which destroyed the Spanish Armada in 1588, for which they were personally thanked by Queen Elizabeth I. (For those interested in royal connections with occult groups start by researching Elizabeth who was believed to have had more than just a passing interest in paganism.)

The most common method of power raising is dancing. Tradition dictates that one dances deosil (clockwise) for spells of increase or attraction, and widdershins (counterclockwise) for decreasing or banishing spells. Start the dance at a steady and stately pace using whatever accompanying music you wish. There are several recordings available of drumming which can be used for power raising. Then slowly begin to speed up the pace, continuing this way until you can literally feel the mass of energy raised above you. Then, concentrating on the goal, release the energy to go to where it is needed, or send it into the world of the unformed to manifest. The cone of power is an extremely ancient and efficacious method of directing energy, so keep in mind the Wittan Rede as you decide where your energy is to be sent.

THE ELEMENTS OF SPELL CONSTRUCTION

In an earth religion a spell can utilize virtually anything which comes from nature. The power is not as much in the object as within the deep mind. Elemental representations are less a concern than the will and force of the magician. In old Ireland the people lived close to nature. The elements were all around them, and utilizing artificial representations of them, as in the form of ritual tools, was unnecessary.

Once you decide to create a spell follow these basic steps:

❧ Clearly understand and define your magickal need.

❧ If you wish to use a special element then decide which one is most appropriate and collect items to represent that energy.

❧ Gather candles, stones, or whatever else you intend to use to focus and send the energy you will raise. Empower those items with your personal energy as you focus upon your goal.

❧ Decide upon your words of power. You may write them out, or simply remember the key phrases you wish to use as you improvise.

❧ If you wish to use a special deity in your magick, decide on who, and on how you will petition and connect with him or her. You may want to write out special prayers and invocations and memorize them.

❧ Plan how you will visualize your goal. This is the essence of the magick and very important to your outcome. The moment you start visualizing the resolution of a magickal need is the moment you begin to create the changes in your deep mind necessary for the magick to manifest. Don't skimp on visualization. Enjoy it!

❧ Decide when and where you want to do the spell. Where will depend largely on your own resources. When can be anytime you like, or you may take into consideration astrological influences.

❧ At the appropriate time gather what you will use and go to the place where you will perform the spell.

❧ Cast your protective circle or utilize some other form of protection which you can count on.

❧ Invite whatever elementals, faeries, spirits, or deities you wish to have present as you work. They should always be welcome, but they are not necessary for spell work.

❧ Clear your mind and begin visualizing your goal.

❧ Raise energy within yourself and pour it into the magickal object(s).

❧ Use your words of power, light your candles, charge your stones, dance or sing. Do whatever you have decided to do to focus your attention and raise energy.

❧ Take advantage of natural phenomena which can help you raise energy. A storm, for instance, is an excellent source of energy which can help feed a spell. Feel yourself becoming a part of the storm, and feel yourself psychically drawing on the storm's vast stores of energy as you seek to raise your own energies or cone of power.

❧ When you feel you have put as much energy into the spell as you can, send the energy out to do your will. Relax, throw up your arms, raise a tool, kneel, or do whatever else makes you feel the energy being sent. Be sure to direct it out from you visually as well.

❧ You should finish your spell with words such as "So Mote It Be." Mote is an obsolete word for "must." These words are synonymous with "Amen," "So It Is," and "It is Done." It is a statement of completion and an affirmation that you know your magick is successful. All magick is worked from the point of view that the desired goal is already manifest—it will not come to be, but IT IS. Always phrase your magickal desires in the present tense such as "I have love in my life now" or "My bills are now paid in full." Talking of magick happening in the future will keep it forever in the future, always just out of reach.

❦ Meditate briefly on your goal. Visualize it as already manifest. Smile, and know the magick is at work.

❦ When you are ready to close the circle thank the elementals and spirits who have joined you, and thank your deities especially. If you have called the quarters then dismiss them in a counterclockwise movement beginning again with the west. Dismiss all whom you have called upon with the traditional phrase, "Merry meet, merry part, and merry meet again."

❦ Always ground the energy from your circle. See it dissipate and return to the earth.

❦ Record your ritual in your Book of Shadows with the date, time, weather conditions and any astrological data you wish to include. This will be useful later when you have done enough spells to look for patterns. For example, you may see that your most efficacious spells were done on Sundays or when it was cloudy or snowing. Everyone has different affinities. These patterns will help you pick the best times for your own spell work.

❧ 4 ❧

RITUALS

Rituals were used in old Witta to observe the sabbats and esbats, to perform magickal spells, to mark rites of passage, and to worship the deities. Modern Wittans use rituals for these same purposes.

In creating your own ritual keep it simple and keep in mind that Witta is a religion and not a magickal free-for-all. Respect the deities and approach your rituals with reverence and joy. No rituals are ever right or wrong, and none are carved in stone. They are flexible and can be changed as you change. There are, however, elements which are recommended in ritual construction, and these will be explored further.

Suggestions and outlines for Wiccan magick rituals and sabbat and esbat rituals can be found in many books, and all of them can be used for Wittan rites by simply replacing the deity names with Irish goddess and god names. Though strongly influenced by ceremonial magick, they are still considered pagan rites.

If you are interested in going back further in time and constructing a Wittan ritual as it might have been several thousand years ago you will have to have a feel for simplicity. Wittans cast a circle and welcomed their deities into them to honor them more often than to petition favors. Candles may have lit the quarters more to illuminate the darkness than to call upon the elements as is done in modern Witta, and altars would have held the bounty of the season rather than a collection of elaborate ritual tools. Either alone, with families, or with whole communities, the beauty of Wittan ritual was its simplicity and sincerity.

Ritual is always symbolic in content. Its function is to trigger responses in the deep mind which which will have a positive and lasting effect on both the physical being and the spirit being of a person. Ritual by its very nature has to involve a certain amount of repetition, but it need not be slavishly repeated to the point of mental numbness. There should always be something new and meaningful added, even if it is only the addition of one single word or movement.

Rituals are highly personal acts, reflecting the worshipper's feelings about god/dess and their place in the universe. Even group rituals (good rituals, that is) make allowances for everyone's self expression so the circle is deeply meaningful for everyone involved.

THE ELEMENTS OF RITUAL CONSTRUCTION

Below is a step-by-step guide for ritual creation which can be adapted to almost any need and can work for either covens or solitaries.

❧ If you wish to use an altar have it set with items of the season. Acorns, apples, and gourds in fall; flowers in spring; herbs, fruits, and greenery in summer; holly and evergreen in winter, etc. The direction your altar faces is up to you. Every coven and solitary have their own views on this. Many change directions with the seasons. If you are undecided, place the altar in the center of your circle facing west until you work out your own system. West is the direction of the crone's cauldron wherein all things begin and end and begin again.

❧ Cast a circle of protective energy with a shillelagh, your creative mind, or with any other ritual tool with which you feel comfortable. See it clearly in your mind as a perimeter of protective blue-white light.

❧ If you wish, invite, but never command, friendly spirits, faeries, or elementals to join you. In Ireland it is common to invite ancestors to join you, especially during the dark days from Samhain to Imbolg when it is believed that the portal between our dimensions is at its thinnest. Face west, the direction of Tir-na-nog, and call upon your ancestors, imagining your voice echoing out throughout the universe and back to you. Be sure to offer any spirits called from the Otherworld food and drink, as this is a basic tenet of Celtic ritual practice.

❧ Call on the directional quarters or faeries if you wish, and light a candle to them. This is often done by ringing a bell in each direction and asking that the spirits of that quarter join you. However, remember that bells frighten away faeries. If you want faeries at your ritual, forgo the bell. Be sure to walk clockwise as you call the quarters. Many pagan traditions begin this call in the north. Witta uses the west, the direction of Tir-na-nog.

❧ Definitely use a candle to honor each deity whom you invite into your circle. Goddess candles are traditionally white, and god candles are orange or red. You also can use a white, red and black candle for the Triple Goddess. Once again, this is a matter only you can decide. If you only have plain white candles available, then use them for both the God and Goddess, marking them with male and female symbols for distinction.

❧ State out loud the purpose of your ritual—sabbat observance, personal enrichment, rite of passage, honor of a deity, magick, or whatever. Sing, dance, chant, meditate, and/or offer praise and thanks to your deities. Let the words come from your heart. Singing (feel free to make up your own words and melodies) can quickly tap your inner states of consciousness, and dancing can raise your personal power and energies. You can write out and memorize your rituals or you can speak spontaneously as would have been customary in ancient Ireland. You can have certain set phrases you use, but be creative and celebrate with feeling. You will get more out of your ritual by being spontaneous than you will with most pre-prepared speeches. And if you find you have done something you really liked, then by all means, write it down after you have closed the circle.

❧ If you choose to work magick have with you whatever materials you need for your spell. Once a circle is cast it is unwise to break it until it is grounded. Making a "hole" in the protective energies allows the energy you've raised to seep out, and can allow who-knows-what to enter. When I began my path in witchcraft I tended to ignore the sanctity of the circle, feeling myself too rational to believe some nasty entity was just waiting to get in. I had a few surprising and unpleasant experiences. Don't learn the hard way. The energy you raise will attract things you don't want around. With your circle properly cast they can't get in, and will go when the energy they are attracted to is grounded. Respect your circle.

❧ If your purpose is a rite of passage then you should have already worked out with the family of those involved just what words, gestures, or materials will be used. Keep these as simple as possible without losing the meaning of the event.

❧ Raise and send your cone of power if you wish. If you have no magickal need for it you might send it out to heal the polluted and ailing Mother Earth. If you have just celebrated a rite of passage then you can send loving energy to the persons or spirit involved. But remember that magick is generally not worked on a sabbat unless absolutely necessary.

❧ If it is a sabbat, enact whatever drama you wish to honor the holiday, and use whatever seasonal rituals seem appropriate. The Great Rite is most appropriate at spring sabbats, but can be done at all of them if you wish. At Samhain many circles enact the death of the God and mourn for him. At Yule we celebrate the rebirth of the God. Adapt seasonal songs for these holidays, and thank the Goddess for the bounty of the earth at all seasons.

❧ There is no rush to close the circle once you have finished your ritual. You may sit inside it and sing, meditate, scry or just feel in communion and at peace with nature and your deities. If you are with a group, you can eat, tell stories, or play circle games. Don't dismiss the circle until you feel ready. Sacred space has a healing effect on the mind and body.

❧ Thank and then dismiss any deities, elementals, and spirits who have participated in the ritual.

❧ Ground your excess energy and open your circle.

BANISHING RITUALS

When magickal self-protection has failed and you feel the presence of a malevolent force it is imperative that you take steps to eliminate it immediately lest it grow in strength and eventually become a hindrance to your magickal work and your peace of mind.

To create a banishing ritual follow the above formula to the point of stating the purpose of your ritual. When you state that you wish to drive a negative influence out of your life say it bravely and loudly as if addressing the negativity itself. Show no fear on which the unwanted energy might be able to feed.

There are several visualizations which can aid in banishment. I like to picture a beam of white light energy coming down from infinity and slowly filling me and my home with a throbbing, pulsating protective force. Then I picture it starting to whirl like a giant inverted tornado and moving into the ground, taking with it all the negative energies. Then the white light comes down again, filling me and my home with a shield of protection which cannot be penetrated. I also put up mental pentagrams around my dwelling and try to remember to feed them mental energy at each new moon. If you make these things real with your mind you will create them astrally with thought-forms and they will indeed exist.

There are many other spells you can do which will put the final cap on any banishing rituals. Use mirrors in front of black candles to reflect the negativity back from where it came, or send it harmlessly away. Name your negativity if you can or draw a picture of it and then ritually cover it with handfuls of earth thereby grounding it. Fill a handful of salt with the essence of the negativity and when it is full put it in a bowl of water. Visualize the negativity dissolving. Later you can pour it down a drain or out onto the earth. Or stand with your arms spread and envision all the negativity forming between them in a great ball. Picture it and feel it there all ugly and gray. When you feel you have cornered it all then throw it away, preferably onto earth where it will be grounded and neutralized.

Your mental state has a lot to do with whether a banishing ritual is successful or not. The idea is to make you realize that you have control of your own life and your own being. To allow negativity to make you fearful or hesitant only gives it more power over you. Before you close your circle spend some time laughing at the source of your problems. Belittle it any way you can and feel your own personal power returning. A curandera (Mexican shamaness) in Texas told me once that the best thing she knew to do was to turn and face the negativity when you felt it and say, "I know who you are and I'm not afraid, so just leave!"

After you conclude your banishment ritual vow never to think about the negativity again. By not giving it your thoughts you rob it of the energy it needs to live. If you find your thoughts steered to it at any time don't worry, just say the words, "Go away." Say this in the same tone of voice as an adolescent would speak to an annoying younger sibling. And like a pesky younger sibling, if the negative energy can't get a rise out of you it will see no point in continuing the game.

SABBAT RITUALS

Most pagans think of rituals in conjunction with the sabbats, and this is indeed probably the time they are most commonly used.

Sabbats in old Ireland were a time when whole communities would come together to celebrate the season. And these old customs have not been entirely forgotten. Though the name of the feasts may be different now in many Irish villages, the sabbats are celebrated with much of their old symbolism still intact. What is even more surprising is that many of the older residents of these small villages seem to know exactly why these ancient rituals continue to be enacted. They know why a maypole is woven at Bealtaine and why jack-o'-lanterns are lit at Samhain, and this curious conflict of old and new theology doesn't seem to bother most of them. This fact has made it easy for modern day Wittans to reconstruct many of the old ways and adapt them into our own sabbat rituals.

At sabbats bonfires were built, and the people feasted and danced. They ate the traditional foods of the sabbats and danced traditional Irish dances intended to act out the meaning of the holiday (the word holiday is a contraction of the words "holy" and "day"). For ideas on how the ancient Irish Celts celebrated read the chapter on the sabbats.

The purpose of a sabbat ritual is to honor the deities and to acknowledge and celebrate the continuous turning of the wheel of the year. Other rituals may be constructed around magick or a rite of passage, or just because the mood to worship and meditate strikes, but a sabbat ritual is purely for worship.

But worship need not be a wholly somber event. In Witta it is also a celebration of life, death, and triumph over death by rebirth.

Every coven or solitary is encouraged to write their own rituals. None are ever written in stone, and none are better, or more correct, than another. Some covens rewrite their sabbat rituals every year, keeping what they love and in doing so creating their own traditions while still keeping their rituals fresh. Others cling to the familiarity of the tried and true.

The point is to write a ritual which you feel best represents the meaning of the sabbat, and the ritual which you feel best gives love and honor to the deities.

The following is an example of a coven ritual for Yule, the second sabbat in the wheel of the year. Use it to inspire your own creativity.

Yule Ritual

When the coven has gathered, place all materials which will be needed inside the area where the circle will be cast. Decorations should already be in place on the altar, and the altar itself set with all the items you wish it to hold. Keep the circle in relative darkness until everyone has gathered. A single candle only (a white goddess candle) is recommended unless more are needed for safety's sake. The single candle is representative of the one creative life force. At this sabbat it also stands for the maiden goddess who is alone, but who will soon be joined by her consort as she gives birth to him again. You will also need plain

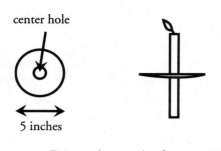

center hole

5 inches

Drip catchers made of
cut-out paper plates

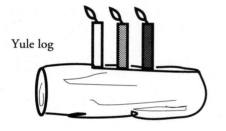

Yule log

white candles for everyone. You might want to cut small circles of paper plates to put the tapers in so hot wax won't drip on anyone.

You will need a Yule log with the traditional white, red, and black candles. This is made from a plain log, usually of oak, which has a flattened bottom, and three holes bored into the top for the candles. Decorate it with Yule greenery (holly, pine, etc.).

You will also need a cauldron, but any cup or chalice may substitute for this item. Put a small amount of salt water in the bottom of the cauldron. The use of any other ritual tools or altar items is up to the coven. Below is one possible Yule altar layout which incorporates the items needed for the following ritual.

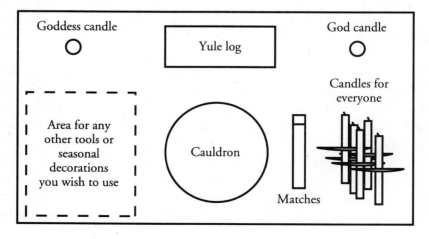

Goddess candle

Yule log

God candle

Candles for
everyone

Area for any
other tools or
seasonal
decorations
you wish to use

Cauldron

Matches

This ritual's leader is identified as the "Acting High Priest/ess" to allow for alternating leadership roles of which Wittan covens should make use.

Before the night of the Yule ritual you need to choose two males to be Oak and Holly Kings, and three females to represent the Triple Goddess. Have fun dressing your players for their parts.

Acting High Priest/ess:

> *Failte!*

(Failte is the Irish word for welcome and is pronounced fawl-t-chay or fawl-t-yay depending upon which region of Ireland one is from.)

Covenors:

> *Failte!*

Acting High Priest/ess:

> *The wheel of the year turns on and on, bringing us to and from each season, and from and to another. What will be is. What was will be. All time is here and now inside this sacred space. We pause briefly to watch the wheel turn, and we gather on this blessed eve so that we might celebrate this season of Yule. In this moment between time, we come to praise the bountiful Goddess and her child-lover who is about to be born again. We wish to give thanks, and to feel ourselves a part of the relentlessly turning wheel of life, death, and rebirth. Let all who would honor the Goddess and her consort enter into her protective circle.*

The coven should now cast the circle in whatever manner has been decided upon. In some covens this honor is given to one person, and in others all participate. If you wish to call upon the directions, faeries, or invite any other entities you may do so now. The Acting High Priest/ess should remove the god candle (usually a red or orange taper) from the altar and hold it up.

Acting High Priest/ess:

> *Tonight we celebrate the longest night of the year. And though it be our season of winter, tonight our darkness will end. Even though all about us appears in slumber and death, we are not forgotten. Our blessed Lady Brigid* (Breed) *carries in her young womb—that womb which has birthed all things into being—a son, her consort, our Lord Lugh.* (Lugh is a sun deity and this is a sabbat which celebrates the sun's return.) *Brigid turns the wheel once more and the sun, her child and lover, our God, returns to warm us anew.*

Covenors:

> *Blessed be Brigid, giver of life! Welcome Lugh, bringer of warmth!*

Acting High Priest/ess:

> *Tonight darkness has reached the limit of its power. Now the light of Lugh is victorious over darkness.*

Acting High Priest/ess lights the god candle with the flame of the goddess candle. It is then set back down in its place on the altar.

Covenors (facing west to acknowledge that the reborn Lugh has come from the cauldron of the Caillech in Tir-na-nog):

> *Blessed be Brigid, giver of life! Welcome Lugh, god triumphant!*

Covenors face the center of the circle again. If the Acting High Priest is male, a female Priestess should have been chosen, if the Acting High Priestess is female, a male Priest should have been chosen. Together they will perform the next part of the ritual. The two of them should now approach the altar and pick up the god and goddess candles according to their gender.

Priestess and Priest:

> *Tonight Goddess and God are reconciled.*
> *Together again these children set out on*
> *another journey through the eternal year.*

The Priestess and Priest place the candles together so the flames merge as one. This is a mimicry of the Great Rite which will be done in sabbat rituals beginning with the Ostara sabbat. The feeling now is that these youngsters are not ready for this type of union and the merging of the candles is performed instead. All covenors will now approach the altar, pick up a candle, and light it from the joined flame.

Covenors (while lighting their candles):

> *Blessed be Brigid and Lugh.*
> *Blessed be creation.*
> *Blessed be Brigid and Lugh.*
> *Blessed be the light.*

The Yule log should now be lit by the three pre-chosen women from the coven. Each one lights one candle—the maiden white, the mother red, and the crone black.

Maiden Aspect:

> *Blessed be Danu* (Dawn-noo) *the little girl goddess, wide-eyed and eager, innocent and fresh.*

Mother Aspect:

> *Blessed be Brigid the mother goddess, lov-*
> *ing and protective, proud and fertile.*

Crone Aspect:

> *Blessed be Badb* (Bayv) *the crone goddess,*
> *powerful and wise, guardian of the great*
> *cauldron of death, life, and rebirth.*

The three goddess aspects dip their right hands into the crone's cauldron which has some salted water in it and they pass around the circle clockwise and touch each covenor as they pass. The maiden touches the feet, the mother the stomach, and the crone the forehead. This is a symbolic goddess blessing with the maiden blessing the pathway of your feet, the mother blessing the reproductive regions, and the crone blessing the head wherein wisdom resides. When the circle is complete all the covenors can extinguish their hand-held candles and place them in a designated spot. Just as this is done the chosen Oak King and Holly King begin to "fight" in the center of the circle. In their simulated struggle they may use whatever ritual tools they choose. Much of this depends on which ones the coven chooses to use, but shillelaghs or staffs are most recommended because these are easy to find or make, and are part of the old Wittan tradition. The covenors should cheer the Oak King until he is victorious. At that time the Holly King will fall to the ground in an imitation of death.

Oak King:

> *I am the Oak King, god of the waxing*
> *year. Fear not on this dark night of winter,*
> *for I have come again to guide us to on to*
> *summer and all its blessings.*

Covenors:

> *Blessed be the Oak King, king of the wax-*
> *ing year.*

Acting High Priest/ess:

> *The Holly King is slain. The Oak King reigns. Our Goddess is young once more. A new young Lugh is born to us. Tonight, on this darkest night of winter, we turn to the light, the sun god reborn, and we say …*

All:

> *Blessed Be!*

Acting High Priest/ess:

> *Who is Brigid?*

Covenors:

> *Brigid is Goddess.*

Acting High Priest/ess:

> *Who is Goddess?*

All Women:

> *I am Goddess.*

Acting High Priest/ess:

> *Who is Lugh?*

Covenors:

> *Lugh is God.*

Acting High Priest/ess:

> *Who is God?*

All Men:

> *I am God.*

Acting High Priest/ess:

> *Who are the Goddess and the God?*

Covenors:

> *All living beings are Goddess and God.*

Acting High Priest/ess:

> *And who are we?*

Covenors:

> *We are the children of deity. And we are deity. We are a part of the creative life forces which move the universe. We are microcosm and macrocosm. We are part of all that is.*

Acting High Priest/ess continues now with whatever seasonal celebrations the coven chooses to have. The reading of ritual or seasonal poetry either borrowed or written by members of the coven is a nice touch. In Witta it has also become something of a Yule tradition to tell the heroic tales of the giant god Finn MacCool whose stories can be found in books on Irish mythology. After the circle is closed in whatever manner has been agreed upon continue with …

Acting High Priest/ess:

> *Though we are apart, we are ever together for we are one in the spirit of our Goddess and our God. Merry meet. Merry part.*

Covenors:

> *And merry meet again.*

All:

Blessed Be!

Now games and feasting can begin. Since this is Yule it is appropriate to give gifts in honor of loved ones who have passed on to Tir-na-nog during the year which ended at the last Samhain. Leave any left over feast food for the faeries and as an offering to the deities.

Wittan rituals need not be any more elaborate or sturdily constructed than this. However, if more formality pleases you then by all means have it. Use special poems, steps, and movements. Make the ritual longer. Do what feels correct for you. Nothing is wrong in a circle if it is done with love and honor.

Remember that honoring the Irish deities and learning to live in balance with nature is what Witta is all about.

❧ 5 ❧

FÆRY FOLK, SPIRITS, AND SPOOKS

Faery beings play a large part in the belief system of the Irish people past and present. More than in any other pagan tradition Witta utilizes, acknowledges, and works with the "wee folk." Today in Wicca and other Western pagan traditions faeries have been relegated to the role of elemental beings associated with the four directions who minimally participate in magickal work or in the everyday lives of witches. They are called upon to be present at circle rituals but are usually accorded no active role. Faeries in Ireland were petitioned to aid and intercede on human behalf. They could not be summoned at will, nor controlled by egotistical magicians. In a departure from all other European folklore, Irish faeries are not merely archetypes, but living, sentient beings with individual personalities.

Irish mythology tells us that faeries were once much more involved with the human world than they are now. Some believe this is because the ethereal faeries cannot fully exist in the rigid and demanding human world. But faeries do inhabit our world, though they remain at its fringe, ever puzzled and intrigued by human folly. Etain, the queen of the Tuatha de Danann, was once a human woman wooed into faery land by her future consort, King Midhir. But later we read of Manann, God of the Sea, who raised a cloak of enchantment between the hero Cuchulain and the faery Fand to erase the memory of each from the other's mind. He decreed that the two worlds, though they lived side by side, must remain forever divided.

The Irish people believe faeries were created by the same life force which created us. They have the right to live freely and to be respected. It was the Irish who were the first to utilize many everyday objects as charms and talismans because they were believed to be gifts of the "little people."

Belief in faeries has been demonstrated in every known world culture. And faeries are still seen and heard throughout Ireland, with even the most educated doubter of magickal ways not risking doing things which are known to upset the wee folk. In the Irish language the word for faery is sídhe (shee) from the Indian word siddhi meaning "something which controls the elements." And it is from the Indian myths, carried across Europe to Ireland by the Celts, that the Irish faery forms were created.

In old Ireland it was the frost faeries who, sent by the Goddess, arrived in winter to bed down the sleepy trees and plants for their winter's slumber. Then they aided the Goddess in bringing winter to the world while she was distracted with mourning for her dead consort. In spring the flower faeries awoke the flowers and trees once more, and helped them dress in their colorful spring finery to honor the young virgin Goddess and her son/lover. In autumn the painting faeries colored the landscape with rich golds and reds and frolicked in the woodlands with the mischievous Great Horned God. In summer these elemental faeries were at leisure, and used the time to enjoy themselves with games, which included playing pranks on unsuspecting humans.

Modern superstition and folk custom in Ireland devotes a large portion of itself to information on the little people and their likes and dislikes. One belief which still persists in rural Ireland is that you shouldn't throw water or other household waste out after dark when the little people are about. Even in the daytime it was considered unwise not to call out a warning to the wee folk before dumping anything out the windows or doors.

Faeries are small beings who love nature and love to hunt and play games. They are fascinated with humans and love to discover all they can about them. Often they will appear unknown to us in shapeshifted forms, particularly in the guise of friendly domestic animals. And their mischievous nature makes playing pranks on hapless humans an irresistible delight.

Though they are mainly creatures of the astral world, faeries can live anywhere within nature, and they are often classified according to the place which they choose to inhabit. Faeries are further divided into two subgroups—those who work and live together in groups, called "trooping faeries," and those who are solitaries.

In the myth cycles the earliest invaders of Ireland were faery races. The most famous were the Tuatha De Danann who were said to make their homes beneath the ground. Another name for Irish faeries is daoine sídhe which means "faery people," and may relate to the Goddess Dana who brought into Ireland these first "people" (literally "people of peace"). After their defeat by the Milesians, the Tuatha stayed underground to become the faeries and gnomes of Ireland, and their underground dwellings became the faery mounds of today.

The most well-known of all the faery folk of Ireland is the leprechaun. The leprechaun guards a pot of gold which is, in fact, a cauldron. If one can gain control of these wily creatures one can have the cauldron, and along with it, three wishes. The origin of this belief is probably rooted in crone worship. Presumably anyone who could get ahold of the crock, or cauldron, could have control over life and death.

Leprechauns are mischievous, but still can be helpful to humankind if approached with respect. They are solitary faeries who do not enjoy working with their fellow creatures. They have been associated with the shoe-making elves, but seem to most enjoy finding lodging in an old barn which they will carefully protect from harm. With leprechauns the Irish share a demonstrable love of horses, and they were the people to first take the upward turned horseshoe as a symbol of luck.

Leprechauns love to dance and are attracted to music. Legend says that if you start them dancing they cannot stop until you quit playing your tune. In this frenzied state it is said that they will gladly lead you to their crock of gold, if you will please only allow them to stop dancing. Also catching a leprechaun's eyes and staring at him unblinkingly will give you power over him. Whatever you do, do not grab the little fellow. Remember that he is a creature of another dimension. If you grab him he will fade, still very much in your grasp, but unseen in our world. You will think you have lost him and inadvertently set him free.

Even if you are sly enough to capture this elusive faery, the lucky leprechaun still has his ways to trick you out of both the crock of gold and the three wishes. If he can trick you into making a fourth wish by sundown you lose all your wishes and the crock too. This is certainly not hard for him to do given the propensity we humans have for wistfully voicing wishes.

Another faery similar to the leprechaun is the clurichaun (klooree-kong). Clurichauns are solitary faeries who are the self-appointed guardians of wine cellars. They will prevent casks from leaking and wines from going bad, and they will chase away all those who come to take a drink uninvited by the master of the house. Clurichauns are almost always drunk, but are impeccably groomed and dressed.

If you wish to attract a clurichaun to your cellars leave a bit of wine out for him. If you have one, know that he is there to stay. If you ignore or mistreat him he will wreak havoc on your cellars and on your home, and he will most definitely sour your wine stock. Once you have chased away your clurichaun by your insensitivity or lack of hospitality no other will ever come to take his place.

The bean sídhe (banshee), or "woman faery," is another well-known and often feared Irish faery, though some term her a ghost. The origins of the bean sídhe have been lost in time, but it is reasonable to assume that she represents a mother form from the land of the dead, Tir-na-nog. In old Ireland Tir-na-nog was also known as the "land of women." It was believed that upon physical death a soul was reabsorbed into the womb of the Great Mother, or into some other woman form, to await rebirth. The mournful keening of a bean sídhe is said to be heard when death is approaching a household. Many who know of one, or who have heard one, do not report their wailing cries as being frightening at all, but oddly comforting. But the majority find her sound bone-chilling and quite terrifying.

Occasionally a bean sídhe is seen at a river washing the winding sheets which will soon become a shroud. The "washer at the ford" is an old Celtic legend which stems from this belief. To see the washer meant that a major life-changing event was about to occur. To the Irish who saw the bean sídhe washing sheets it was a fearsome sight which portended a death in the community. If later that night any of your candles burned in a winding pattern you would know that the death was to be in your own household.

The lamentations of the bean sídhe are still heard all over Ireland when death is near. Usually they are attached to a particular family or locale, though the latter is not so common. Many believe the bean sídhe to be attached only to the old noble families of Ireland, those directly of Milesian descent. This idea probably evolved from the old larger family units called clans. Each clan would have its own bean sídhe. But when under patriarchal influence the clans broke up into smaller family units, the bean sídhe became attached only to the clan chief's immediate family.

Dryads are tree-dwelling spirits for whom the female Druidic order is named. They are thought to be useful in human attempts to connect with deity if they are approached properly. The Druids were supposedly on good terms with the Dryads who helped them to achieve much of their power by teaching them the secrets of divination and astral travel.

Elves or gnomes were mostly known to Scotland, though northern Ireland had its fair share. These trooping faeries were beings who lived within the earth among the tangled roots of sacred oak trees. They went abroad during the night to aid woodland animals, and occasionally would reward a virtuous or unselfish human being with some act of kindness. The faery tale of the kindly old cobbler who was assisted by elves bears out this belief. Elves and gnomes do their good deeds out of the joy of giving, and any act of overt thanks will drive them permanently away.

Murdhuachas (mer-oo-khas), sea faeries, are often mistaken for merpeople (mermaids and mermen). They can be helpful in locating fish or in finding one's home port on a fog-shrouded night. Or they can turn nasty and lure sailors to their death on coastal rocks, like the Germanic Lorelei, with her haunting songs.

Merpeople in Ireland are referred to as merrows and they can be either harmful or helpful depending on where they live. Those in inland lakes are generally friendly while those of the open sea are more mischievous or even harmful. Irish sailors used to believe dolphins were friendly merrows.

Another sea faery race is one banished from the island by the Tuatha de Danann. The Formorians, when driven out of Ireland and into the sea, became grotesque sea monsters which prey on ships and fishing boats.

Phookas (pook-ahs) are the hobgoblins of Ireland. These nasty faeries delight in working harm to human beings, especially to children and crops. The phookas lay claim to any crop which is not harvested by Samhain eve, and to risk cutting a plant after this time is to invite these dangerous faeries into your life. In spite, for taking what they believe to be theirs, they have been known to kill herd animals, particularly cattle. In Ireland a cow which has died mysteriously is sometimes said to have been "poofed" or "pooked," a term derived from belief in the phookas.

Phookas, unlike most of the solitary faeries of Ireland, are trooping faeries, though these particular creatures tend to run in destructive packs. They are said to be extremely ugly and ill-tempered and to have frequent quarrels among themselves. They especially love human babies and are always on the lookout for a newborn which they can steal. In its place they leave a changeling, or faery baby. One remedy for this is to place garlic or dill weed in a baby's crib, and to not call the child by his or her truthful name until it is six months old. When a baby is a helpless newborn it is especially vulnerable, therefore many Wittans will give a child a craft name, or true name, which they keep secret until their coming of age.

Well spirits are another popular faery form. It is to the spirit of a well whom you make a petition when you drop a coin in a wishing well. Well spirits are water sprites who are very sympathetic to human needs. Often they are said to take the form of human beings, whose form they envy, and are then dangerously beautiful. If you allow a well spirit to embrace you, you risk being dragged into the well to live forever as his or her consort.

PROTECTING YOURSELF FROM FAERIES

There are several ways of protecting yourself against mischievous faeries, and one of the most popular is to discover a faery's true name. Recall the story of Rumpelstiltskin, the baneful faery who wished to take the son of a queen whom he had helped. When she discovered his name the earth opened up and swallowed him.

If one fears he or she is being pursued by a faery, or any ill-meaning spirit, one should cross over running water. The water acts like a grounding element and diffuses the baneful power.

Sharp noises, especially snapping fingers and clapping hands, are said to hurt the ears of wee folks and they will flee. The more recent custom of tolling a church bell at a funeral was derived from this belief. Better still is to do protection rituals or hang protective herbs, such as basil or garlic, in your home.

Iron is something that all European folk cultures tell us will protect us from faeries. For some reason we cannot understand, anything astral cannot come into contact with metals—especially iron—without having its energy negated. The only exception to this seems to be an iron cauldron. Many spells tell us not to allow metal to touch our working tools or talismans. There is a recorded account of a young Irish mother who placed a needle on her baby's night clothes each evening knowing it would thwart any faery seeking to exchange the child for a changeling (faery baby).

In line with the taboo on iron, many farmers would hang their scythes over the front doors at night to prevent faeries from entering.

Faeries love a warm fire but they cannot tolerate excessive smoke. Smoke has been used in Ireland as well as elsewhere as a purifying force. Anyone smoking a pipe will keep faeries away for as long as it burns. It was traditional in Celtic lands that when a fire was banked for the night that prayers of protection be said as the smoke of the waning blaze began drifting upward.

Nettles are hated by faeries and they will not travel where nettles grow. Other protective herbs especially useful against faeries when either worn or hung in the home are clove, mistletoe, pepper, hazel leaves, garlic, and mandrake. A faery will not enter any garden where tomatoes grow. And mints taken as teas will guard your sleep and your dreams from prowling faeries.

Clothing worn turned inside out is another protection against faeries, and a turned-out glove thrown into a faery ring (circle of dark grass unexplained by science) will dispel the faeries and render the ring safe to step inside.

Carrying the herb St. Johnswort was another old Irish charm against faeries. Tying up twigs of sacred trees, such as rowan, thorn, and ash, in a red thread was another.

SEEING FAERIES

There are times when you might wish to see or contact faery folk, especially if you have a request of them. In the first two decades of this century it became a fad among occultists to claim faery contact and several elaborate hoaxes were staged. The most famous was the Cottingly Grove hoax in which two young girls were photographed frolicking with faeries. The "faeries" turned out to be cut out drawings taken from children's books. However, at the time many people were fooled, and flocked to Cottingly, England, to see the faeries and talk with the young girls about them. Among those fooled was the eminently logical Sir Arthur Conan Doyle, the famous occultist who wrote the Sherlock Holmes stories.

You need not imagine or make up your faeries. Faeries can be found and contacted, and occasionally in magick rituals one might wish to ask their aid. While in the protection of a circle you may call upon a faery. Ask, but never command, its presence. The faery, if interested in what you have to say, should appear to you just outside of your circle. If you don't see one, then try to sense its presence and make your request. Under no circumstances should you ever permit a faery to come into your circle. You have no way of knowing the faery's true intent and since many of them can be quite nasty it is prudent to be cautious.

If you still have trouble judging the presence of a faery try using bluebells to help you. Bluebells, a traditional adornment of an Irish witch's garden, are said to ring when faeries are present. Plant some near your circle, either in the ground or in a portable flowerpot. The bluebells can be heard "ringing" when faeries are present. Remember that the ringing can also warn you when a faery is present when you don't want one around.

Faeries are sensitive creatures and enjoy your gratitude, but while profuse gratitude is not appreciated, bits of fresh food and milk are. Some faeries will even undo all their good, or leave and never return if they hear spoken words of thanks.

In Ireland if one wants to contact faeries it is customary to offer them some inducement to inhabit your property. Leaving them food, water, and milk is the best method. Faeries are also reputed to adore fresh strawberries and leaving some of these out for them will definitely win their hearts. In old Ireland it was obligatory to give any left over sabbat feast foods to the faeries who in turn would bless your home—or at least not make mischief there—until the next sabbat.

If you don't live in an appropriate place for them to come to you find a faery mound and leave your offerings there. Respectfulness of their dwelling places is a must.

Do not desecrate a faery mound or you risk the eternal ire of the wee folk. Legends abound in Ireland of families still reeling under the curses of indignant faery folk who were thwarted in some way by ancestors long dead.

Beware of faery rings, dark circles of grass among a lighter lawn. These are said to be the magick circles where faeries dance. Irish legend says if one is caught inside a faery ring at dawn or dusk one will be forever trapped in the faery world. Also faery mounds, boroughs ("burghs" in Irish) of earth where the faeries who are descended from the Tuatha De Danann live, can be opened for a cautious peek inside. The safest time to do this is at Midsummer while wearing protective charms. Go to a mound and tap on it lightly three times and request it to open for you in the name of the Goddess Dana.

A grass-covered
faery burgh

Primrose and cowslip are known as faery flowers and having them in your garden or window box may attract them. They also are said to be fond of catnip. Faeries are attracted to most of the Druidic sacred trees especially oak, elder, willow, birch, and ash, and will often make their homes in the branches or among the roots. But their favorite trees are thorn trees, especially blackthorn from which Irish leprechauns make their little shillelaghs. Just who copied the shillelagh custom from whom may forever be a mystery.

Faeries are notoriously delicate of feeling. One must constantly watch out for them underfoot and not carelessly hurl insulting remarks. And most of all, if you see faeries, believe in them. After all, they are really creatures of the astral world. They visit the earth plane from time to time much as we visit the astral realms. And if they find your dwelling to be a hospitable place to come they may be induced to come more often.

How Faeries Can Help You

Remember that faeries cannot be summoned at will, nor controlled by egotistical magicians. They are sentient, living beings who are extremely sensitive, and they deserve our respect. When you are in the protection of your circle try calling on faeries while keeping their individuality in mind rather than thinking of them as merely elemental energies to be used only if needed.

To summon them, open your circle in your usual way, then face each direction in turn as your tradition prefers, and say:

Hear me now, oh powers of the (name
direction). *With an open heart I invite all
the friendly spirits and faeries of the* (name
direction) *to come to the edge of my circle,
this sacred space, to witness and participate
in the worship of our Goddess and our God.
At the side of this sacred space you are welcome. We shall work together for our mutual
good in accordance with our free wills.*

If your tradition calls for bells to be intoned as the directions are
invoked you must avoid this if you wish to bring faeries. Bells have
long been used as a deterrent to frighten faeries away. Any sharp sound
while you are in your circle, including whistling or hands clapping,
will frighten them away, leaving you only the mere raw energies of the
directional elements.

Faeries love to dance. While you are in the protection of your circle you can dance with the faeries to help in raising energy or a cone of
power and they will be glad to help. Just politely state your intention
to them before you begin and ask their help. If they wish, they will join
in. Another helpful hint might be to explain to them why what you are
doing is important to you, especially if it is a spell for something personal. Faeries loathe human greed and treachery, but will gladly help
you if eradicating these things is your goal.

As much as you do, household faeries such as gnomes or
clurichauns want to keep your home peaceful and happy. They will
gladly lend their energies to raising a shield of protection around your
dwelling. Again, just ask them politely and then see if you can feel
their added energy as you raise your defenses. The elflike gnomes are
the only faeries known to Celtic mythology to be reliable around children, and you can safely call on them to guard your babies.

The Dryads were said to be able to be implored to aid ailing
humans, especially female children for whom they have a great love,
probably because they are so childlike themselves. To contact Dryads,
cast your circle under one of the Druidic sacred trees and call to them
in the usual way. They can be especially helpful if you need healing
energy or are working in your circle with divinations.

Some faeries are known to be friendly to animals and will come immediately to stand guard over them if need be. Again, it is a matter of calling the faeries to the edge of your circle and stating your intention. After you ask the faeries for help in looking over your livestock or pets you should follow up your request with a protective spell and/or a talisman. (Faeries hate human laziness and will turn on you if they think you expect them to do all the work.) Call upon gnomes, the healers of woodland creatures, or gruagachs, goddess faeries who care for livestock, if you want someone to aid your animals.

If you are ill and wish to be directed to a proper herbal medicine faeries can help. Go to a wild wooded place and put yourself into a light meditative trance by relaxing and concentrating upon your goal of finding an appropriate herbal cure. After a time, open your eyes and look around for signs. A wiggle of a branch or the sparkle of a ground leaf might be a sign. When you feel you have been led to an herb, *do not* immediately consume it. With gloves on, talk to the plant and tell it why you need its sacrifice. Cut it clean without allowing it to touch the ground. Wrap it in a clean cloth and take it home, to a library, or to the biology department at a nearby college for identification. *Never* eat any plant you can neither identify nor understand how it will effect you.

Once you know what it is you can look up its healing properties in an herbal medicine guide. Chances are excellent that if a kind, rather than a mischievous, faery aided you in your find, that it will be just the cure you are looking for.

FÆRY TALES

Faery tales are not stories of faeries but folk stories which were created to keep pagan lore alive after the entrenchment of Christianity. Though some (such as Rumpelstiltskin) do offer insights into the mind of the faeries, most do not. They simply were ways of passing along the old traditions in the midst of persecution. Some of these stories were discovered for what they were by the clergy and rewritten to take into account the view of the old gods that they wanted us to have, especially where the crone was concerned.

Diabolization of the crone into a hideous old woman who poisons young girls and eats children alive was a major faery tale theme. Note the stories of Hansel and Gretel and Snow White.

One story which escaped church detection was the tale of the Three Little Pigs, whose crone image was so well-hidden that it escaped discovery. Pigs are sacred to the Goddess, and three of them together represent the Triple Goddess. The principal power of the crone is wisdom. The first two pigs, the virgin and the mother, built houses of materials which could easily be destroyed by anyone wanting to enter them. No doubt the Big Bad Wolf was representative of the early clergy who sought to "huff and puff and blow" the houses of practicing pagans away. It was the last of the three pigs, the wise crone, who was able to thwart the wolf with her superior wisdom and wits and in the process save the lives of the other two pigs. Note that the wolf's end comes while trying to enter that magickal portal known as the chimney. As he climbs down he is destroyed when he lands in a boiling cauldron—the cauldron of death and rebirth which is always presided over by the crone.

Though much of the deeper meaning of faery tales has been forgotten and re-formed in our minds with archetypes which the patriarchy wants us to identify them with, faery tales still have strong and deeply meaningful messages for our children. In the same way that the mythic heroes of old Ireland gave strength and inspiration to Wittans long ago, the modern faery tales help children now to learn how to deal with today's adults, and give them a sense of personal strength. It is no accident that most of the protagonists of these stories are children.

Please remember that these faery stories, like the older myths of humanity, have often been deliberately altered over time. Be cautious of stories which denigrate women or women's abilities, and of stories where the monster, or antagonist, is the victor.

In his classic work on faery tales, *The Uses of Enchantment*, child psychologist Bruno Bettelheim outlines how faery tales give guidance and understanding of the larger world to children too young to cope with adult life. He unlocks the messages which our children receive. The story of Sleeping Beauty, for instance, is not merely a tale of a pretty princess who pricks her finger and sleeps. It is a tale of first blood, or first menses, the coming of age of a young woman, a time which would have been celebrated by an ancient pagan community. In the new tale, first blood is rendered as a "curse," a nasty pejorative for monthly bleeding. Yet, as Bettelheim contends, facing fear helps children liberate their emotions. Though, as Wittans, we should teach our children to face the fears of growing up in a slightly more positive way.

The study of faery tales and nursery rhymes by a Wittan is well worthwhile. Reading again these treasures of childhood with a newly opened mind will bring about many interesting insights into how they were crafted to conceal pagan mysteries. And if we read them to our children we have a duty to point out these mysteries—the children will understand the rest.

IRISH GHOSTS

Ireland is an old land and many old energies refuse to die away. The Irish love their ghosts and enjoy sitting around a balefire or hearth exchanging spine-chilling tales of their encounters with restless spirits.

Many metaphysicians have sought to find an answer for just what a ghost is and why it, or its residual energy, remains long after a physical shell has died. The most popular theory seems to be that a haunting is a repetition of an electromagnetic recording in air waves. High energy emitted during a traumatic or frightening event gets trapped in the air and is played back at times when those waves are stimulated by another energy force such as a human presence. Others claim that these shades are truly the discarnate forms of those passed over who have not yet reincarnated, or who have, but their former astral aspect remains intact and attached to the place of its life.

In any case, it is clear that Ireland is over-populated by ghosts, with nearly every old house, castle, ruin, and village claiming at least one or two resident specters. And virtually every coastal town has its own sea ghosts which make some of the better blood-chilling stories.

One of the most persistent ghost legends involves the sinking of the American steamship *Lusitania* which was torpedoed by German U-boats off the coast of Kinsale (County Cork) in May of 1915, taking 1500 American and British lives. Irish folklore tells a slightly different version of the story. Once upon a time the King of Kinsale stood on Great Sovereign Rock, a rocky projection which juts out defiantly into the cold north Atlantic Ocean, and he tossed a spear out into the sea as far as he could. He decreed that this represented the outermost boundaries of his kingdom and that no one dared cross through it without his permission. On dark nights people have claimed to see the king standing on the rock watching without mercy as the great ship sank into the cold waters.

A similar ghost story involves the Spanish Armada which came to its end off the rocky coast of County Sligo with 1100 lives lost.

One need not venture into the far rural reaches of Ireland to seek ghosts. Dublin is overrun with them. Nearly every old theater, church, and manse has one or two. Dublin Castle and the old Shelbourne Hotel are said to have more than a few. Ask around. With typical Gaelic pride, the Irish love to talk about their ghosts.

How to Initiate Spirit Contact

Spirit contact has always been a part of paganism, especially so in Ireland which has a history of matrilineal ancestor worship due to the Wittan belief that one must re-enter the womb of the Great Mother to enter the Land of the Dead.

Some Wittans choose to shun spirit contact as a dangerous practice, one in which they see no value. While it is true that just because someone is dead does not mean he or she has inherited all the answers for a universe of questions, contact with a passed over relative can be a meaningful experience in itself. And the Irish seem to have a natural affinity for contacting passed over loved ones.

Though I had been a practicing pagan for a good number of years when my grandmother died, I had not sought spirit contact, nor did I feel it was of any value to me. My grandmother and I were very close, often more like good friends than relatives separated by more than fifty years. Yet several days after her passing I was suddenly jolted out of a book I was reading by the clear awareness that she was in the room with me, 1500 miles from where she had lived, in a place she had never visited. So strong was her presence that I feared to look up from where it emanated.

At first I found the episode rather disturbing, though eventually I grew used to her presence. She stayed with me for several days and I found it oddly comforting. Friends who knew how close we had been commented that I seemed not nearly so upset by her passing as they would have expected. The reason was that she was with me, a fact that made it very hard to mourn.

Eventually she moved on to the Land of the Dead, but that experience she gave me taught me not to be afraid of spirit contact, and that it does have its purposes. It said clearly that the esoteric belief in spiritual survival of physical death is no mere fancy of humans who fear death as an ending, and not as a natural continuation of being. Something of human existence does most definitely transcend earthly life.

Many methods are given in various texts for how to contact spirits. This is the one I use. It is simple and relatively easy to perform.

❧ Find a quiet place where you know you absolutely will not be disturbed.

❧ Relax and cast a protective circle around yourself, then cast two more. When calling for spirits it is best to have this added protection just in case the energy you radiate attracts things you don't want around. You can call for a spirit guide or helpful entity, or you can contact a loved one. It is best to have someone specific in mind rather than throwing yourself open to just any energy which happens to be in the neighborhood. If you are contacting a loved one try to hold in your hands something which belonged to him or her to help you focus on his or her energy. When choosing a place to relax many Wittans prefer to sit so they can face west towards Tir-na-nog. Also doing this at sunset when the sun itself is "dying" in the west will aid you in getting the proper feeling for this ritual.

❧ Breathe deeply several times and go into a receptive, meditative state of mind, focusing your attention on whom you wish to contact. Call out with your mind, inviting that being to come to the edge of your circle. This may take some time, but eventually you will feel a presence. Most people who engage in spirit contact don't actually see anything, they merely sense someone's presence. In some cases they might even faintly smell a perfume associated with their loved one. Enjoy being in each other's presence again without making demands on each other. Messages are rarely exchanged, and I would be leery of any message you do get which is hateful or demanding. If you get such a message shut the contact off *immediately* and mentally surround yourself with a protective white light. Performing a banishing ritual of some kind is also a good idea.

Another method of spirit contact is scrying. In a room lit by only one candle, gaze into a magick mirror used only for scrying and other rituals. Concentrate on the face you want to see while chanting something like:

> *Candle, candle burning bright,*
> *In the darkness of the night.*
> *Mirror shining with your light,*
> *Bring the one I seek to sight.*

A note of caution: spirit contact is not for everyone. Some people do not find themselves comfortable with this practice. It is not an essential part of Witta. It is done for your, and/or your loved one's, personal enrichment. If you feel afraid or feel it won't enrich you, *don't do it!*

❧ 6 ❧

THE ESBATS

The esbats are the thirteen times of the full moon in a solar year during which Witta celebrates the Great Goddess in her mother aspect. Commemoration of these events is common to virtually all pagan religions.

It was easy to see how the moon became intimately linked with the image of primal womanhood. The moon went through a twenty-eight-day cycle, very similar to the menstrual cycle. The moon was never born and it never died, it merely showed different faces, as it is with the Triple Goddess in her guises as maiden, mother, and crone. The moon had a profound effect on the tides, and because of its likeness to blood, water was already a feminine symbol. The moon affected planting and growing cycles just like a woman's state of being affected a growing life inside her. The moon was a creature of night and of mystery, and until the male fertilizing principle was discovered, new life was the greatest mystery of all. Some ancient peoples even believed it was the moon itself which had the power to impregnate.

For centuries men and women gathered alone or in groups to honor the moon at her fullness long before rituals to her were codified or the word "witch" was spoken. The moon was simply part of the larger life, and like her counterpart the sun, she was necessary for life to continue.

After the advent of patriarchal religions there was for a time a marked division in family religious life. The men of Europe worshiped the god of the new religion, and women gathered to worship their goddess at the esbats as they had always done. Kele-De, an Irish goddess surrounded by mystery and almost lost to history, was one such deity with an all female following. Her worshippers were known as kelles, and it was their right to take any and all lovers they chose. Oddly enough, Kele-De was probably a crone image in this early Christian period of Ireland. To the kelles' minds it was not the mother aspect, but the crone aspect which was seen as the lover and consort of the God. Kele-De's cult was wiped from Ireland by the witch hunters of the early Christian Church who soon realized they needed women's participation and consent (albeit a forced consent) to make the new religion work. And they knew most profoundly that they had to do away with the idea that women were free to accept lovers other than the husbands bound to them by the laws of the new religion.

Going skyclad, or ritual nudity, is most often a part of esbat observances, when utilized in Witta at all. Many people come to paganism attracted by this practice and by the reputedly loose bonds of pagan marriage. Contrary to popular belief, paganism is *not* a sexual free-for-all. Anyone who tries to present paganism this way is sorrily misled or else is looking for something which the religion simply does not offer.

The idea of going skyclad was more practical and prevalent in the long past than it is now. I have met few people who can get into a coven and honestly look at the nude human beings around them as earthly incarnations of the Goddess and God, which is how they are to be viewed. Sadly the patriarchy has caused us to fetishize human body parts, and has forced us to accept the standard of beauty as an artificial state of thinness and youth which requires faces be made-up and bodies unblemished. Crones hardly fit this concept, as does anybody who is overweight, large-busted, small-penised, or too short or tall. It has been my experience with several covens that those most ready to shed their clothing are very attractive people who are anxious to seek approval for the state of their physical being. They inevitably taunt those who do not wish to disrobe, insisting to them that they are simply not comfortable with their bodies. Who could be comfortable in such a situation?

Studies have repeatedly shown that when Western people are asked to describe their Goddess or God an overwhelming majority— over ninety-five per cent—view their deity as a robed figure. Even the modern day clergy of the patriarchy don robes as vestments of heavenly power. For these reasons I find that when working with others those groups that choose to wear robes work best together. There are exceptions to this of course and everyone should do what feels right. But be warned that any group which coerces or cajoles you into doing anything you do not wish to do is the wrong group for you. Get out fast! These people violate and defile the free will tenet of Witta.

Robes are fairly easy to make if you are reasonably handy with a needle. They can be of any color and can bear any design which is of meaning to you or your coven. Traditionally robes are black because this is the color of the night and of secrets. Here is a step-by-step guide to making your own. You will need fabric, a needle, pins, matching thread, scissors, chalk, and a partner to help you cut your pattern.

🌿 Measure yourself from head to toe and then purchase two times that amount of durable, washable material. For instance, if you are five feet, four inches you would need ten feet, eight inches of material which is approximately three and one quarter yards of fabric.

🌿 Iron the fabric and then cut it in half so you have equal amounts of yardage in each section.

🌿 Take one of the sections and lay it out flat on the floor or on any other hard surface which can support your weight. Make sure the wrong side of the fabric is facing up, that is, the underside of the cloth, not the front. Then lay the other piece on top of this one making sure they are lying as even as they can be. Pin them so they won't slip and so they will be easier to cut out later.

❧ Lie down in the center of the fabric and have your partner trace your outline with chalk. Make sure you trace about five to seven inches away from the body to allow for the fabric to meet around you and to allow for seams. Larger people will need to allow more room and very petite people will need somewhat less. Do not trace the head.

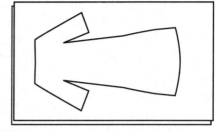

Robe traced on fabric with chalk.

❧ When you are satisfied that you have drawn a pattern which will fit you, cut both pieces out. They should look something like this:

After you cut out your pattern, you will have two pieces which look exactly the same. They resemble this.

If you wish to have a V neckline in your robe, cut a V in ONE piece of the fabric ONLY. A V is a nice touch and makes an attractive frame for any necklace you wish to wear.

❧ Turn the pieces so that the right sides of the material are facing each other and pin them together.

❧ Sew the two pieces together leaving a seam of about one half inch. Be sure not to sew over the neck hole, arm holes, or the bottom.

❧ Hem the neck and arms with a hand needle and thread. The bottom can be turned up and hemmed either by hand or machine. Have your partner pin up the hem for you at the proper length.

❧ If there is enough material left over (you can purchase extra) you might want to try and make a hood for your robe. Lay out two pieces of fabric and pin them as you did in the third step above.

❧ Cut two pieces that look like this:

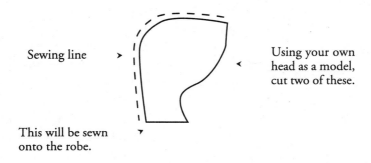

Sewing line →

Using your own head as a model, cut two of these.

This will be sewn onto the robe.

❧ Again, with the right sides together, sew up the long side, curving over to the pointed edge.

❧ Hem around the part which will be around your face.

❧ Sew the end of the long part into the back neckline of your robe. The finished product should look something like this:

A finished robe with hood

THE ESBAT CIRCLE

The belief that the moon induces madness is derived from the reports of people who accidentally stumbled upon witches reveling at their esbats. The word esbat comes from the old French esbattre meaning to gambol or frolic. Though many esbat rituals can be solemn and even awe inspiring, they are a time of rejoicing.

Wittans tended to work as solitaries during the esbats, even though they would gather in covens or as entire communities for sabbat celebrations. They would cast their circles and petition their deities alone on hillsides, in groves, and at their own hearthside.

Wittans who do have access to covens and choose to use them for esbat rituals should remember that this is a celebration of the creative life force which birthed and sustains the universe. Make your gatherings fun and joyful. Feast, play games, and tell stories, especially old Irish stories of goddesses and heroines.

Wittan esbat altars hold simple symbols of the Mother Goddess which are found in nature, though a complete set of ritual tools is fine if one feels a need for them. A cup or chalice of water is all that is really needed. Altars can be further decorated with night blooming flowers or goddess figurines, or white or red candles. Decoration is up to you, do what feels right.

The ceremony of cakes and ale is an old one in both the Wiccan and Wittan esbat traditions. The cake, or bread, symbolic of Mother Earth, and the wine, a symbol of water and the moon, is blessed and ritually consumed. Some of the cake is left for the birds and some wine is poured onto the ground as an offering to the Goddess. Thus earth and water, the two feminine elements of the four quarters, are utilized. Wittans who work in covens at esbats have developed a tradition of passing the chalice and allowing each covenor to make a toast and honor the Goddess in his or her own way. No one should be pushed. Remember that some people will not wish to drink wine. Others might be ill and do not wish to contaminate a communal cup. Allow everyone the freedom to express him or herself in his or her own way. Some might raise the cup to the moon, others pour some on the ground as an offering, others might offer a blessing or make a toast, and others might choose to kiss the cup. All are fitting honors to the Goddess.

Within an esbat circle is the time to link psychically with the Mother Goddess and to feel a part of her and of her earth. Offer her blessings, pledge to work for environmental causes, or spend some quiet time sending healing energy to a nearby woods. Magick of all types is worked within the esbat circle, especially magick for fertility. Whether you are a solitary or part of a coven, you can use the esbat to do magick for people who have requested it of you. Do as much as you can without depleting your personal energy stores.

DRAWING DOWN THE MOON

This is one of the most ancient rituals in Western paganism, and is practiced among the Wittans today much as it was thousands of years ago. This is the act of drawing the Mother Goddess into the physical body of a woman or priestess. It can be done by a solitary or within a group. Some prefer to watch, and others to participate. It is a moving and awe inspiring experience not everyone wants to have.

The purpose of drawing down the moon is threefold. One, it creates a time to merge with the Goddess so that her mysteries might be better understood. Two, the essence of Goddess which is present through this rite adds to the efficaciousness of all other circle workings. And thirdly, it is an ancient fertility aid because the full moon represents the midpoint of a woman's monthly cycle, the time when she is most fertile. To draw a part of the mother Goddess into yourself at this time is a form of sympathetic magick designed to promote human fertility.

Wicca uses the athame as the tool with which to draw down the moon. Wittans are more inclined to use a water-filled silver cup or a branch cut from a sacred willow tree on the night before the full moon.

Cast a circle in your usual way. You may place here whatever esbat rituals you like. But before you start on the drawing down the moon ritual, spend some time in meditation connecting with nature and with the full moon energies. When you feel ready, ask the presence of the Goddess to be with you that you might easily merge with her for a brief moment in earth time. Raise whatever tool you choose (be consistent in which one you choose to use, as the energies absorbed by it will make each subsequent drawing easier) and point it at the moon. You should have an unobstructed view of it, and the end of your tool should be directly in the center of your view. If you are using a water filled chalice hold the cup before you and see the moonlight dancing on the water.

Mentally fill the tool with moon energy. Visualize it happening and know that it is real. Open yourself to the Goddess' presence, and, when you feel her essence has entered your tool, pull the tool to your breast. Feel her spirit enter you as you become one with the mother Goddess. You may begin to feel a little different. If you are in a coven, others will notice the special charge in the air too.

You may speak as the Goddess if you feel moved to do so, or you may go through a prescribed ritual such as the Great Rite while in this state. As the Goddess you are now the priestess of the circle and can better direct magickal workings, power raising, communication with discarnates or faeries, or any other circle working.

Within a coven it happens occasionally that some unscrupulous types use their guise as the Goddess to lash out at fellow coven members or air their personal grievances. This should be stopped at once. Anyone who would stoop to this type of disruptive and hurtful behavior is definitely not filled with Goddess energy, and his or her actions defile the sacred space. Remember that merging with the Goddess is not an experience done just for the sake of gaining power. It is an act of spiritual fulfillment which enables you to better understand the Goddess and to ethically work your magick for mutual good.

When you have finished with the drawing down the moon ritual, simply hold your tool against your breast and feel the Goddess energy flow out of you and back into the tool. Raise the tool back towards the moon and feel yourself returning to normal consciousness.

Most women who perform this ceremony alone are moved to tears by the surge of emotion it produces. Take some time to sit quietly in the circle and contemplate on what has taken place before you move to close your circle. In a coven others may wish to talk about what took place and how they feel about it. All those feelings should be aired before your circle is closed. Be sure to thank the Goddess for her presence and her aid before dismissing your circle.

MOON MAGICK

Though magick can be worked at any of the moon's phases, most people feel best casting spells with the energy and completeness of a full moon. The full moon also lends its energies to the raising of the cone of power (described in Chapter 3).

Full moons relate to matters of motherhood, fertility, manifestation, money and prosperity, empowerment, full growth, protection (especially of children), and completeness. So virtually any magickal need can be worked during a full moon. Unlike the sabbats, work is not prohibited at the esbats, in fact magickal working is encouraged during these times. Like a kind mother the Mother Goddess has trouble denying her children.

Moon baths taken by lying under the light of a full moon, or by capturing moon beams in water and pouring them into a tub have been popular in Witta. This is a method of immersing one's self in the energy of the moon to gain the goal of a magickal working.

Full moon water can be gathered by setting a silver cup or chalice out under the moon and letting it absorb the energy. If you don't have a silver cup then use a glass container with a piece of silver coin or jewelry in it. This water can be poured into baths, charged towards a specific magickal goal, or have a magickal oil added to it. This water can be kept and used when the new moon appears at which time you have the natural waxing moon energy available to you again. (The old water should be discarded on fresh earth.)

Certain herbs are best collected at the full moon, and her light makes the task almost as easy as in daylight collection. Any herb intimately associated with moon energies should be collected now. Jasmine, a night blooming plant, is one of these. Moonwort, willow, mugwort, potatoes, and Irish moss are others.

If you enjoy the Celtic tree symbolism and wish to make a wand or a staff for each of the thirteen lunar months it is best to cut your branch just before the full moon of the corresponding month. Be sure to get the tree's permission for a cutting, then thank it, and leave a gift at its base.

If you wish to banish something from your life, do spells at the waning moon to take advantage of those decreasing energies. If you can mold a representation in clay of a bad habit, your bills, or something else you wish decreased, set this sculpture out every night from the full to the new moon while visualizing it vanishing from your life. When the moon is ready to wax again, bury the sculpture.

Likewise, if you wish to increase something, make a representation of it (money, love, health, etc.) and leave it out every night from the new to the full moon. Bury it when the moon is ready to wane again. And be sure to keep up your visualization at least once a day all through the moon's cycle until you get that which you seek.

While not overly concerned about moon phases for use in magick, Wittan tradition nonetheless holds that the influence of the full moon is felt for a seven-day period from three days before until three days after reaching fullness. It is generally thought best to take advantage of waxing energy and do magick just before the exact moment of fullness.

Magick can also be worked on the waning and waxing phases of the moon; but, except for special workings, covens do not regularly meet then. Many happy solitaries worship and work with the new crescent moon and with the last sliver of the waning crone moon.

Remember that moon phases have their uses and special energies, but if you need magick now—don't wait!

THE CELTIC TREE CALENDAR

The lunar tree calendar of the Celts has been a source of much controversy among scholars. Some contemporary mystics have attempted to take the tree calendar into new realms such as divination and Goddess manifestations. In essence, it was a method of keeping time by the thirteen yearly cycles of the moon. Each moon phase was assigned a corresponding tree, each tree being sacred to either the Goddess or the God.

The Druids are given credit for creating this system and there seems to be no scholarly evidence to prove otherwise. The twelve sacred trees and one plant (ivy) make up the thirteen months much like a traditional coven of twelve plus a High Priest or Priestess.

The trees the Druids chose for this were already trees which were sources of Celtic folklore. Several of the trees are said to be attractive to faery folk. And some of them were used in magick spells and herbal medicine, especially the trees which were thought to be feminine in character. After all, healing was an art practiced exclusively by women until the Druids came to power.

There are two major systems of tree calendars, each popularly credited as the "true" one, but both can make good academic arguments for themselves. The one beginning with the sequence birch-rowan-ash is probably the most widely used today. In reality both (and maybe several others) may have been used simultaneously in various regions of Celtic lands. Those interested in a more in-depth look at this calendar and rituals associated with it should read Pattalee Glass-Koentop's *Year of Moons, Season of Trees* (Llewellyn Publications).

The sacredness of trees in Ireland was a given in early Witta, but tree magick practice and calendar codification was the work of the Druids. Magick, divination, and rituals concerning trees were devised by the Druids and much of that knowledge was held secret. Some of the correspondences survive today in the form of nursery rhymes and popular Irish tree lore.

There is a popular misconception in the West that the Druids worshiped trees. This is not any more true than saying that Christians worship the cross. Both are merely symbols of deity and concepts which are held sacred in each religion.

Why trees? Trees were a physical representation of the old mystical belief "as above, so below," meaning that what is in the world of the unseen is manifest in the physical world. (This is the basic principle behind all magick.) A tree has two equal parts, a top which reaches into the above, and an equally complex and virtually identical part which reaches deep into Mother Earth—the below. Around the world many cultures have had a religious archetype or map known as the Tree of Life which explained the nature of the universe and all it contained. Nordic and Chinese pagans used theirs extensively and their lore remains to be studied by those who are interested.

Trees physically unite the heaven and the earth making Goddess and God one. It is no accident that the leaves or bark of most of the trees in the Celtic calendar are also used as fertility herbs. Like human clans, trees branch off with one limb begetting another and another.

Many pagan gods sacrificed themselves on trees, most notably Attis and Odin. Because of the all-reaching symbolism of the tree, this act united them with the "all that is" which contains both male and female energy. This is especially true in Witta because of the Irish belief that only women forms enter the afterlife of Tir-na-nog. Men must first be reabsorbed into a womb, and a tree, which takes in both sky and earth in a sort of great rite, would fulfill this symbolism.

In early Celtic myths it was believed one could see the Mother Goddess if one simply asked to, and then looked high into the branches of a tall willow tree. I was once in a circle with someone who tried this and the result was astonishing.

Other spirits were believed to dwell in trees, especially ones disposed to aiding humans or petitioning the deities on human behalf. In high branches lived the tree faeries who watched over children and laughed at human folly, but who, when approached through the proper rituals, could be beseeched to aid ailing or hungry humans. These Dryads were thought to have a special affinity for female Druids to whom they gave their name. And gnomes, the kindly earth elementals native to northern Ireland and Scotland, were said to make their homes within the roots of large oak trees and watch over all woodland creatures.

The counting of the Celtic moons begins with the full moon nearest Yule (which already places the calendar in a later period since Samhain was the original beginning of the Celtic new year). It must be remembered that this system was devised by the Druids who served as a link between the matriarchal and patriarchal periods of Irish history. The thirteen moons of the lunar year are as follows:

❧ Birch Moon: Moon of Inception; Moon of Beginning

❧ Rowan Moon: Moon of Vision; Astral Travel Moon

❧ Ash Moon: Moon of Waters

❧ Alder Moon: Moon of Utility; Moon of Efficacy; Moon of Self-Guidance

❧ Willow Moon: The Witches' Moon; Moon of Balance

❧ Hawthorn Moon: Moon of Restraint; Moon of Hindrance

❧ Oak Moon: Moon of Strength; Moon of Security

- ❧ Holly Moon: Moon of Encirclement; Moon of Polarity
- ❧ Hazel Moon: Moon of the Wise; Crone Moon
- ❧ Vine Moon: Moon of Celebration
- ❧ Ivy Moon: Moon of Buoyancy; Moon of Resilience
- ❧ Reed Moon: Moon of the Home; Hearth Moon; Moon Which Manifests Truth
- ❧ Elder Moon: Moon of Completeness

The trees were also used for magickal purposes, and working with them within their special months was believed most efficacious. The leaves, and sometimes even the bark, were used like herbs and made into talismans or thrown onto magickal fires. The following is a list of the magickal properties generally associated with each tree:

- ❧ Alder: completeness, spirituality
- ❧ Ash: prosperity, protection, healing
- ❧ Birch: protection of children, purification
- ❧ Blackberry vines: prosperity, protection, healing, inspiration
- ❧ Blueberry vines: protection, spirituality
- ❧ Elder: exorcism, prosperity, banishing, healing
- ❧ Grape vines: fertility, inspiration, prosperity, binding spells
- ❧ Hawthorn: fertility, peace, prosperity
- ❧ Hazel: manifestation, protection, fertility
- ❧ Holly: protection, prophecy, magick for animals
- ❧ Ivy: healing, protection, cooperation, exorcism
- ❧ Oak: all positive purposes
- ❧ Reed: fertility, protection, love
- ❧ Rowan: healing, empowerment
- ❧ Thistle vines: courage, protection
- ❧ Vine: dependent on the plant
- ❧ Willow: love, healing, protection, fertility

There are several types of herbal spells you might try if you wish to use the leaves or bark from these trees.

If you want to bring something into your life try tying the herb in a small bag around your neck or waist. As you make the pouch be sure to pour your own energies into the herb, clearly visualizing your goal.

If you wish to get something out of your life pour your energies into the herb while concentrating on your goal. Do this as if you were telling your problems to the herb and feel it absorb your negative energy. When that is done bury the herb to ground and diffuse the negative power.

You can also bring the influence of the herb into your circle or dwelling by burning it as an incense. Toss small bits of the bark onto charcoal incense blocks after empowering it with your need.

In the case of exorcism use the incense first while visualizing the harmful entity or energy being broken up and absorbed safely into the earth. Then take the smoking incense around your home or other place you wish to cleanse while chanting something like:

Smoke of power at this hour,
Clear this place of all things sour.
Now depart all ill and harm,
By the blessing of this charm.

After you have done this, make a small talisman of the tree herb by either carving on the bark or placing some in a small pouch and wearing it around for a while to ensure that the harmful entities will not return.

You can also bathe in the tree essence by boiling the leaves or the bark for thirty minutes or so while concentrating on your goal and empowering it with your energies. Pour the liquid into a bath. Be sure you are not allergic to the juice of the tree by making a test patch on your arm twenty-four hours before you wish to use it.

A note about cooking herbs: metal has always had a negative effect on magick. The only exception to this seems to be a cauldron. Any time you wish to use something as a catalyst for magick it cannot come into contact with metal. Therefore, a glass cooking pan is a good investment.

THE OGHAM ALPHABET

The ogham alphabet was in existence several centuries before the Druids came to the height of their power, some say as early as the fourth century B.C.E. But it came into its own when the Druids, who claimed it was revealed to them by the god Ogham, standardized it and made it workable.

The alphabet consists of a series of straight and slanted lines which rest either above, below, or across a central line. Each set of lines and their positioning on the larger line represent phonetic sounds rather than letters. The straight lines made it easy to work these characters on stone, wood, or other carvings. The ogham alphabet is known today because of stone carvings found in Ireland and Scotland, and not from any samples of writing on paper or parchment.

The most famous example of ogham writing in Ireland is the Ogham Stone in Coolmagort, County Kerry. This large phallic-shaped stone has one squared edge which is used in lieu of a line. The carvings are believed to date from the first century C.E.

Wittans today can use the ogham to carve names or words of power onto wands, staffs, cups or other magick tools. It can even be used to write in the Book of Shadows, but unless you work with the ogham on a regular basis, reading your Book may be difficult. Ogham characters can be used on stones or benches at your circle site, and as decorative borders for any certificates for rites of passage which your coven uses. And if you decide to make a separate wand or staff for each of the thirteen moon calendar trees, you might consider carving the name of the wood on the wand with ogham lettering so you can tell them apart. After all, once your wands are stripped of their bark and varnished, they will look maddeningly alike.

The Druids were said to be able to manipulate the alphabet to create sounds that brought about creation or manifestation. This idea that words create was familiar in India and the Middle East from where it may have traveled to Europe. These sounds were correlated by the bards of music (Druids who specialized in the study of music) to correspond to musical notes which were said to cause inanimate objects to move at the Druids' will. Many people have attempted to recreate these sounds, but so far no one has been successful.

The ogham has been found reading both left to right from the top of a piece, and from top to bottom from the top left corner of a piece. Either way is correct, and if you wish to use this writing within your Book of Shadows it is probably best to use a left to right method to which English speakers are more accustomed.

The ogham has thirteen consonants, one for each of the lunar months, five vowels, and symbols for Ng and Sh. The following examples show both the left to right and top to bottom forms of the alphabet.

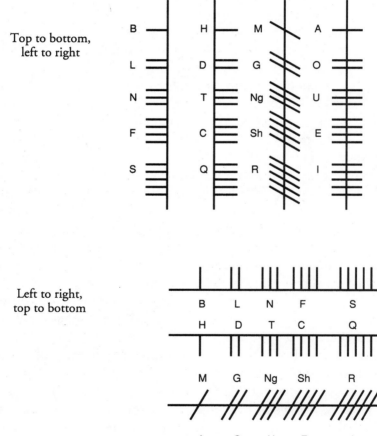

Top to bottom, left to right

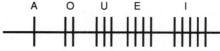

Left to right, top to bottom

7

The Sabbats

The eight sabbats which are now known to Western pagans were not always the eight sabbats of Ireland. Once Bealtaine, Midsummer, Lughnasadh, Samhain, and Yule were the only actual sabbats, and even then the Roman and Nordic invaders had a profound influence on the prominence and significance of Yule. The sabbats are given different spellings and pronunciations within different traditions. Here, I use the Irish spellings and give the Irish Gaelic pronunciations.

The word sabbat is from the Greek word sabatu meaning "to rest." And since to perform an act of magick is work, it is customary that no magickal working be done on a sabbat unless there is a pressing, life-threatening need. Sabbats are for relaxing, enjoying friends, and celebrating life.

The eight solar sabbats represent the turning of the wheel of the year, and each of them honors a stage in the eternal life cycle of the Goddess and God. Their stories and lore have been acted out in community plays and in Wittan circles for thousands of years. And remnants of these stories survive in folk songs, faery tales, children's games, and nursery rhymes.

By some accounts the dates for the sabbats in the old Celtic lands are given as roughly ten to fifteen days off what is commonly observed within the rest of Western paganism. I find no evidence for the persistence of this idea other than some confusion which logically might have arisen when Great Britain switched from the Julian to the Gregorian calendar in 1752. In that year eleven days were removed from the year with September 2 being followed by September 14. Since the dates of the sabbats are figured in times of solar astrology it stands to reason that the autumn sabbats in 1752 were thrown off. Whether this reasoning has any validity or not is up for debate, but it is one theory for why some insist that the true Celtic Samhain is around November 11 and the Celtic Bealtaine around May 15.

To the Celts the "day" begins with sundown the evening before. This idea originated not in Celtic lands, but in India and the Middle East. Even today the Jewish calendar begins counting each day this way. In Witta, for instance, the beginning of the Samhain sabbat officially begins at sundown on October 30.

The following is a model of the wheel of the year which begins with Samhain and flows clockwise.

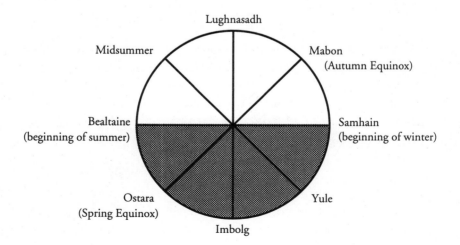

Samhain marked the beginning of the old Celtic new year and it is with this sabbat that we Wittans begin our journey through the wheel of the year.

SAMHAIN
(Sow-in or Sah-vin)
October 31

Samhain, also known as Halloween, still retains much of its original form and meaning in Ireland despite the efforts of the Church to turn it into a massive observance of feasting and prayer for its vast pantheon of saints. When the Church diabolized paganism and its deities they began a campaign of fear among Ireland's Christians concerning Halloween. In many parts of rural Ireland leaving the safety of hearth and home is still discouraged on this night.

The idea that evil spirits walk the earth at Samhain is a misinterpretation of the pagan belief that the veil which separates the land of the living from the land of the dead is at its thinnest on this night, and in Witta deceased ancestors and other friendly spirits are invited to join the sabbat festivities. These spirits, especially those of the recently departed, are asked to help in divinations, and it was considered a propitious time to strengthen karmic ties with those whom you wished to be with again throughout another lifetime.

However, if good spirits could walk the earth, a few bad ones could also sneak in. After all, death would not suddenly turn someone who had lived a mean and parsimonious life into a joyful and helpful ghost. Just in case of this, the idea of the jack-o'-lantern was born. The first ones in Ireland were carved turnips which could be easily carried if one needed to be abroad during the night. All these carved faces are probably relics of the even earlier custom of placing candles in windows to guide the spirits along their way. Today it is still a Wittan custom to place candles in the windows and to leave plates of food for the visiting spirits.

Halloween bonfires are lit across the island even in modern Catholic Ireland, and it is generally considered unadvisable to throw water out a window or let the cat out as the little people are especially active on this night and one would not wish to anger them. Sídhe mounds, or faery hills, were dangerously opened to the world of humans on this night, and if one were careless he or she risked falling under a faery spell never to return to the human realm.

An old Celtic custom states that one will have good luck all year long if a dark visitor is the first caller of the new year. This may have been a form of sympathetic magick whereby one hoped any ill-meaning spirits would see a dark presence already upon a dwelling and not be bothered with it. It was also believed by the fair-skinned Irish that dark people were gifted with special occult powers. As Samhain marked the beginning of the new year it was a certainty that on November 1 the darkest people in town were paraded around the countryside as token visitors.

Samhain also marked the beginning of the Irish winter, as Bealtaine marked the beginning of summer in May—the only two recognized seasons. In Witta, Samhain began "the dark of the year," though most other pagan traditions mark the Autumn Equinox as the turning point into darkness. Field work and herding were put aside for winter, and people turned their thoughts and lives inward.

The predominantly herding culture of Ireland slaughtered much of its stock before Samhain rather than try to feed the animals on the sparse land through the long winters. Fresh meat was always served at sabbat feasts, as was colcannon. Colcannon is a mashed potato, cabbage, and onion dish still served in Ireland on All Saints' Day. It was an old Wittan tradition to hide in it a ring for a bride, a button for a bachelor, a thimble for a spinster, and a coin for wealth, or any other item which local custom decreed. As this was the new year, the person who got these items in their portion had his or her fortune told for the coming year. If you serve colcannon, please exercise caution. More than a few people have choked on their good fortune.

Recipes for colcannon vary slightly depending upon which region of Ireland one comes from. The following recipe is from the Galway region.

Colcannon

4 cups mashed potatoes (don't use artificial potato flakes)
2 1/2 cups cabbage, cooked and chopped fine
1/2 cup butter (don't use corn oil margarine)
1/2 cup evaporated milk or cream
3/4 cup onion, chopped very fine and sautéed (traditionalists sauté in lard or bacon grease, but butter is acceptable)
1/4 teaspoon salt
1/8 teaspoon white pepper

Place all ingredients, except the cabbage, in a large pan and cook over low heat while stirring.

Turn the heat up to medium and add the chopped cabbage. The mixture will take on a pale green cast which will look inherently Irish.

Stir occasionally until the mixture is cool enough to eat. Drop in the thimble, button, ring, and coin and stir well. Serves about eight.

A similar Irish dish called champ is more popular in the north of Ireland and is served in individual bowls with the butter on top rather than mixed into the dish. Champ is more heavy-handed with the onions than is colcannon, but it still uses the four traditional divinatory items.

So ingrained in the Wittan mind was the Samhain feast that the Church could do nothing to halt the practice even among converts to the new faith. In an attempt to disguise the meaning of the sabbat, the Catholic Church made the day after Samhain the Feast of All Saints followed then by a day to honor the dead. This feast was later renamed Harvest Home, and much of its pagan significance returned. In rural England and Wales this feast is still observed complete with a Harvest Queen and King which at one time would have represented the Goddess and God.

In Western paganism Samhain marks the third and final harvest, and so it is also in Witta. All crops had to be gathered by sundown on October 30. To dare to harvest anything after this night was risking the worst luck since the phookas, the nasty-tempered Irish hobgoblins, claimed for themselves whatever remained uncut in the fields.

The Norse invaders probably brought the idea of blood sacrifice to the Samhain observances, a custom not unfamiliar to Ireland because of Druidic practices. Blood sacrifice was a logical adaptation to this sabbat since this is when the God dies, waiting to be reborn of the Goddess at Yule. Royal sacrifices, other human offerings, and then animal sacrifices were a common theme in the very old days of Witta. They not only symbolized the God's demise, but sought to offer a substitute for him in death so that he could soon be reborn. Fortunately the Wittan Rede of "harm none" also applies to animals, and we have happily evolved out of our need to make a blood sacrifice of any kind to our deities.

With October comes the apple harvest, and the idea of wassailing the apple trees (ritually drinking to their health with levity) was a Samhain ritual which was later moved to Yule (and then to Christmas) through Roman and Nordic influence. Wassailing has come to mean the drinking to the health of anyone with a spiced punch prepared especially for the holiday. This custom is still seen in parts of Ireland, and is common practice in nearby England and Wales. In Witta it is traditional before Samhain to take an apple, carve it in half, pour your illnesses or bad habits into it, put it back together, and bury it in the ground. This is a direct ancestor of today's new year's resolutions.

Bobbing for apples, a common Halloween activity, evolved from the idea of capturing the spirit of the dormant Goddess who will grieve for her consort until Yule. To capture the fruit sacred to her was to ensure her continued presence and good will even though she was virtually "incommunicado" for the next six weeks.

At Samhain sacred hazelnuts were taken and tossed in divination patterns and then buried to honor the old gods. They are also consumed at this time of year to induce mystic wisdom, and the Druids used them this way, even barring their use to the common folk.

To divine with hazelnuts draw a small circle about one foot in diameter on the ground in front of you. Take thirteen nuts and shake them around in your cupped hands while concentrating on your question. Gently toss the nuts in front of you. Those that land directly in the circle have the most bearing on you. If more land in the circle than out of it, you have a right to be concerned about the question you asked. Study the nuts for patterns which you can interpret. For example, if the nuts are all pointing in one direction this could be an indication of a direction you need to take your problem. If they appear in the form of a familiar object use that information to apply to your question. Occasionally they may appear as letters of the alphabet which you can relate to your question. A letter N might mean "no" and a Y "yes." Or they might be the initials of someone you know.

The cauldron, so intimately linked with the crone who is in her full aspect at Samhain, features prominently in this sabbat circle. The cauldron, representing the primal melting pot where life begins, ends, and is reborn, is often the centrally featured item during Samhain worship. Cauldrons are used as centerpieces on altars and in circles, and wine, representative of spirit and of blood, is often poured into them so the crone can stir them to new life. Some Wittans even wish to have the Samhain bonfire burned within the cauldron's confines.

Samhain sabbat circles usually involve an invitation to, and blessing of, the crone, called the caillech in Ireland and Scotland, and mourning for the dying God. It is a time to reaffirm our belief in the oneness of all spirits, and in our firm resolution that physical death is not a finality. Acorns representing the harvest god, Lugh, usually adorn the altar along with the bounty of the harvest for which we thank the Goddess. Yet the observance is not all somber. Like its secular counterpart, Halloween, Samhain is a time for pranks, circle games, and merrymaking which could be teasingly blamed on nearby spirits.

Indian corn and decorative bouquets prevalent throughout the harvest months are a holdover from when such stalks of corn, wheat, or barley were chosen to be stored away to become the grain dolly (corn dolly in North America), a symbol of the Great Mother used at Imbolg. Barley was the grain of choice in Ireland since corn, indigenous to South America, was unknown there until the sixteenth century.

Masks have been used in all cultures of the world to invoke animal or totem energies, as aids to sympathetic magick, to raise power, and to imitate the deities. The first known mask dates from the Paleolithic period and is represented in a cave drawing in southern France.

The tradition of masking one's face at Samhain goes so far back in antiquity that it is difficult to know just what the original significance was. Some say it was originally a form of sympathetic magick for witches to dress as the Gods and Goddesses, and that it was done at all sabbats. By masking one's self as deity the Goddesses and Gods were believed to be more readily present, and also in this way participants could truly be viewed by their fellow covenors as deities incarnate. Others claim that it was a ploy to scare away faeries and mischievous spirits, but this has overtones of a custom of a much later period. During the Burning Times masking hid the identity of witches while in circle so they might escape detection.

It was believed that when masking was representative of a certain deity or goal it was also a form of sympathetic magick which would ensure a good hunt, vital to survival through a winter for which Samhain is the beginning date in old Ireland. Therefore it is conceivable that the earliest Samhain masks were of game animals.

All masks once served ritual purposes, usually those of sympathetic magick. If one wished to achieve something one would take on the persona of the thing wanted. For example, if your goal was a successful hunt you would mask yourself as your game and seek to think and be that game. If you wished to take on a deity form for the purposes of bestowing blessings and favors on yourself or your family, you would wear a mask which you believed to look like the deity you wished to temporarily become.

Many masks are available commercially in October including some which might interest Wittans. Or you can make your own. There are many methods to use and some are so simple a child could make them. Almost everyone has made a mask in school using a paper plate with eyeholes cut in it and a rubber band to hold it in place.

More elaborate masks can be made from papier-mâché. This requires cutting many strips of newspaper which will form your mask. To bond them you must dip them in a large bowl which contains a thick paste made from water and flour. Begin with three cups of flour and one and a half cups of water. Mix them, varying the proportions slightly, until you achieve a nice thick goo.

As a base for the papier-mâché mask you might try a cardboard box or a wig stand. Any of these things will be big enough to allow you to place your head in them. Be sure to cut eye holes first and any holes you feel you need for breathing. Work your paper strips around these openings. Once the paste dries it will be virtually impossible to cut the holes.

You can shape the mask any way you like by molding the strips of paper. The elderly and dying Great Horned God, with his proud antlers, is the god form honored at Samhain, and you can make a Horned God mask by taking two sections of rolled up newspaper and placing wet papier-mâché strips around them. Then you can add more wet strips to attach the horns to the body of the mask to look like the antlers of a deer.

When you have finished with the body of the mask, you can paint on facial features, color, words, etc. You can also glue on sequins, beads, buttons, hair, or any other decoration which pleases you and suits your purposes.

Papier-mâché can be molded into almost anything and you will find lots of uses for it once you start working with it. Many of the props you might wish to make for your seasonal circles can be crafted in this way.

Because of the closeness of the spirit world, Samhain was the prime night of the year to conduct a regression—a trip into the collective unconsciousness for a glimpse at a past life. Various trance methods are used to transport a person back in time. Common methods were guided meditation, concentrated relaxation, and herbal aids. This, and divination, are still popular Samhain pastimes. Some of the clearest regressions have been performed at this sabbat.

Drumming is more commonly heard at this sabbat than any other. Ritual drumming had been used worldwide to summon spirits, and the rhythmic pounding induces a quick altered state of consciousness necessary for several traditional practices including spirit contact and astral projection.

In matters of spirit contact the Wittans of medieval Ireland could not resort to the use of tools such as Ouija boards and Tarot cards because the practice was condemned by the all-powerful Church. By owning such things one risked death. Methods which could be done with common household items were used.

Scrying into a fire, glass, or dark bowl was a popular method of contacting the dead, as were meetings on the astral plane achieved through astral projection, the expulsion of the subtle body into a different realm. Simply sit before the object you want to look in, preferably one with a reflective surface, and gaze into it while concentrating on the person you wish to see.

With the death of the God, the wheel of the year turns again, bringing us to Yule and his rebirth.

YULE
circa December 22

At Yule the God is reborn of the virgin Goddess. The God represents the sun which "returns" after this night to again bring warmth and fertility to the land. The profusion of lights on every house and tree at Christmastime is a carry-over of the candles and fires lit in sympathetic magick to lure back the waning sun. Today it is still an Irish custom to leave lights burning all through the house on midwinter night to honor the sun's return.

Interestingly enough, the word "virgin" is another term mistranslated and misrepresented by the early Church. Even those of us today forget that the term had absolutely nothing to do with the hymen, a bit of useless flesh which is now evolved away from most women. The term "virgin" was applied to priestesses in European temples, particularly during Rome's pagan period. The term identified a woman who was a complete entity unto herself. She was not bound by secular law, had no husband, and she was free to take all the lovers she chose. In other words, she was "intact"—she needed nothing else but herself for completeness. Eventually the idea of being "intact" was applied to the hymen, the thin layer of tissue covering an unentered vagina.

The Goddess, in a virgin form but hardly sexually innocent, gives birth to her son who will be her lover at the spring sabbats (as he was the previous spring), and the father of his next Yule incarnation.

Yule in both old Roman paganism and in the Norse tradition was the start of the new year. The word "yule" comes from a Nordic word meaning "wheel." In the tenth century Nordic pagan influence moved the date of the accepted Celtic new year from Samhain to Yule, where most pagans now observe it, though die-hard Wittans will still insist on Samhain for this.

The tradition of Yuletide gift giving also comes from Rome. The celebration of Saturnalia was a new year's festival of pagan Rome where gifts were given in honor of loved ones who had died during the previous year. Early Roman explorers brought this tradition to Ireland where it remained as part of the Yule celebration.

Yule altars throughout paganism show the influence of Ireland and the Druids with their holly, pine, and mistletoe coverings. Yule rituals enact birthing rites, ask for the sun god's return, and beseech the Goddess to turn the wheel of the year again. The wooing "back" of the sun is a symbolic act in itself, a carry-over from an earlier period of time when people lived in fear of betrayal by the divine elements which sustained them. By the Druidic period, Wittans were not ignorant of astronomy and were fully aware that the sun was right where it always had been, but ancient rhythms compelled them to enact the old rituals. In some covens it is still traditional to fast during Yule, with feasting and celebration to begin the following day when the sun was on its way back to the earth, an image interpreted as the rebirth of the sun god.

Two sets of images fight for supremacy at Yule. One set of battlers is the Holly King and the Oak King, and the other is the birds, wren and robin.

The Holly King and the Oak King are probably constructs of the Irish Druids to whom these two trees were highly sacred. The Oak King (king of the waxing year) kills the Holly King (king of the waning year) at Yule. The Oak King then reigns supreme until Midsummer when the two battle again with the Holly King the victor. Vestiges of the Holly King's image can be seen in our modern Santa Claus. He wears red, dons a sprig of holly in his hat, lives but one night a year, drives a team of eight (number of solar sabbats) deer, an animal sacred to the Celtic gods.

The other battle image is probably much older and was observed in Ireland as soon as they became aware of which animals were prevalent through which seasons. At Yule the robin, the bird symbolic of the waxing year, kills the wren, the bird symbolic of the waning year. At one time it was a certainty that at least one wren per family or community was slain in an act of sympathetic magick on midwinter eve.

In their book *Eight Sabbats for Witches,* Janet and Stewart Farrar relate that in County Mayo "wren boys" still go door to door carrying an effigy of a dead wren on a bed of holly while soliciting coins to bury it. In terms of sympathetic magick, to "bury the wren" would mean to bury winter.

Pine trees were decorated at this time of year with images of what one wished the waxing year to hold for them. Images of items to be used at future sabbats, fruits for a successful harvest, love charms for happiness, nuts for fertility, and coins for wealth adorned the trees. Even on today's Christmas tree many of these images remain intact, though their original meaning is long forgotten. Pine trees are sacred to the Goddess. Because they don't "die" from year to year as do deciduous trees, they represent the eternal aspect of the Goddess who never dies. And their verdant greenery was symbolic of the hope for the sun's return to make the earth green once more.

When Norse influence moved the new year from Samhain to Yule, the practice of new year's divination came with it. Looking into the future was a favorite pastime on Yule night. Asking a question, throwing nuts into a Yule fire, and watching how they popped foretold the future. If they jumped high your answer was favorable, sputtering indicated a negative reply.

The Yule log was probably a custom of the Druids, though some scholars feel the practice predates them. The log is a phallic symbol and is inherent in fertility magick. A log, usually of the God-related oak tree, is carved into a small section which can be brought easily into a dwelling. Three holes, to represent the Triple Goddess, are bored into the top and the log is "impregnated" with three candles. Sometimes the candles are all virgin white, but most often they are the Goddess' tri-aspect colors of white, red and black. The entire log is then decoratively covered with holly and evergreens to represent the intertwining of the God and Goddess who have been reunited on this sabbat. Hopes for fertile crops, herds, and families are invested in the Yule log image.

Later in Irish history a curious custom grew up around Yule. It became traditional for stories of the heroic giant and god of Irish mythology, Finn MacCool, to be remembered on this night. Finn was the giant who protected the island from invaders and who initially drove the invading Firbolgs back into the sea. Scottish pagans sometimes refer to Yule as Finn's Eve and tell similar tales of the exploits of the Scottish version of Finn MacCool.

Finn's tales can be found in most books on Irish mythology, several of which are listed in the bibliography. To add a different flavor to your Wittan Yule observance you might want to try setting aside some time to honor Finn.

Many common Christmas carols contain pagan images that are not so subtle. "Deck the Halls" contains not one Christian religious image. In this carol we sing of decorating with holly, singing Yuletide carols, dancing ("merry measure"), and the telling of pagan myths ("Yuletide treasure"). Look into other Christmas songs for hints on how to adapt them to your own Yule rituals. You will find you need make very few changes.

Feel free to have a lighted tree in your home, hang a wreath (a symbol of the wheel of the year) on your door, and give gifts in memory of loved ones. Remember that Yule is a pagan festival.

IMBOLG
(Em-bowl/g)
February 2

Imbolg (Imbolc in Wicca) was not a sabbat in early Ireland, but this was a special day to honor the Great Mother Goddess Brigid. By Imbolg the waxing year is assured and thanks were given to her for turning the wheel of the year once more. So ingrained in Ireland was this festival that the church was forced to name it Saint Bridget's Day.

Grain dollies, often called corn dollies in other traditions, are woven into human or symbolic form. Weaving straw, corn, wheat, or barley to form an image was an old form of fertility magick. Any form of grain was acceptable, but barley was the grain of choice in Ireland.

In Ireland the straws were often woven not into human form, but into an equilateral cross known today as Saint Bridget's cross, but which is actually a sun wheel sacred to the god Lugh. Wittans cherish these dollies which are kept throughout the year in a cradle known as a bride's bed, from the name of goddess Brigid which is spelled Brid (pronounced breed) in Gaelic. The figure is usually dressed in white at this sabbat, or in something else related to marriage, with her garb updated as the wheel of the year carries her on into cronehood. Sometimes male fertility symbols such as nuts are tossed in the cradle with her. The dolly should be stored in a place of honor in your home. Even in modern rural Ireland elaborate welcoming rituals accompany the bride, and she is sometimes paraded down a village street.

To make a grain dolly all you need is some stalks of wheat, corn, or barley which you have kept from your last harvest. In many places dried corn shocks are sold as decorations and make excellent dollies. You also need some string and scissors.

The dolly does not have to take a human form; many people are uncomfortable making a human-shaped grain dolly. You might want to consider weaving a mat which will be rolled up and used as a dolly to be dressed and honored.

The mat is easy. Just count out about a dozen grain leaves about eighteen inches long, and about two dozen that are half that size. Lay the longer ones side by side in a row. Taking a strip of the shorter ones go *over the first leaf and under the second* and so on until you have woven the strip in and out of the entire layout of grain. The next short length will be started by going *under the first grain.* Continue this way until the next leaf has been woven in. Push it up against the first one you wove and it should be opposite in form—where the first one goes under, the second should go over, and vice versa.

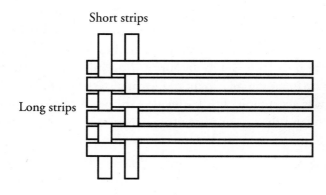

Short strips

Long strips

When you have woven all the grain leaves in, roll up the dolly in either the long or short direction. With your string, tie the top and bottom of the mat loosely so that it will not unroll. You might want to add a third string in the center for extra strength, and to represent the Triple Goddess.

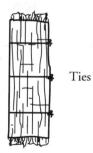

Ties

The mat-style dolly can be dressed as easily as a human-shaped one, perhaps more so because it is sturdier. But if you wish to try a more realistic dolly try wrapping some of the grain leaves around some quilt batting or a polystyrene ball available at craft stores. Leave the loose ends free to represent the body.

A grain dolly made with grain strips over a polystyrene ball. Tie securely under the "neck" and allow the rest to hang loose.

If you wish to go a step further you can take leaves and wrap them around the center and bottom of the loose part to become arms and legs. But the legs will probably be covered with clothing and not seen anyway.

To dress your grain dolly as an Imbolg bride you can do this by simply wrapping it in lengths of white natural fabric, or you can purchase commercially made doll clothes, or, if you are good with a needle, you can try making a dress yourself.

Imbolg is also the sabbat where magickal wells (cauldron images) are visited and coins thrown in them in Brigid's name to grant wishes. Many of the ancient magickal wells were usurped by the Church and either covered over or encased within church walls. But a few can still be found. If you are in Ireland looking for one, ask the locals who will enjoy telling you the lore of their community, especially if you are a descendant of their region.

Outside of Ireland you can mimic this custom with any well or body of deep water. Go to it when you can be alone and throw in three coins while stating and concentrating on your wish for the coming year. Before you leave ask the guardian spirits of the well to look after the energies you have left behind and to bless them until they manifest.

Crossroads also figure prominently in this sabbat. This is a night that spirits of the dead are said to walk among the living, and for centuries the Irish have seen them at the safety of a crossroads. The crossroad also represents an equal-armed cross which throughout ancient Europe was seen as a symbol of balance and protection.

Saint Bridget's cross, Brigid's cross, or the sun wheel, is also represented by a perfect intersection. Since the cross is a protective symbol, the Irish often went on the eve before this sabbat to bury negativity at a crossroad so it couldn't escape, much in the same way a Latin cross on a coffin was designed to keep vampires contained. But Wittans know that Saint Bridget's cross is a symbol of the sun god and of their beloved Brigid. Both Wittans and Christians in Ireland weave them for home ornamentation. They can be used to decorate an Imbolg circle, and kept to use year round in your celebrations. We even hang ours on our Yule tree.

Crossbars of sun wheel

To make your own sun wheel go to a craft shop and purchase approximately six to eight yards of unbroken dried grape vine. When you get home place the vine in a tub of warm water for several hours until the vine becomes pliable. Aim to make your sun wheel about six to eight inches in diameter. Take two or three yards of vine and cut into strips about ten to twelve inches long. Make two such lengths of these and lay them crosswise. You can weave them in and out of each other if you like.

About six to eight inches from the center of the design, anchor one end of the rest of the unbroken vine. While trying to keep the vine going in a perfect circle, take the vine on down to the next crossbar and intertwine one strand of the crosspiece in the vine to hold it. Move on to the next crosspiece and repeat.

A finished grape vine
sun wheel

Keep moving around the perimeter of the sun wheel weaving the vine in and out so that it holds. You may find that you need to cut it off in places and start over to get a true woven effect. Weave a strand of each of the long crosspieces into the circle each time you pass it.

In Witta, as in other pagan traditions, Imbolg is a festival of lights. Candles are lit in profusion, and even worn in crowns on young girls' heads, a custom which also came from the Norse invaders, and is intended to be a representation of the virgin aspect of the Goddess. At Imbolg, spring is not far away and the lights act again as a sympathetic magickal draw for the sun and its warmth. Guessing how long until spring shows itself is a common pastime, absorbing much space in the annals of ancient folk lore. In America, Groundhog Day, also on February 2, is a weather divination ritual which tries to predict when the warmth of spring will show itself. Depending on whether or not the groundhog sees his shadow foretells if spring will come early or have to wait for six more weeks until the Spring Equinox.

In Ireland it was considered a sign of an early spring if one heard a lark singing on Imbolg. Larks are sacred to the God, and this belief may have stemmed from a conviction that the God was coming early, in a hurry to find his Goddess bride.

An Imbolg altar might contain a profusion of candles (as many as are safe) to represent increasing warmth, the bride's bed, sun wheels, a cup of melted snow, and any symbols of the coming spring which can be found in your climate.

OSTARA
(Oh-star-ah)
circa March 22

Ostara is a Latin name, and comes from the name of the spring goddess Eostre for whom Easter is named. In old Ireland this sabbat was virtually overlooked until Nordic invaders brought it into prominence. In Celtic Cornwall and Wales, Ostara was known as Lady Day, and was the official return of the Goddess after her winter hibernation. Though most branches of the tradition refer to the old Latin name, in Witta it is usually just called the Spring Equinox.

As a result of this Nordic influence most of the myths associated with Ostara are of Greek, Roman, or Nordic origin. Many of them concern trips by deities into the underworld, and their eventual struggle to return from the land of the dead.

Many of the fertility rites associated with Bealtaine were transferred to Ostara where they happily co-exist today. The balance of night and day made this association easy to make. The Great Rite, an often misunderstood pagan ritual, began to be enacted on this sabbat. This rite symbolizes the sexual union of Goddess and God and of all living males and females, and from this union comes all creation, both the physical and the spiritual. Many pagan traditions enact the Great Rite at every sabbat, not just the spring ones. The rite is performed by one male and one female who were representative of the male and female polarity of the God/dess. They usually unite "sexually" in a symbolic manner by placing a knife (phallic symbol) in a chalice (primal female image), though some traditions allow for everyone to leave the circle except the two participants, and no one knows how the rite is enacted.

As the growing and mating seasons approached in Ireland, whole communities would celebrate the enactment of the Great Rite and the positive effects such sympathetic magick would surely have on the crops, the animal populations ... and the people.

Patriarchal religious teachers have often criticized paganism's use of the Goddess' son as her lover, using this imagery of "proof" of the "sinfulness and immorality" of pagan religions. Remember that these stories are symbolic, and represent the eternal existence of the deities rather than concrete familial relationships.

In keeping with the Church's practice of grafting saintly feast days onto any pagan festival it could not eradicate, the feast day of Saint Patrick, Ireland's patron saint, was assigned near the time of the equinox. After being repeatedly driven out of Ireland, Patrick's procession was said to have arrived at Tara to present his new faith to the high king on Easter Sunday, which not coincidentally also falls near Ostara.

The practice of decorating eggs is as old as the first human who saw life miraculously come from them. Eggs were held as sacred objects of life, carried as fertility amulets, decorated to honor the deities, and given as cherished gifts. The concept of a rabbit delivering decorated eggs comes from the legend of the goddess Eostre, who figures largely in the Teutonic and Greek pantheons. So much did a lowly rabbit wish to please his goddess that he laid the sacred eggs in her honor, gaily decorated them, and then humbly presented them to her. So pleased was she that she wished all human kind to share in her joy. In honoring her wishes, the rabbit went through all the world and distributed these little decorated gifts of life.

In decorating eggs, many pagans like to use natural dyes derived from flowers and herbs. To make the dyes, boil a large handful of an herb or flower until the water is well colored. Place the water in a glass heat-resistant cup or other non-metal container, stir in a teaspoon of vinegar, then place a hard boiled egg into the mixture. Getting the color to take requires a bit more time than the commercial chemical dyes, but most feel it is worth the effort to have this contact with the old ways. The dyes do tend to be less stable though, so protect the eggs from being scratched.

Here is a list of the most commonly used natural dyes. But feel free to experiment and find your own combinations with any non-toxic herb, vegetable, or flower:

❧ Yellow: carrots, turmeric, fenugreek

❧ Orange: onion skins, paprika

❧ Red: red onion skins, madder root, cayenne

❧ Red-violet: purple grapes

❧ Green: carrot tops, bracken

❧ Blue: blueberries, red cabbage, black raspberries

❧ Blue-violet: blackberries, beets

Eggs can also be painted with brushes and non-toxic water color paints. With this method you can freely express your creativity and design eggs to personally represent yourself, loved ones, the sabbat, and/or your favorite god/dess aspects. With a few trinkets and some non-toxic glue you can add yet other dimensions. Try using sequins, feathers, synthetic hair, glitter or commercially made doll accessories to add a humorous touch.

An Ostara altar might contain early spring flowers, symbols of balance such as sun wheels (Brigid's crosses), or painted eggs. Ostara rituals may include the Great Rite and celebrate the waxing to maturity and the newly discovered sexuality of the youthful deities.

BEALTAINE
(Beel-teen or Beel-tawn-uh)
May 1

Bealtaine falls opposite Samhain in the wheel of the year. These were the two greatest sabbats in the Irish calendar, marking the beginning and ending of the two recognized seasons. As Samhain marked the start of winter, Bealtaine marked the start of summer. The Goddess and God are in full youthful bloom, she as Mother and he as her lover who will impregnate her with his next incarnation which will be born again at Yule. And because this is above all a fertility sabbat, the eggs also used for Ostara make a comeback, and observance of the Great Rite is a given.

Even though this is a fertility sabbat, one which above all celebrates life, it is interesting to note that some scholars believe the holiday takes its name from the Irish death god, Beltene. Another possible derivative might be the Scottish god Bel, but he appears to be more of a sun deity, such as Lugh, who would be honored at Midsummer or Lughnasadh rather than in the spring. Wittans prefer to believe the sabbat name of Bealtaine is derived from a word meaning "balefire." Balefires, or bonfires, are lit all over Ireland on May Eve, just as they were in the past.

It is traditional to take home a smoldering piece of the Bealtaine balefire to bring summer blessings into your home. The first cookfires of the summer season were once lit with part of this sabbat fire. And note that the custom asks that you "take" part of the balefire home. No one in Ireland would have given this to you because of a prohibition against giving fire away on Bealtaine. It is a basic belief of most European faery lore that faeries cannot start their own fires, but must obtain them from human sources. Wittans feared that faeries, active at this sabbat, would come to the celebration disguised briefly as humans to ask for a part of the fire which, when freely given, would give the faeries some measure of power over the fire giver.

Another custom of Bealtaine which has never died out is that of the May Day maypole. In Ireland, Britain, and the United States, people are still encouraged to grab the ribbons and dance.

The original maypole was the pine tree which had been decorated at Yule, with all but its uppermost branches now removed. Stripped of its goddess-like greenery, it now functions as a phallic symbol. The ribbons attached to it are traditionally white and red, white for the Goddess and red for the God. Female dancers take the white ribbons and males the red. Then they do a morris dance, the Anglo name for May Day dances, and interweave the colored ribbons into a pattern. It is not hard even in North America to find such a celebration going on at May Day. My Indiana elementary school celebrated May Day every year under the label "Health Day," with festivities culminating in a maypole dance in the school gym. Through the morris dance has evolved somewhat, its Irish form still retains all the symbolism of uniting the God and Goddess in a fertility rite (see Chapter 2).

Bealtaine circles were once constructed with the maypole at the center, and a balefire at a distance at one of the cardinal points. The altar consisted of fertility symbols such as holey stones, shillelaghs, flowers, and spring time greenery. The rituals were erotic in nature, symbolizing the union of God and Goddess. Just as the newly impregnated Goddess ensured that life would continue, so did her blessing ensure that earthly

185

life would be blessed with the abundant sustenance needed for survival.

Because the Irish were primarily a herding culture, the welfare of livestock figured prominently at Bealtaine. Special summer pastures set aside for cattle and sheep were opened for the first time each year only after May 1. Before May Eve the fields were still the province of the nasty phookas who claimed them after Samhain. Driving the animals through or over the balefire when the blaze wanes is a Bealtaine ritual.

Smoke was always seen as a cleanser and a purifier, but so much more so was the smoke from the waning balefires. People were willing to risk injury to themselves and their animals to pass them over the nearly extinguished fire for the benefits of the magickal smoke. A safer method consists of taking the animals three times around the fire in a clockwise circle.

Anything you wish to have ritually purified can be done so over the balefire smoke. Pass ritual tools, cherished possessions, heirloom jewelry, newly acquired items whose history you do not know, or yourself.

May also marked the beginning of the lambing season, and the condition and color of the first born lamb to a clan or community was indicative of how the rest of the year would go.

Taboos which began at Samhain were now lifted. Certain plants which could not be eaten or used for fear of the phookas were now available, and planting could be done on the freshly sun-blessed earth. Hunting of summer animals was now permitted, and the hunting of winter game such as the deer was prohibited. The traditional faery tree of Ireland, the hawthorn, could now be used and approached without fear. While many of these taboos seem silly now and are often written off as control measures, they were merely a way of living in harmony with nature. In common with other pagans, Wittans knew they were dependent upon nature and sought to live in balance with her, not taking more than they needed, and putting back whatever they could.

Goats and rabbits were sacred to the Bealtaine sabbat both because of the goat's horns, which symbolized the Horned God, and for their reputed randiness. Goats and rabbits (the latter sacred to the Goddess) were prolific breeders who could be relied upon year after year to provide food and clothing.

The goat also provided milk, and dairy products figure heavily in the Bealtaine feast. Sweets were also an important part of the feasting. To combine the two elements, a rich dairy cream pie was baked for the celebrants. This simple cream pie recipe was my grandmother's and I have no idea how old it is. Warning: this is not a dessert for the diet conscious!

Bealtaine Cream Pie

Prepare and pre-bake a pie shell and have it ready in the pie dish. The pie filling will be warmed but not baked.

    1 cup whole milk
    1 cup rich cream
    1/2 cup or one stick of butter (don't use margarine)
    3 tablespoons cornstarch
    1 1/2 cups sugar
    1 1/4 teaspoon vanilla
    ground nutmeg

Melt the butter in a wide cooking pan. (The mixture heats more evenly in this than in a taller more narrow pan. Traditionalists will use a heavy cast iron pan.)

In a separate bowl slowly add the milk to the cornstarch making sure it is fully dissolved and absorbed before adding more milk. When the cornstarch is fully blended add this and all the other ingredients, except the vanilla, to the cooking pan.

Stir constantly over medium heat until the mixture becomes thick like a pudding. Remove from heat and stir in the vanilla.

Pour the mixture into the waiting pie shell and sprinkle with nutmeg. The pie may be eaten while it is still warm as long as it has cooled just enough to set. Or the pie may be chilled and eaten later.

Wittans decorated for Bealtaine with much the same frenzy with which people decorate today for Christmas. Greenery, flowers, and other symbols of spring were placed on doors and hearths. Wreaths, symbolic of the wheel of the year, were gaily festooned with ribbons and flowers. Occasionally a flowered wreath is still seen topping a modern day maypole. Another form of wreath was a leafy crown woven by elders of the clan for the May King and May Queen. This "royalty for a day" idea is still practiced in modern May Days, and is derived from the custom of having a young lass and lad represent the priestess and priest who would perform the Great Rite within the Bealtaine circle.

Women rode besoms hobbyhorse-style over fields and through pastures. Women riding phallic symbols over areas where any animals or plants were meant to multiply was a fertility symbol. Menstruating women were the most sought after for this act, as the sacred blood of which all life was made was clearly present with which to saturate crop land and animal feeding grounds.

In old Ireland, meade made the year before was taken from its cask and drunk in celebration. Meade is a savory honey ale rich in tradition and folklore in the British Isles. In the Celtic tradition it is an aphrodisiac—a direct gift of the Great Mother Brigid. Meade, akin to the Irish word midhe meaning center, represented spirit, and drinking this potion of the deities made one more attuned with that elusive fifth element, spirit. Connoisseurs of meade cultivate their brew as carefully as makers of fine wine, jealously guarding their special family recipes.

Making meade is not easy. Like wine it requires a fermentation period and much care. Here is one of the many recipes for meade which can be found if you are willing to dig around.

Meade

> 1/2 gallon water
> 1 1/2 cups raw honey
> 1/4 cup lemon juice
> 1/8 teaspoon nutmeg
> 1/8 teaspoon allspice

Heat all ingredients together in a large stock pot. As the honey melts, an oily crust will form on top of the meade. There are two schools of thought about that. Some say to leave it for it adds to the flavor of the meade, others will tell you to skim it off. I am of the mind to leave it there.

When it is well-blended remove it from the heat. Stir in one package of brewer's yeast and pour the meade into a wooden cask or some other receptacle where it can ferment.

It is perfectly acceptable to drink the meade as is without the fermenting process, but it will not have any alcoholic content. Like this it will taste like a sweet honey-lemon tea. The meade needs to ferment for a period of at least six months. During that time the casks must be aired daily to allow any built up gasses to escape, and at least once a month it should be poured into a fresh cask. At the end of the six months you should have a workable meade.

I confess to preferring a meade short cut. I stop before the fermentation process and add just a touch of grain alcohol to the mixture before I bottle it. You don't get the full bodied flavor or euphoric intoxication that meade is famous for, but you still get the taste and the idea.

Another popular Bealtaine drink, though less pleasant, was a mixture of cow or sheep blood which was mingled with their milk. (The animal was not killed.) This was thought to ward off evil faeries, though it may have been born of an earlier belief that what one consumes is born of them. Hopeful mothers may have drunk this mixture for fertility at this strongly symbolized fertility sabbat.

Bealtaine is a time for feasting, rejoicing, frivolity, and celebration. No solemnity is permitted. It is a time to look outward and forward, a yearly re-enactment of the primal joy all creatures and plants of the earth feel at spring after a long cold winter's rest.

MIDSUMMER
circa June 22

The Goddess is heavy with pregnancy just as the earth is pregnant with the coming fall's bounty, the animals in the field await calving, but the fertility rites continue. As any expectant mother knows, just being pregnant is not an assurance that all the fuss is over. Just as a human baby can be miscarried or born blighted, the Wittans knew the same was true for crops and animals.

Because of the sun's obvious role at Midsummer this was a time of fire rituals throughout western Europe. Balefires figure as prominently at Midsummer as at Samhain or Bealtaine, and this sabbat is second only to them in importance in the Wittan year. For every mother there is a father, and so it is in Witta. The sun is at his peak in the sky, and we celebrate the God's approaching fatherhood.

The Irish had several sun goddesses as well. Even today, Irish Gaelic is one of the very few languages in which the word for "sun" is a feminine noun.

Animal blessings were popular at Midsummer, and it has become a Wittan practice to take familiars and beloved pets into the Midsummer circle for a special protection blessing. People whose livelihood depends on their livestock would bring in a token animal from their herds to receive the blessings. In some areas the blessings conclude with the animals being passed through or over the smoke of the balefire.

A blessing for a household pet might go something like this:

> (Hold the pet) *Blessed Brigid, guardian of all creatures, I ask that you enfold your loving arms of protection around my cherished friend* (state pet's name). *Blessed Horned God, ruler of the wildwood, king of the creatures of the forest and the hearth, give my beloved friend* (state pet's name) *the blessings of strength, health, and long life.* (Address the rest to the pet) *May I always know how to aid you when you are in need. May I always see to your comforts as well as I see to my own. And may I be as good a friend and companion to you as you are to me. In accordance with your free will I bless you on this sabbat ... So Mote It Be!*

You might then wish to anoint the pet's head with some salted water or pass a stick of incense around it three times, or anything else which signals blessing and protection to you.

If you wish, this would be a good time to present your pet with a special talisman of its own to wear on its collar. If you are talented at carving wood or metal you can carve a small charm for your pet. The design is up to you—whatever signals protection and love to your own mind. You might want to put a traditional pentagram on one side. On the other you might carve a heart, a knot, or a sun wheel. Another idea might be to buy or borrow a wood burning wand to make a wooden talisman. These wands have pointed tips and produce directed heat. All you have to do is draw your design and it will be burned into the wood by the wand point. Drill a small hole in the talisman and attach it to the pet's collar with an S hook available at any hardware store, or put it on the same hook with the pet's I.D. tag or license.

Human conception was as much of a concern to the Wittans as was that of animals, and Midsummer was the last sabbat until spring-time where the blatantly obvious fertility imagery could be utilized. Several folk magick grimoires advise a woman to squat naked in her garden on Midsummer night if she wishes to conceive.

Ashes from the Midsummer balefire were often scattered over fields or mixed with animal feed to ensure fertility as well as protection. The modern science of botany has discovered that ash contains rich nutrients, such as nitrogen, which are necessary for the healthy growth of many food crops.

Pieces of unburnt balefire wood were kept as powerful talismans of light during the ever-darkening waning year. They ensured the presence of the sun god, just as capturing an apple at a Samhain game ensured the Goddess' presence until Yule. It was also traditional to use nine different types of wood for the Midsummer fire. Nine is the traditional number symbolizing the moon, and this may have been another way in which to bring the Goddess into this very God-oriented sabbat. Because paganism seeks to balance the male and female aspects, it was considered fortuitous if a full moon coincided with the sabbat. The full moon is the moon phase associated with the Mother Goddess aspect, which is also the aspect of the Goddess at Midsummer.

In Ireland, as in other herding cultures, animals were not only relied upon to provide meat, but also to provide milk. As a pregnant woman begins to lactate, so does the Mother Goddess, and Midsummer sabbat rituals often substitute milk for wine or water. Rituals are done just prior to the sabbat to insure the continued milk production of their goat and cattle herds. Offering a bowl of milk to the faeries was a way many Wittans shared their good fortune with the little people, and remained in their good graces for the rest of the year.

Menstruating women were pressed into service to bleed onto the fields. These customs came down from the time when the male role in conception was unknown and there was a prevalent worldwide belief that the blood was what created life without any outside help. The menstrual taboos of the patriarchal religions stem directly from this awe of the female power of procreation, a power which made goddess worship hard to eradicate.

In Ireland as well as in America, June has been a traditional month for weddings. The reason given is that this is when school lets out and many young people marry at the end of their schooling. For the old Wittans this would have been highly impractical. It was considered unlucky to marry during the dark of the year, which by the Irish calendar didn't end until Bealtaine. Because of the joining of God and Goddess at Bealtaine, May was considered a sacred month in which no mortal should marry. It was also a Wittan practice (one that came after women's clan groups were broken up and families became more like what we know now) to wait until a woman was pregnant to marry. Young men and their pregnant women married at the first opportunity which was June.

The Oak King and the Holly King who battled for supremacy at Yule now fight again. This time it is the Oak King who is slain and the Holly King, king of the waning year, who now reigns, gaining in power and strength until Yule.

Two Irish Christian holidays occur very near Midsummer. One is Saint John's Day, also a time of lighting bonfires. Some authorities believe this day was instituted by Saint Patrick to occur just before Midsummer to draw attention away from the Midsummer reveling. The other is the Celtic-Anglo-Christian observance of Whit Sunday.

Commonly called Whitsuntide, it is the fiftieth day after Easter and corresponds to Pentecost on the Jewish and Roman calendars. Perhaps to discourage the pagan ways, patriarchal Irish superstition has deemed this a very unlucky day, especially for one's animals. Threats of faeries carting off prized stock and unsuspecting human revelers was a common scare tactic to keep Midsummer festivals inside and away from the larger community.

Because this is a sabbat which glorifies the sun, and the sun is a symbol of protection, many Wittans make protective amulets which are later charged and consecrated in the Midsummer circle. One Wittan I know of has routinely done this for years. She buries the old one near an oak tree just prior to Midsummer each year as she begins construction on a new one. Rue, rowan, and basil make a good trio tied up in a gold or white cloth which can be carried in your pocket year round. Or you might search for a special stone which represents protection to you. It might be golden-white like the sun, or in the shape of a phallus.

Many herbs and wild plants are fully mature by Midsummer and this is a fine time to begin gathering magickal and medicinal plants to dry and store for winter. The Druids gathered their sacred plants at Midsummer, especially their important and revered mistletoe.

Many pagan traditions insist that magickal herbs must be cut with a special, curved, white-handled knife commonly called a "bolleen." It is a good idea to cut magick herbs with a knife which is only used for ritual purposes, but one need not be so specific. It is also essential that the herbs, once cut, not be allowed to touch the ground. The earth is a grounding force often used in rituals to absorb excess energy. Magick herbs which touch the ground will have their power drained back into the earth. Take along a cloth of natural fabric in a neutral white or black on which to lay the cut plants. They can be taken home, tied in bundles, and hung up to dry in a kitchen, an attic, or near a fireplace.

Lavender is an aromatic herb which figures prominently in many British and Irish folk songs. Just the smell of it was once believed to be a catalyst to love magick and it is still sought out as an aphrodisiac. Lavender in full flower was commonly used as a Midsummer incense to honor the divine parents-to-be.

Beloved pets are brought into the circle to be blessed and to join in the celebration and feasting. Look for pets which seem attracted to the energy and comfortable with it if you are looking for a familiar. A familiar is a psychic animal helper who is not a pet, but an equal working partner in magick.

A Midsummer altar might contain a chalice of milk, a besom, summer herbs, or young food plants. The rituals are again full of fertility images celebrating the mother and father aspects of the deities.

LUGHNASADH
(Loo-naas-ah)
August 1

Called Lammas in Wicca, Lughnasadh is a sabbat in honor of the Celtic god Lugh, and represents the first of the three harvest sabbats. In Gaelic, Lunasa means August, and the name may also have some association with Luna, the Roman moon goddess. In Western paganism it is a grain festival sometimes called the Sabbat of First Fruits. Corn and barley are ready to be picked by August, as are many other grains. Native Americans celebrate early August as a grain festival in honor of the Corn Grandmother. Western paganism notes that the Irish tradition is responsible for most of the practice and symbolism of this first harvest sabbat.

Lugh was a god of harvest, fire, light, and of the sun. He was the king of the Tuatha De Danann and the consort of Dana, the first Great Mother Goddess of Ireland; some later versions of the myths make him her father or brother. Much of the mythology surrounding him is open to varied interpretations, reflective of erosion over time of the original stories by the patriarchal culture. At this sabbat his stories and heroic exploits are retold, in whatever version the storyteller prefers.

Though this sabbat is named in honor of Lugh the god, the goddess aspect figures prominently. Dana, as Lugh's queen, is also honored and her stories told round the circle. Some Wittans enact Lugh's sacrificial death and rebirth as a sheaf of grain at Lughnasadh, which symbolizes the older Wittan belief that a god must eventually bow down to his goddess through whose benevolence he is reborn.

Because there is more yet to be harvested in the coming months, Lughnasadh is not void of fertility imagery, but these are downplayed. The Goddess, as Dana or Brigid, is honored and thanked for bringing forth the first fruits. She is revered and treated with the respect and care shown to any new mother. Yet this Goddess is still pregnant with the future harvests of autumn. This is a time when Wittans who work within a coven often choose three women to represent each aspect of the Triple Goddess within the circle.

In the continental United States this is a season of storms, making it a great time to tap into those powerful energies which symbolize fire (male) and water (female). Doing a ritual or spell during a storm lends an extra charge of energy to them. In Ireland threats of rain so late in the growing season could irreparably damage a crop, and pleas went out daily to the deities to protect the fields.

Threshing of the grain, separating the grain and the straws, was considered a magickal task. Threshing houses were believed to be guarded by Lugh and Dana and their symbols could be found carved into the walls of the threshing room. The practice of carrying a new bride over a threshold (the wooden floorbeam across a doorway which held the grain inside the threshing house) was an old fertility custom now kept alive in Witta by having a newly handfasted couple jump over a broomstick.

Grain ales were made around Lughnasadh and dedicated to the God in his aspect as Harvest Lord. Whiskey was once sacred to this sabbat. Ales were made around Lughnasadh and dedicated to Dana or Brigid to be kept for esbats.

The feast of Lughnasadh is the largest of any sabbat. All first fruits of the season are consumed, especially any and all grains which have been harvested. The cakes and ale ceremony which accompanies the esbats may also be observed now, only instead of having the cakes act as moon symbols, they are sun symbols. Cut cookies or flat sheet cakes into pentagram or disc shapes. They can be frosted orange or yellow, and even topped with sun-gold sprinkles in honor of the sun god. Breads, especially ones made with newly harvested grain, are very appropriate. In North America, August is the time of the corn harvest, and corn bread, with its bright yellow coloring, is a fitting symbol of this sabbat. Serve breads with honey, another sun-associated food.

Potatoes, long a staple crop of Ireland, are also harvested at this sabbat and should be featured at the sabbat meal. The following recipe for Irish potato pie belonged to my grandfather who refused to give it to me until I was grown. He said it was an Irish original which belonged to his grandfather. I can't account for how they may have altered it to taste over the years, but here it is.

Irish Potato Pie

$1/4$ pound melted butter (margarine will work just as well)
1 medium onion, well chopped
3 cups shredded potatoes (if you want to save time and energy, pre-cut hash browns are available in your grocer's dairy case)
3 well beaten eggs
1 cup milk
1 $1/4$ cups grated cheese (colby varieties are preferred)
1 teaspoon prepared mustard
1 tablespoon dried parsley
salt and pepper to taste
paprika

Place all of the ingredients, except the paprika, in a large mixing bowl. Also save out $1/4$ cup of the cheese to use later as a topping. Mix very well. Place in a well-greased, deep pie pan.

Bake at 375° for 40 minutes. Remove from oven and sprinkle on the remaining $1/4$ cup of cheese. Bake for another 5-10 minutes, or until the cheese is melted. Remove and sprinkle on a bit of ground paprika. Serve immediately. Serves four to six.

Rituals contain enactments of growth and birth, and honor and thanks to the Goddess from whose earth womb they grew. Thanks are given to Lugh in his aspect as sun god for blessing and impregnating the earth womb with heat and light. The grain dolly made at Imbolg is taken from her bed and given a position of honor on Lughnasadh altars, along with milk, corn, barley, and other first fruits of the season. Some Wittans choose to make a new dolly and bury the old one in the fields. This new one will be with them during all the harvest sabbats and will be buried at Samhain when the materials for a new one are gathered.

MABON
(May-bone)
circa September 22

Called simply the Autumn Equinox in Ireland, Mabon is named for Mabon, the Welsh god-son who symbolized the male fertilizing principle in the Arthurian myths.

As a day of balance between light and dark it was not unnoticed by the Wittans, but as a sabbat it went unobserved until the Norse invaders brought it into prominence and placed it between Lughnasadh and Samhain as the second of the three harvests. With the number three being associated with the Goddess and with the act of completeness for so long, the Irish adopted this addition whole-heartedly.

It became customary in old Ireland to visit burial mounds, or cairns, at Mabon to honor dead ancestors, particularly female ones. Early Wittans had a cult of female ancestor worship which based its beliefs on the notion that men were reabsorbed into the wombs which bore them and therefore only women inhabited Tir-na-nog, the Wittan land of the dead which was also known by the name "The Land of Women." It was believed the balance of light and dark would act like an equilateral cross and offer protection from any negative spirits attracted to the mounds. Fires were lit at the mounds or carried in gourds and other ripe vegetables to further frighten these baneful spirits, and to honor the ancestors.

Wines from the autumn grape harvest have always figured prominently in pagan harvest rites. But Ireland is not a land known for its grape industry. What is common in Ireland and other Celtic countries is a heather wine made from the native flowering plant. And though the end product doesn't have the deep sacred significance of grape wines in other lands, it is a tribute to the bounty of nature and very appropriate for Mabon.

Blackberries, which are sacred to Brigid, ripen in late summer and early fall, and gentle blackberry wines are made and dedicated to her. In Ireland there was, and still is, a folk taboo against eating blackberries after Mabon, but all berries made into wines for a Goddess were permissible to keep and use. Occasionally wines were poured onto the ground to honor the aging Goddess as she moved swiftly into her crone aspect. Blackberry pies were also featured items on this sabbat.

Heather Wine

You will need to gather at least a pound of fresh heather. Use the upper stalks and flowering heads.

In a large stock pot boil the heather in a gallon of water until you have a heavily colored tea. You may need to add more of the plant to the water if the color is weak. When it is right you shouldn't be able to see through it in a clear drinking glass.

Remove the mixture from the heat and scoop out the plant material which is still in the water. A colander can help with this process.

When the mixture has cooled slightly add:
4 cups sugar
1/4 teaspoon nutmeg
1/4 teaspoon allspice
1/4 cup lemon juice

Pour the mixture into casks and allow to ferment for about six months. Heather wine has a gentle, grassy flavor.

Blackberry Wine

2 1/2 pounds fresh blackberries
3 cups sugar
2 cups hot water

Let the berries set out in a large bowl for about four weeks, stirring them occasionally. The berries will get a rank smell and may begin to mold.

With mortar and pestle, crush the berries into as smooth a pulp as possible. Stir in the sugar and then the water.

Pour the wine into casks to ferment for eight to ten months. The longer it is kept the better it will be. The wine will have to be aired every few days to allow building gases to escape. This wine has a gentle port-like flavor when finished.

Brigid's Blackberry Pie

Line a deep pie dish with an unbaked pie crust (to save time and energy, you can purchase ready-made pie dough at the grocery store).

4 cups fresh blackberries (thawed frozen ones will do as well)
1 1/2 cup sugar
1/3 cup flour
1/4 teaspoon cinnamon
1/8 teaspoon salt

Mix all ingredients together in a large bowl. If it appears too "wet," mix in a little more flour (about 2 tablespoons). Pour the mixture into the pie shell and dot with some butter or margarine. You can bake the pie as is, or cover it with another pie crust. If you do this, pinch down the ends to hold it to the other crust. Then score the top several times with a sharp knife. Bake at 325° for 1 hour, or until the top crust is a golden brown.

It is interesting to note how the fermented juice we know as wine figures in history as a drink of the deities. Many cultures limit the making and use of wines to a priestly class, or to certain time periods. Wines have nearly always been dedicated to a particular local deity when finished. This ancient practice is the reason Jewish law insists on the use of kosher (ritually correct and pure) wine. To ensure that their wines are not inadvertently consecrated to a pagan deity, they carefully guard the making of their wines, then dedicate them to their own god.

Vines also figure heavily in Mabon symbolism. They are used as decorations for altars, as raw material for the making of wreaths, and for head crowns for Mabon worshippers.

A little-known Irish festival known as Garland Sunday was observed on the first Sunday in September, and still is in some parts of rural Ireland. Garlands were constructed of native vines and apples by a village's unmarried women and taken by them and the unmarried men to a churchyard. If an apple fell during the procession it was an ill omen. At the churchyard the garland was then broken apart and strewn over the graves with loud keening. Feasting and dancing followed, and it was obligatory to show hospitality to strangers on this evening. This seems to be a carry-over from the fertility and death symbols of the harvest sabbats. The traditions surrounding Garland Sunday no doubt grew out of the older Mabon tradition of making pilgrimages to burial grounds to honor the dead.

You can make your own garland out of any greenery you like if you have access to it without harming any trees. Otherwise, you can go to a craft store and purchase several yards of dried grape vine. The length will depend on how many people you wish to have in your procession. Estimate that you will need three feet, or one yard, per person. You will also need some small wires such as those that are covered with paper and used to seal bread packages. These can also be obtained at craft stores and will be used to attach the greenery and apples to the vine.

Gather your greenery and your apples and, with the wires, begin attaching them to the vine until it is as full as you like.

Another idea, and a much saner one in this time of environmental concern, would be to purchase an artificial garland from a store which specializes in supplying artificial flowers and foliage. There is absolutely no reason for this garland to be all natural since it is not being used as a direct catalyst for magick. An artificial one would harm no living thing and could be used again. To attach fresh apples to this garland you can use the same wire twists, or thread string through the apples and tie them on.

Except for a few items still in the fields, Mabon is the completion of the harvest. After this night of balance, darkness will again over-come the light. In many Wiccan traditions this is the official turning point to the dark of the year. Wittans mark the day as a pre-sager of the dark of the year which begins at Samhain, and many divination and nature walks are done to ascertain whether one's life in the last year has been pleasing to the Goddess.

Druids honored the willow tree, a tree associated with death, which was also sacred to the Goddess. New wands and magickal staves were traditionally cut from willow branches just before Mabon.

Mabon altars can contain a fiery bouquet of autumn leaves, wine, berries, gourds, and other fruits of the season. Rituals enact the elderly period of the life of the God and Goddess. The God is dying and preparing for death at Samhain, and the Goddess is entering cronehood, though deep inside her maiden aspect the impregnated seed of the God lives on to be born at Yule as the wheel of the year eternally turns.

✣ APPENDIX I ✣

IRISH GODDESSES AND GODS

To become truly familiar with the Irish pantheon, one must read the mythological literature of Ireland. The list presented here is far from exhaustive. Some of these figures are not deities by normal standards, but because many of them are of a non-human race, and because of their prominence as heroes or heroines in the myths, they are included.

The rules of pronunciation for Irish Gaelic are extremely complex, and are made even more confusing due to variations in regional dialect. If one wishes to learn the language fully, a university class is recommended. Irish Gaelic is the oldest of the Goidelic group of Celtic languages, a group shared by speakers of Manx and Scots Gaelic.

AESUN (Aee-son): Early Irish god whose name means "to be."

AIFA (Aw-fah): Goddess and queen of the Land of Shadows who has a son by the warrior Cuchulain.

AINE (Awn-ee): Irish cattle goddess popular in her native Munster. She was raped by Ailill Olum, a king of Munster who was the consort of Madb. Aine's magickal arts destroyed him for his violation of her.

AIRMID (Awir-meet): Irish goddess of medicine and all healing arts.

ANGUS MAC OG: Harpist of the Tuatha De Danann. Son of Dagda and Boan. God of love.

ANKOU (Awn-koo): Death. This word comes from the Celts of Brittany and literally means "death." The Irish word for death, Bas, is rarely used to refer to the being called Death. When a death occurs in Ireland, Ankou's black cart can be heard rattling along rural roads as he comes to take the dying soul on the first leg of its journey to Tir-na-nog.

ANU: Synonymous with Dana and Danu. Eriu was her virgin aspect, and Macha her crone name.

BADB (Bayv): A crone aspect of the Triple Goddess. Her names means "one who boils," as in boiling the cauldron of death and rebirth. Later she was seen as a sister to the crone Macha.

BALOR (Bay-lear): Sometimes called the grandfather of Lugh, he was the king of the Formorians, early invaders of Ireland in the myth cycles. He was for a time Dana's consort, later replaced by Lugh.

BANBA (Ban-na): A warrior goddess who protected Ireland from invaders. One of a tri-form with Eriu and Fotia. Her story is a later addition to the myth cycle when the god Dagda was seen as having birthed the Triple Goddess rather than the other way around.

BELTENE: Irish god of death. Some scholars claim it is he who was originally celebrated at Bealtaine, and for him that the Sabbat was named.

BLATHNAT (Blay-net): King of the Underworld.

BOAN (Bo-ann): Water goddess for whom the River Boyne is named. Her name is also spelled as Boann or Boanne. In later myths she was relegated to the sea where she was queen of the ancient Formorian invaders, a race driven into the sea by the Tuatha de Danann where they became sea monsters.

BRIGID (Breed): The Great Mother Goddess of Ireland. Her Irish name is spelled Brid. Other forms of her name are Brighid or Bridget. At one time in history most of Ireland was united in praise and worship of her. In the fifth century her shrine at Kildare was desecrated and adopted as a holy site by Christian missionaries. Brigid represents the supernal mother, fertility, and creative inspiration. She has also been worshiped as a warrioress and protectress, a healer, and a guardian of children. Other sources say she was also the goddess of agriculture, animal husbandry, medicine, crafting, and music.

THE CAILLECH (Call-y'ac): Death goddess who presides over the cauldron of death and rebirth from her home in the Land of the Dead. She is the crone form of all Celtic goddesses.

CERNUNNOS (Ker-noon-noes): A Greek name, and one of the many names of the European Great Horned God. His Irish name has been lost in history. The Horned God is probably the most widely worshiped god-form in paganism. He is the master of the hunt and comes into his full power in late summer and early fall. He is the primal fertility god, consort to the Great Mother. He is depicted as god of the woodlands, animals, revelry, and male fertility. He is thought to be the Celtic form of the Greek god Pan whose name means "all."

CESSAIR (Keshar): A member of the faery race known as the Partholans who were the first to occupy Ireland. She is considered the first queen of Ireland.

CIAN (Key-awn): Sometimes a son and sometimes the father of the sun god Lugh. He was taught the art of shape-shifting by a woman.

CLEENA: She escaped Tir-na-nog with her mortal lover before the Caillech was ready to send her back. The Caillech sent faeries to lull her to sleep on an Irish beach while a giant wave washed her back to the Land of the Dead. She has since existed in Irish mythology as a minor sea goddess, doomed by the Caillech never to return to Ireland in mortal form.

CONNLA: Son of Cuchulain and Aifa. Connla grew up with Aifa and later came searching for his father in the mortal world.

CREDNA (Krin-nah): Irish god of metallurgy and smithing.

CROM CRUIACH (Crom Croo/k): An ancient sacrificial god about which little is known. His name may be associated with the popular Irish festival loaf called "bram brac." His feast day has been Christianized in Ireland.

CUCHULAIN (Coo-cul-lan): Great warrior of Ulster, elevated to a demi-god of Ireland. He fell in love with the faery woman Fand. Manann, God of the Sea, separated them forever, decreeing that the faery world and the human world should never mix. His stories are recorded at length in the Book of the Dun Cow. For his heroism on behalf of his country, modern Irish lore says that Saint Patrick rescued his soul from hell.

DAGDA: A later addition to the myth cycles has him as the father of Brigid and her sisters (the Triple Goddess). In the early traditions all male deities are born of females. His name means "the good god." He was originally associated with the Tuatha De Danann as the son of the Goddess. In the early Christian period when patriarchy was establishing itself in Ireland and disrupting the matriarchal clans, he replaced Lugh, Cernunnos, and Brigid as the principal deity in what was left of pagan Ireland.

DANA (Dawn-na): The name literally means "great queen." She was the first Great Mother Goddess of Ireland, later renamed Brigid. Today Dana's tri-form usually assigns her the name Danu, the virgin aspect of the Triple Goddess with Brigid as mother and Badb as crone.

DEIRDRE OF THE SORROWS: Prophetess who drew her own horoscope and charted her fate which was to be separated always from love. She is finally forced to wed against her will and she dashes herself to death on rocks in an act of defiance. This is a popular Irish legend and one of the Three Sorrows of Irish mythology. The name Deirdre is common in Ireland.

DHONN (Theen): Lord of the Underworld, consort of the crone Macha.

DYLAN: Guardian of the mouth of the River Conway.

EOCHY (Y'oh-kee): The Firbolg's high king.

EPONA (Ee-pone-ah): British horse goddess vigorously adopted by conquering pagan Rome, and also by Scottish and Irish pagans. Her Irish name is Mare, and she is the bringer of dreams.

ERIU (Air-ee-oo): Protectress of Ireland, a daughter of Dagda. She is often part of the Triple Goddess in her maiden form. The native form of her name, Erinn or Erin, has been the poetic name for Ireland for centuries.

ETAIN (Ae-dawn): Sometimes spelled Edain. She was queen of the Tuatha De Danann and a superb horsewoman. She was wooed out of the human world by her consort, King Midhir.

FAND and LIBAN: Twin goddesses of health and earthly pleasures. Fand, a woman of the faery race, fell in love with the hero Cuchulain.

FINN MacCOOL or McCUAL: Legendary giant being of Ireland who foresaw the coming of the Formorians, and banished an invading giant from Scotland. He married Grainne, a master herbalist who was the daughter of King Cormac. In many circles he is considered a god and his memory is often honored at the Yule sabbat. He was the leader of the Fianna warriors.

FINVARRA: A faery king who used games of chess to gain power over his enemies. He was a close friend of Oisin.

FLIDIAS (Flee-daws): Shape-shifting goddess of the woodlands. Sometimes depicted as the consort of the Horned God, she is believed to get about on deer back or in a sleigh pulled by deer.

THE FOUR SWANS OF THE SORROWS: The four swans were the semi-mortal children of the god Lir who were turned into swans for nine hundred years by their jealous stepmother. Their beautiful voices sang the praises of the Irish deities and won them honor in their exile. Their story is one of the Three Sorrows of the Irish myth cycles.

FRANCONIAN-DIE-DRUD: A Druidess later associated with the horse goddess Mare, the bringer of dreams.

THE GREAT HORNED GOD: Though paintings of him have been found on cave walls and Egyptian hieroglyphs, his modern incarnation is Celtic in origin. He is probably the most persistent and common of god images in European paganism. He has been called by the names Pan and Cernunnos, but his old Irish name has been lost. Most Wittans simply refer to him and worship him as the Great Horned God. He is most fully honored at Bealtaine, Lughnasadh, and Samhain.

GRIANNE (Gree-awn): A sun goddess.

IUCHAR and IUCHARBA (U-char and U-car-bah): Along with Brian were said to be the three sons of the goddess Dana. Their epic tale of an impossible quest is recorded in the Yellow Book of Lechan.

KELE-DE (Kay-lay-day): Mysterious Irish goddess whose followers formed an all-female cult known as the kelles. The early Church once allowed the cult to flourish for a time in remote areas of Ireland. She and her high priestesses reserved the right to take any and all lovers they chose. Oddly enough she was probably a crone image in Ireland, and was linked as a counterpart to the male principle. Some scholars believe she is a corruption of the Indian goddess Kali.

LIR: Welsh sea god whose name is sometimes adopted into the Irish pantheon. He can be compared with Oceanus, Neptune, or Poseidon in the Greek and Roman pantheons. In Ireland he is most well-known by the name Manann, though some accounts make him Manann's father.

LUCHTAIN (Lock-teen): An Irish god of war.

LUGH (Loo): Literally, "the shining one." The Irish sun god, or god of light, who is celebrated at the sabbat Lughnasadh. Like Brigid, he was a god of many skills and was even said to be able to come into human form to worship among the Druids for whom he was the primary deity. He is also worshiped as the god of metallurgy, crafting, weaving, harvesting, and as a protector of the weak.

MACHA (Maax-ah): Death goddess of Ireland, a crone aspect of the Triple Goddess who is synonymous with the Caillech. She rules over the cauldron of death and rebirth. Her home is in the west in Tir-na-nog. The faeries are said to do her bidding. One word of baneful utterance from her can destroy the world. She is credited with mingling attributes of the deities within the human race.

MADB (Mayv): Faery queen of Ireland, also a legendary warrioress high queen of Connacht who reigned for eighty-eight years. She was sometimes viewed as a goddess of war in the early patriarchal period.

MANANN (May-nan): A chameleon-like sea god. The Isle of Man was named for him. It is he who decreed that the world of faeries and the world of humans must forever remain separated.

MARE: Irish horse goddess of the night who brings dreams. The word "nightmare" is derived from her name. She is the equivalent of the Pan-Celtic goddess Epona.

MIDHIR (My-ter or Myah-ter): First king of the Tuatha De Danann. He seduced Etain out of the human world and took her as his queen.

THE MORRIGU (Mor-ee-goo): Known in Britain and Wales as the Morrigan, this Triple Goddess consists only of crone aspects and is symbolized by the carrion crow. Celtic scholars believe she made her appearance in Irish mythology about the time of the Nemedian invasion. The Morrigu's names are Neman (patron goddess of the bean sídhe), Badb (arbiter of life and death), and Macha (goddess of war).

NUAD (New-ag): Last king of the Tuatha De Danann. He was forced to abdicate his throne to the Milesian invaders.

OGHMA (Ohg-mah): His name is often spelled Ogham. He is the god of writing, communication, and poetry who gave the ogham alphabet to the Druids.

OISIN (Oh-sheen): Son of Finn MacCool and Saba who traveled to Tir-na-nog and back. Only Dagda and he traveled to the Land of the Dead and were able to return again. As a result of his travels he was on very good terms with the faery folk of Ireland. Faeries would seek him out for company, especially to play the Irish game known as hurling.

OLLAV FOLA (Oh-lahv Foh-lah): A powerful high king in the line of Eremon. A poet.

THE RED BRANCH: A chivalrous order of the warriors of Ulster who were taught their battle skills by the goddess Skatha. Their fortress was called Emain Macha (Ae-meen Maax-ah).

SABA: Wife of Finn MacCool.

SINEND (Sheen-en): She went to a magickal well to do a ritual, but she came unprepared and irreverent. Worse yet, this well was the great well of knowledge, sacred to the Caillech. Sinend's actions so outraged the well's waters that they rose up and sucked her into themselves. She was washed up on the banks of the River Shannon, the river named for her. For her effrontery she was denied entrance to Tir-na-nog. She is now a queen of the well spirits of Ireland.

SKATHA (Scah-yah): Warrioress of the Underworld. This Goddess was said to have a school on an island in the Irish seas where the greatest of Ireland's warriors came to be trained. Cuchulain, Ireland's greatest warrior hero, was one of her students. Skatha didn't train women because of a Celtic belief which stated that only women could teach men battle skills, and only men could teach them to women.

TEA (Tay) and TEPHI (T'py): Co-founders and protector goddesses of the sacred site at Tara.

TETHRA (Tate-rah): King of the Formorians after they were banished into the sea where they became grotesque sea monsters.

THE TRIPLE GODDESS: The three aspects of the feminine principle of deity: maiden, mother, and crone.

TUAN MacCARELL (Toon Mc-Carel): He was a god created by Dana. He is king of Irish deer herds, and is occasionally seen as another form of the Great Horned God.

✾ APPENDIX II ✾

PAGAN AND IRISH TERMINOLOGY

Pagan terms from all traditions and cultures would make an index which would constitute a book in itself. For this work I have chosen to list only those pagan terms of particular interest to Wittans.

ABRED: In the Irish tradition this is the innermost of three separate magick circles. This concept was expanded on by the Druids who used it to create a model of the universe.

AMULET: An object which is reputed to give protection to the carrier. Amulets are objects found in nature such as stones and are not to be confused with manmade talismans.

ASPECT: The particular principle or part of the creative life force being worked with or acknowledged at any one time. For example, Brigid is a mother aspect of the one Goddess.

ASTRAL PROJECTION: The art of "leaving one's body" or "lucid dreaming" whereby someone in a trance state visits other locations and realms. This is thought of as traveling into the astral plane which is generally conceived as a parallel world unseen in our own world of form.

ASTROLOGY: The belief and study of the effects which the movements and placements of planets and other heavenly bodies have on the lives and behavior of human beings.

ATHAME (ath-ah-may): The ritual tool associated with the element of air and the direction of the east. This most likely came into Irish Witta through contact with ceremonial magick. The knife in ceremonial magick is traditionally black-handled, but Wittans, not bound by the teachings of Kaballah, should consider having natural wood handles.

B.C.E.: Abbreviation which stands for "before common era." A term scholars often use to denote time synonymous with B.C., but without the religious implications.

BALEFIRE: The traditional fire of Samhain, Bealtaine, and Midsummer sabbats. It is in reality what we would call a bonfire, derived from the word "boon" meaning a gift or extra. Even in modern day Ireland balefires play a major role in holidays and folk celebrations.

BEALTAINE (Beel-teen): Called Beltane in Wicca. This sabbat is rife with fertility rituals and symbolism, and marks the beginning of summer in the Irish year. Along with Samhain, it is the primary sabbat of Witta.

BEAN SÍDHE (ban-shee): Means "woman faery." The shrieking spirit that visits a house wherein death is imminent. The keenings of bean sídhes are usually attached to one particular family.

BESOM (bay-shum): The witches' broomstick. European folklore tells of witches riding their brooms through the sky which may be an uninformed explanation of astral projection. As a tool the broom is used to sweep a sacred area, ground a circle, or to brush away negative influences. Besoms were mounted and "ridden" over crops in a fertility rite.

BOOK OF SHADOWS: Also called Book of Lights and Shadows, this is the spell book, diary, and ritual guide used by an individual witch or coven. Some say the name came from having to hide the workings from Church authorities, and others say it means that an unworked spell or ritual is a mere shadow, not taking form until worked by a witch.

THE BURNING TIMES: The time from the Spanish Inquisition through the last outbursts of persecution and witch killings (usually by hanging) in the mid-nineteenth century (though actual persecution began as early as the twelfth century). The last known capital sentence for witchcraft in the West was in Scotland in the mid-1800s.

C.E.: Abbreviation which stands for "common era." A term scholars often use to denote time synonymous with A.D., but without the religious implications.

CAULDRON: Linked to witchcraft in the popular mind, this is a primal goddess image used like a chalice or cup. This was a common magickal instrument in old Ireland because it was a practical object as well, one which could be used for cooking or washing as well as making brews and magick potions. In Witta, the cauldron of death and rebirth is in possession of the crone in Tir-na-nog.

CELTIC KNOT: The drawings and carvings of the Celts often resulted in elaborate intertwined lines known popularly as Celtic knots which were said to be inspired by sacred black snakes. Many Wittans will use complex knots in spells of binding.

CELTIC TREE CALENDAR: Druidic system of reckoning the thirteen lunar months of the year by assigning each a sacred tree which represents the character of the month.

CHALICE: In Wicca the chalice or cup as a ritual tool represents water and the west, and it is also representative of the feminine principle. In Witta chalices are also used, but a cauldron is preferable.

CHARGING: The act of empowering herbs, stones, or other magickal objects with one's own energies directed towards a magickal goal. Charging is synonymous with enchanting.

CIRCLE: The sacred space wherein all magick is to be worked. The circle contains raised energy and provides protection for the witch. It is created and banished with his or her own energy. Many books on magick include in-depth discussions on circle lore and practice, and it is recommended that students of Witta study these carefully.

COLLECTIVE UNCONSCIOUSNESS: A term used to describe the sentient connection of all living things, past and present. It is synonymous with the "deep mind" of each individual. This is believed to be the all-knowing energy source which is tapped during divination.

COMING OF AGE: At age thirteen for boys, and at the time of a girl's first menses, pagan children are considered to be spiritual adults. They join with other pagans to celebrate their new maturity with rituals and celebration.

COVEN: A group of witches who worship and work together. A circle may contain any number of witches, both male and female. The traditional number of members is thirteen.

COVENSTEAD: An obsolete name for the area encompassed by an individual coven. In the days when Witta was the only religion of Ireland one met in covens with persons who lived within a particular covenstead.

CROSSROADS: Crossroads figure heavily in the lore of Ireland and Britain. The Celtic goddess Epona (envisioned as half human and half white horse) was said to appear at crossroads for those who would come to invoke her aid. Crossroads were also thought to be protective because they form a natural X, a symbol which is used in protection rites. An X is also represented by division of the four elements in a magick circle.

DEVIL: The Christian and Islamic opposite of God. The Devil as an entity was the result of the mistranslation of a Hebrew word appearing in the Old Testament, ha-satan, which simply means "adversary." The term was personified by the early Christian Church and its image taken from the Celtic Horned God as a means of frightening people away from the religions of witchcraft. Some Christians contend that all pagans worship the Devil, but since he is a creation of Christian theology, and adopted whole-heartedly by Muslims, one must necessarily be of those faiths to believe in or worship him.

DEOSIL (jes-l): The act of moving clockwise.

DIVINATION: The act of foretelling the future by reading potential currently in motion. Divination can be done through meditation, astral projection, with cards, stones, or any one of a myriad of means.

DRAWING DOWN THE MOON: Ancient pagan ritual enacted at the esbats to draw the powers of the full moon, in her aspect of Great Mother Goddess, into the body of a female witch.

DRUIDS: Much speculation still continues on the role of Druids in Ireland. They were the priestly class of Irish society, the magicians, writers and poets, and royal advisors. Their power flourished from the second century B.C.E. to the second century C.E.

DRYADS: Female Druids, the priestly class of Ireland. Scholars are divided on their role and function. This is also a term for tree dwelling spirits which the Druids believed inhabited the sacred trees.

DUALITY: The opposite of polarity. Duality separates two opposites such as good and evil and places those characteristics into two separate god-forms.

ELEMENT: One of the four alchemical substances—earth, air, fire, and water, plus the element of pure spirit in and of them all—once thought to make up the entire universe. In Witta, earth corresponds to the direction north, air to east, fire to south, and water to west.

ELEMENTAL: Archetypal spirit being associated with one of the four elements.

ENCHANTING: See CHARGING.

ESBAT: The time of the full moon which is celebrated monthly in Witta and most of Western paganism. The word is from the French esbattre meaning to gambol or frolic.

EVOCATION: The act of summoning the presence of deities, friendly spirits, or elementals to your circle.

FAERY RING: Also called a sídhe ring, it is a circle of grass which appears darker than that surrounding it. This dark grass can also take the shape of a faery path, and often leads to a faery mound wherein some of the faery race dwells. It was once believed that to be caught inside a faery ring after dark meant that the faeries would whisk you off to their kingdom.

FAMILIAR: A witch's coworker that is of a non-human existence. Animals are the most common familiars, thus the popularity of the witch's cat. But familiars can also be discarnate spirits, spirit guides, or elementals. The choice of having a familiar or not is a personal one.

FILID (singular FIL): The divisions of the Druids according to their specialized craft. For example, musicians were one fil, poets and craftsmen were members of different filid. Special schools were set up throughout Celtic lands to train Druids in their special craft. The English term for fil is bard.

GEIMHREADH (G'yim-ray-ah) Winter, one of the two recognized Wittan seasons. It begins at Samhain.

GEISE (gay-sh): In the Irish myth cycles this was an obligation which bound someone to do something or to not do something. This bond had magickal connotations and to break it brought horrible misfortunes and even death. A geise is often the point on which hangs the conflicts in the mythic stories. In modern Witta coven members are often bound by a geise requiring them not to reveal the names of their fellow coven members nor discuss with outsiders the inner-workings of the coven.

GOD: The masculine aspect of deity.

GODDESS: The feminine aspect of deity.

GRIMOIRE (grim-warr): A book of magickal spells and rituals. Some claims to antiquity are highly suspect, and those that are ancient contain much apocryphal material. However, this does not invalidate the spells or rituals, it just means they are not old. Old is not always better.

HANDFASTING: Pagan marriage, traditionally contracted for a nine-year period, then renewed if agreed upon by both parties.

HERBALISM: The art of using herbs to facilitate human needs both magickally and medically.

IMBOLG (Em-bowl/g): Also known as Candlemas or Imbolc, it is the Wittan sabbat honoring Brigid which is observed on February 2.

INCENSE: Herbs, oils, or other aromatic items which are burned to scent the air during acts of magick and ritual. This ancient practice survives in Ireland where the smooring of peat fires has been ritually used for magick since before recorded time. Incense is associated with the element air.

INITIATION: Modern practice of admitting a witch to a coven. Every tradition has its own method, but it is quite acceptable in Witta to initiate yourself by personal dedication to the deities.

INVOCATION: The act of drawing the aspect of a particular deity into one's physical self. The rite of drawing down the moon is an example.

KABALLAH: Also Cabala or Qabala. This is the mystic Hebrew system of spirituality. Ceremonial magick which derives from this work has had a great impact on both Wittan and Wiccan practice and ritual.

KARMA: A Hindustani word which reflects the ancient belief that good and evil done will return to be visited on a person either in this life or in a succeeding one.

LEPRECHAUN: The most popular of all the world's faeries is the Irish leprechaun, reputed to guard a pot of gold which can be had by a mortal if he or she can capture one of these elusive faeries. As a group they correspond to the Scottish brownie, and they tend to be helpful rather than malicious. The word leprechaun comes from the Irish lu, meaning "small," and chorpan, meaning "body."

LIA FAIL (Lee-ah Fawl): The Stone of Destiny which was used in the crowning of the high kings of Ireland. Many regard it as the Irish equivalent of Excalibur in the Arthurian myths.

THE LITTLE PEOPLE: A popular Irish colloquialism for the faery races of Ireland.

LUGHNASADH (Loo-nas-sah): Also known as Lammas. This sabbat, observed on August 1, celebrates the first harvest and in Irish tradition honors the Irish god Lugh.

MABON (May-bone): Named for a Welsh god associated with the Arthurian myth cycles, this is the sabbat observed at the Autumn Equinox. Mabon was of little importance to the very early Celts, but was later added between Lughnasadh and Samhain as the second of the harvest festivals.

MAGICK: Spelled with a "k" to differentiate it from the magic of stage illusions. According to the infamous ceremonial magician Aleister Crowley, "Magick is the science and art of causing change to occur in conformity to will."

MATRIFOCAL: Also matricentric. This is a term used to denote pre-patriarchal life when clans, especially Celtic ones, centered around and lived near one clan matriarch.

MERROWS: An Irish name for the water faeries known in English as mermaids or mermen.

MIDSUMMER: The sabbat observed at the Summer Solstice.

MONOTHEISM: The belief in one supreme deity who has no other forms and/or displays no other aspects. Judaism and Islam are monotheistic religions.

MYTH CYCLES: The body of lore about any land or people which makes up their mythology. Ireland recognizes five major myth cycles.

OGHAM ALPHABET (oh-gom): Runic writing of the ancient Celts. Credit for the inception of this phonetic writing system is given to the Druids.

OSTARA (O-star-ah): The sabbat observed at the Vernal Equinox. Referred to simply as the Spring Equinox in Witta, Ostara was not an important part of the Irish calendar until Nordic pagan influence brought it to prominence in the ninth century.

PAGAN: Generic term for anyone who practices an earth religion. Witta is one tradition of paganism. Not all pagans are known as witches, only those of the Anglo-Brythonic and Celtic traditions.

PANTHEISM: The belief in many deities who are really one because they are all merely aspects of the single creative life source. Witta is a pantheistic religion.

PASSING OVER: A ritual observed when a loved one has died. In the Wittan tradition this ceremony includes keening and candle lighting, then feasting and revelry.

PENTAGRAM: The five-pointed star which has come to symbolize both Witta and Wicca. It is an ancient symbol with multiple meanings. It is always used with an upward apex. Not a "Devil symbol" as modern Christianity teaches, it represents the four elements plus spirit, it represents a human being with arms and legs spread, and it stands for spirit over matter. Satanist cults often take the pentagram and invert it to signify matter over spirit.

PHOOKA (pook-ah): Malicious Irish hobgoblins who reach the peak of their power from Samhain to Imbolg. One tale relates that an old Irish god generated these beings into existence.

POLARITY: The opposite of duality. Polarity means that everything has two sides or two forces within it that are not wholly separate. For example, we can draw power from our gods for either good or evil as these diverse powers are not contained in two separate entities, but in one.

POLYTHEISM: The belief in the existence of many unrelated deities with their own dominion and interests that have no spiritual relationship to one another.

REINCARNATION: The belief that the souls of living things return to the earth plane in another body after death. A basic tenet of paganism.

RITUAL: A systematic, formal, prescribed set of rites. In Witta a freeform ritual is also acceptable.

SABBAT: A great festival or observance of the pagan year (there are eight sabbats per year). The word is from the Greek sabatu meaning "to rest."

SALT: Often used in Western paganism to represent the element of earth and the direction north. Salt may be used interchangeably with clay, earth, or stones.

SHAMROCK: Seamrog in Irish. A green, trifoliate clover which has long been one of the principal symbols of Ireland. It has been associated with the Triple Goddess. In its rare form with four leaves it represents the four elements, and is considered extremely lucky.

SAMHAIN (Sow-een, Sow-in, or Sav-ain): Celebrated at what is now called Halloween, October 31, this sabbat marked the beginning of winter in the Irish year. It was also the Celtic new year until Roman and Nordic influence pushed that distinction to Yule. Along with Bealtaine it is the primary sabbat of Witta.

SAMHRADH (Sav-rah or Sow-rah): Summer, one of the two recognized Wittan seasons. It begins at Bealtaine.

SATANIST: One who purports to worship the Christian anti-God, Satan or the Devil. Witches do not believe in the existence of this entity and therefore cannot worship him.

SCRYING: The act of gazing at an object or candle until prophetic visions appear.

SÍDHE (shee): Literally, "faery." Also Daoine sídhe (Theen-ah shee), and sídh. The name is generically applied to all the faery races of Ireland. Common names for them include the little people, the wee folk, the gentry, and them that prowl.

SKYCLAD: Ritual nudity, a common practice within the Gardnerian tradition of Wicca. In Witta, going skyclad is a personal choice.

SOLITARY: A Wittan or other pagan who works and worships alone without the aid of a coven.

STAFF: Ritual tool which corresponds to the wand in Wicca. A staff is usually used in the Wittan tradition, especially one made to resemble the Irish walking stick known as the shillelagh (shuh-lay-lee).

THE SUMMERLAND: The Wiccan land of the dead, somewhat similar to Tir-na-nog in Witta.

TALISMAN: An object which is reputed to offer protection or some other magickal service to the carrier. It differs from an amulet by being constructed and charged by the witch.

TARA: The palace and hill in County Meath which was the home of the high kings of Ireland. A gathering place for the Druids. A spiritual center and the seat of old Irish law.

THREEFOLD LAW: The karmic principle of Wicca and Witta. It states that any energy sent will return to the sender three times over.

TIRN AILL (Teern Eel): Literally "Other Land." Another name for Tir-na-nog.

TIR-NA-NOG (Teer-nah-nohk): "Land of the Forever Young." This is an Irish version of heaven. Tir-na-nog is presided over by the crone and her cauldron to which all life returns to await rebirth. In the Celtic traditions of Wales and Cornwall this is roughly the equivalent of the Arthurian Avalon.

TRADITION: The branch of paganism followed by any individual witch or coven. The word is synonymous with "path." Witta is one tradition of paganism.

TRIPLE GODDESS: The one Goddess in all of her three aspects: maiden, mother, and crone. This theme of triple feminine deity has been found in nearly every known culture.

TUATHA DE DANANN (Too-ah day Dawn-nann): Literally, the "People of the Goddess Dana." A semi-human race of people who are now some of Ireland's faery folk. They were one of the groups of invaders of Ireland in the Irish myth cycles. The Cauldron of Abundance which holds the secrets of life and death was one of their treasures.

WAND: A ritual tool brought to the craft through ceremonial magick. In Witta wands can be made from the branch of any sacred tree except oak and holly. Often the popular Irish shillelagh is substituted for the wand to symbolize the element of air and the direction of east.

WARLOCK: Often misused as the name for a male witch. Warlock is a Scottish word akin to the word "sorcerer" and is generally not used in modern paganism.

THE WEE FOLK: Irish faeries of all types—leprechauns, gnomes, merrows, etc. Some are helpful to humans and others mischievous.

WICCA: A tradition of witchcraft. Wicca is an Anglo-Saxon term for the craft as it was practiced in England, Wales, and Brittany. Wiccans are also known as witches.

WIDDERSHINS: This word is from the Teutonic tradition. It means to go backwards, and is the act of moving counterclockwise.

WITA: The witchcraft tradition of Scotland which shares much of its lore, language, and customs with Irish Witta. Witans are also known as witches.

WITCH: Pagans of the Wittan, Witan (Scottish), or Wiccan traditions of the craft. Witches trace their roots primarily to Celtic lands.

WITTA: The witchcraft tradition of Ireland. Wittans are also known as witches.

WITTANING: Also called Wiccaning. In Wittaning, a baby is presented in circle to the Goddess and God, and given a craft name which the child will keep until around the age thirteen when he or she can choose a name at his or her coming of age celebration.

WITTAN REDE: Also called the Wiccan Rede. This is the basic tenet of witchcraft. "As ye harm none, do what thou will." The rede prohibits witches from harming any other living thing, or from violating the free will of any living thing.

YULE: Sabbat celebrated at the Winter Solstice. Most of its traditions come from the pagan Roman holiday, Saturnalia.

❧ APPENDIX III ❧

Resources

When addressing the businesses listed below it is a good idea to include a self-addressed, stamped, business-sized envelope. Some smaller businesses can't afford to operate unless you provide this courtesy. All of these companies were in business at the time of this writing.

Herbs and Oils

Companion Plants
7247 N. Coolville Ridge Rd.
Athens, OH 45701
(catalog: $2.00)

Herbal Endeavors
3618 S. Emmons Ave.
Rochester Hills, MI 48063
(catalog: $2.50)

Indiana Botanical Gardens
P.O. Box 5
Hammond, IN 46325
(free catalog)

Leydet Oils
P.O. Box 2354
Fair Oaks, CA 95628
(catalog and price list: $2.00)

IRISH MUSIC

Southern Music Company
1100 Broadway
San Antonio, TX 78212
512-226-8167

This company publishes and sells printed music, including the complete *Roche Collection of Traditional Irish Music.* They are often better contacted by phone.

Postings
P.O. Box 8001
Hilliard, OH 43026-8001

This company sells videos and off-beat audio tapes and CDs. Their audio catalog usually includes a good selection of folk music. Any recording by the Irish group The Chieftains is excellent *(one year of video and audio catalogs: $3.00)*.

The Music Stand
1 Rockdale Plaza
Lebanon, NH 03766

This company sells gifts and novelties inspired by the preforming arts. The Music Stand sells the Clark pennywhistle with an instruction booklet and cassette tape for a very reasonable price *(catalog: $2.00)*.

ANIMAL RIGHTS GROUPS

People for the Ethical Treatment of Animals
Box 42516
Washington, DC 20015
202-726-0156

PETA works to eliminate inhumane treatment of animals and animal exploitation.

The Humane Society of the United States
2100 L Street, NW
Washington, DC 20037

HSUS seeks to stop abuse of all domestic and wild animals.

ENVIRONMENTAL GROUPS

Clean Water Action Project
317 Pennsylvania Ave., SE
Washington, DC 20042
202-745-4870

This organization has chapters all over the country seeking to clean up and protect water resources.

Earth First!
P.O. Box 5871
Tucson, AZ 85703
602-662-1371

This organization publishes *Earth First! Magazine,* and is involved in many environmental causes.

Greenpeace
1436 U Street, NW
Washington, DC 20009
202-462-1177

This worldwide organization is concerned with all aspects of the environment and has increased awareness of our environmental woes.

Book Catalogs of Pagan Interest

Llewellyn's New Worlds of Mind and Spirit
P.O. Box 64383
St. Paul, MN 55164-0383
(one year subscription: $10.00)

Pyramid Books
35 Congress Street
P.O. Box 4546
Salem, MA 01970-0902

Pyramid also sells beautiful pagan jewelry *(catalog: $2.00).*

RITUAL TOOLS AND OTHER PAGAN ITEMS

Craft of the Wise
45 Grove Street
New York, NY 10014
(free catalog)

Isis Metaphysical
5701 E. Colfax
Denver, CO 80220

Isis carries books, jewelry, incense, oils, herbs, and periodicals. It is also a pleasant gathering center for local pagans and other "New Age" thinkers. Be sure and obtain a list of their upcoming workshops, lectures, and classes *(catalog: price varies)*.

Moon Scents and Magickal Blends, Inc.
P.O. Box 1588-C
Cambridge, MA 02238
(free catalog)

Sacred Spirit Products
P.O. Box 8163
Salem, MA 01971-8163
(catalog: $3.00)

COUNSELING AND LICENSED PAGAN CLERGY

Circle Sanctuary
P.O. Box 219
Mt. Horeb, WI 53572
608-924-2216

Address your inquires to Selena Fox and be sure to include a self-addressed, stamped envelope. Selena is a Wiccan priestess as well as a psychologist. She does phone consultations for a $25.00-per-half-hour donation to Circle. Sliding scale fees are available for people of low income. Call to set up a counseling appointment. Circle may also help you contact licensed pagan clergy and offer aid if you have been denied your legal rights due to the practice of your religion. To obtain a sample copy of their excellent publication, *Circle Network News*, send $4.00 to the address above.

IMPORTED IRISH GOODS

Before you try mail order which can be costly when shipping products overseas, try finding an Irish import shop in a city near you. Most major cities have them. Look in phone books at your local library or phone company office.

Blarney
373D Route 46 West
Fairfield, NJ 07004-9880

This company imports Irish goods including Waterford crystal, Belleek china, coats of arms, and woolen clothing *(catalog: $4.00)*.

IRISH CULTURAL SOCIETIES

Look in your phone book or the phone book of a nearby city for a contact number. More often though you will have to keep an eye on the local newspaper for news about where and when the local Irish organization meets. If you have no luck there ask a librarian to help you locate them. Most cities of any size have some type of active Irish cultural organization which sponsors events to teach Irish dance, language, and culture.

❧ APPENDIX IV ❧

A REFERENCE GUIDE TO HERBS

For thousands of years certain herbs have been thought to have energy properties which lend themselves to certain types of magick. There are a number of good, detailed books on magickal herbalism on the market. I recommend any written by Scott Cunningham. In my mind there is no better teacher for a beginning herbalist.

Be aware that some herbs are toxic, especially to children and pets, if are ingested. I have tried to place an asterisk (*) by all known toxins. Also remember that it is possible for you to have an allergic reaction from handling, inhaling, or ingesting an herb. Don't ingest any herb you when are not absolutely sure of its safeness or of your own reaction to it.

Throughout this book many herbs were mentioned in conjunction with various spell workings. On the following page is a list of those herbs with their corresponding magickal properties.

❦ Anti-gossip: clove

❦ Astral projection: ash, dittany of Crete, jasmine, lavender, lettuce (contains opiates), mugwort, poplar, rowan, sage

❦ Faery attraction: broom, catnip, cowslip, elder, primrose, straw, strawberries, thyme

❦ Divination: apples, beans, holly*, nuts, mistletoe*, moonwort, oak, rowan

❦ Exorcism: beans, elder, ivy*

❦ Fertility: barley, bistort, grape vines, grass, hawthorn, moonwort, mugwort, oak, pine, potatoes, primrose, reed, rice, saffron, wheat, willow leaves

❦ Healing (magickal, not medicinal): ash, comfrey, elder, lavender, rosemary, rowan, vervain, violet, willow

❦ Love: apricots, apples, apple blossom, birch, dogwood flowers, gardenia, Irish moss*, lavender, myrtle, orris root, parsley, reed, rose, vanilla, vervain, violet, willow, yarrow*

❦ Mental powers: rosemary

❦ Money and prosperity: ash, barley, blackberries, cowslip, dill seed, elder, grape vines, hawthorn, hay, nuts, oats, peas, pine needles, potatoes, reed, rice, sugar beets, turnips, wheat

❦ Past lives: ash, catnip, ginger, hyssop, lilac, mugwort, orange peel, peppermint, rowan, valerian

❦ Peaceful home: burdock, huckleberry root, St. Johnswort*, vanilla

❦ Prophetic dreams: broom, jasmine, heliotrope*, holly berries*, mistletoe*, mugwort, oak leaves, rose, shamrocks, willow

❦ Protection: apples, ash, basil, blackberries, bluebells, blueberries, broom, clove, frankincense, garlic, gorse, hazel, holly leaves*, Irish moss*, ivy*, mandrake*, nettles, oak, orange peel, pepper, potatoes, rosemary, St. Johnswort*, thistle, turnips, willow

❦ Purification: birch, burdock, camomile, elder flowers, frankincense, heather, linden, peat, St. Johnswort*, vervain

❦ Spirituality (induced by incense): alder, blueberries, mugwort, saffron

❧ APPENDIX V ❧

TRADITIONAL IRISH MUSIC

The true folk music of Ireland, like folk music anywhere, is not owned by anyone. It is in the public domain, meaning that anyone may copy it, print it, distribute it, use it, and perform it publicly without violating any copyrights.

The four songs which appear here are representative of several types of Irish music. The first is the very familiar "Londonderry Air." The popular song "Danny Boy" is set to this ancient tune. The second, "The Gallants of Tipperary," is a quick jig. The next tune is a hop jig, also known as a hornpipe. This tune has several names, but here it will be called "The Two Hop Two Jig." This piece should be played with a spritely dance beat which can be used to aid in the raising of energy. The fourth tune is an old set dancing tune called "Make Haste to the Wedding." Because of the title you may wish to incorporate this tune into handfasting ceremonies.

All the tunes here are written in either the key of D or G which will make them easily adaptable to the pennywhistle.

LONDONDERRY AIR

slowly

THE GALLANTS OF TIPPERARY

lively

THE TWO HOP TWO JIG

spirited

MAKE HASTE TO THE WEDDING

dance beat

❧ BIBLIOGRAPHY ❧

Whenever spiritual systems are written about, be they pagan or mainstream religion, there is much opportunity for dilettantes to abuse the free press. Many books on paganism and witchcraft are mediocre at best, at worst they are uninformed and misleading. But there are a number of writers who are quite sincere and knowledgeable, and it is worth a little effort to seek them out. In general, steer clear of authors and teachers who try to tell you that their ways are the only ways, belittle your questions, or encourage you to do things which make you uncomfortable. These people are not sincere teachers, but charlatans bent on feeding their egos through your need of them.

The best teachers will occasionally have to answer your questions with the words, "I don't know." And these sincere teachers will remember that you also have talents and knowledge to share. When I was an undergraduate student I became friends with a young man who developed an interest in paganism. He was a classics major and therefore had in-depth knowledge and understanding of Greek and Roman mythology, their accompanying pantheons, and their influence by and on other cultures. He contributed as much to my learning as I did to his.

This is the list of texts I consulted while writing this book. It is by no means an exhaustive list of all the good material which is available on either Irish history, Irish mythology, Witta, or on paganism in general. One could fill a good-sized library with all the works compiled on these topics alone. But, hopefully, it is a solid starting point which can steer you in the right direction. In my opinion Wittans could not go wrong in studying the works of any of the following: Margot Adler, Raymond Buckland, Scott Cunningham, Pauline Campanelli, Joseph Campbell, John and Caitlin Matthews, Diane Stein, Barbara Walker, or Marion Weinstein. But listen to your own nature-given intuition and read everything with an open mind and a critical eye, deciding for yourself which pathway is best for you. Good luck in all your endeavors in the Old Religion. Blessed Be!

Bettelheim, Bruno. *The Uses of Enchantment: The Meaning and Importance of Fairy Tales.* New York: Vintage Books, 1977.

Bonwick, James. *Irish Druids and Old Irish Religions.* New York: Dorset Press, 1986.

Campanelli, Pauline. *Ancient Ways.* St. Paul, MN: Llewellyn Publications, 1991.

This work, illustrated by her husband Dan, offers an enticing analysis of the modern folk and religious practice which surrounds the sabbats, and explains how these were adapted from western Europe's old pagan ways.

Campbell, Joseph. *The Masks of God: Primitive Mythology.* New York: Viking Press, 1959.

All of Campbell's books on mythology are expertly written and very thought provoking. A mini-series was made of *The Power of Myth.* Occasionally it is re-run on your local PBS stations, and many of the larger video rental stores carry the complete series.

_____. *The Mythic Image.* Princeton, NJ: Princeton University Press, 1974.

Colum, Padriac. *A Treasury of Irish Folklore.* New York: Bonanza Books, 1967.

Cunningham, Scott. *Cunningham's Encyclopedia of Magical Herbs.* St. Paul, MN: Llewellyn Publications, 1986.

_____. *Earth Power.* St. Paul, MN: Llewellyn Publications, 1988.

This is a collection of very simple earth spells. Their deep earth connection and simplicity make them valuable for Wittan students who are trying to recapture the essence of the old ways.

_____. *Magical Herbalism.* St. Paul, MN: Llewellyn Publications, 1982.

After years of stumbling around trying to find reliable information on herbal lore I thankfully discovered Cunningham. His many books on earth magick are beautifully written and offer the student of natural magick many methods for expression. I heartily recommend every one of his books.

_____. *The Truth About Witchcraft Today.* St. Paul, MN: Llewellyn Publications, 1988.

This and *Wicca: A Guide for the Solitary Practitioner* are probably the two best primers available on the basics of witchcraft.

_____. *Wicca: A Guide for the Solitary Practitioner.* St. Paul, MN: Llewellyn Publications, 1988.

Cunningham, Scott and David Harrington. *The Magical Household.* St. Paul, MN: Llewellyn Publications, 1987.

This is an enchanting collection of household lore, superstition, and magickal practice, with many of the concepts dating from antiquity.

de Paor, Maire and Liam. *Early Christian Ireland*. New York: Frederick A. Praeger, Inc., 1958.

This is a work by Irish historians which concentrates on the Christianization process. Historically it is a solid work, but editorially it is heavily biased from the dominant cultural viewpoint.

Evans-Wentz, W.Y. *The Fairy Faith in Celtic Countries*. New York: University Books, 1966.

First published in London in 1911, this is an enlightening look into the role of faery folk in Celtic lands, particularly Ireland. While Dr. Evans-Wentz has an open mind and was willing to give credence to the existence of faeries his editors did not, the later addition is full of commentary which is somewhat condescending, and the portrayal of witches leaves something to be desired.

Farrar, Janet and Stewart. *Eight Sabbats for Witches*. Custer, WA: Phoenix Publishing, Inc., 1981.

_____. *The Witches' God*. Custer, WA: Phoenix Publishing, Inc., 1989.

_____. *The Witches' Goddess*. Custer, WA: Phoenix Publishing, Inc., 1987.

The Farrars' brand of witchcraft has an admitted Gardnerian influence. But the fact that this couple lives in and loves the land of Ireland makes them a valuable source for those seeking the Wittan path. Their books are very intelligently researched and written, and would be recommended reading for any pagan.

Frazer, Sir James. *The Golden Bough*. Abridged ed. New York: Macmillian, 1956.

While this work has become known as something of a classic in the field of pagan studies and folk magick, one must read it while being fully cognizant of Frazer's world view. In his travels and studies he no doubt witnessed many miraculous events, felt their power, and was probably tempted himself to worship a balanced male-female deity. Yet being a white, upper-class male fully steeped in the mindset of his culture he felt it necessary to add disclaimers to every other paragraph. Nonetheless, being a native of Britain, much of his writings concern the thinking and practices of the rural peoples of Britain and Ireland.

Froud, Brain and Alan Lee. *Faeries*. Ed. and illus. by David Larkin. New York: Harry N. Abrams, 1978.

Glass-Koentop, Pattalee. *Year of Moons, Season of Trees: Mysteries & Rites of Celtic Tree Magic*. St. Paul: Llewellyn Publications, 1991.

The Druidic system of tree magic has been both criticized and applauded by those who have sought to reconstruct it. This is probably the most easily readable source on the subject, and she freely gives credence to her detractors.

Graves, Robert. *The White Goddess*. New York: Farrar, Straus and Giroux, 1973. (First published 1953.)

This work is an acknowledged classic in the field of goddess studies and covers varied world cultures (though much of it is Celtic in origin). Appearing just before Gerald Gardner's 1954 book, *Witchcraft Today*, it was equally influential in re-introducing goddess worship to the modern world. A must-have for every pagan's library.

Gimbutas, Marija. *Goddesses and Gods of Old Europe*. Berkeley, CA: University of California Press, 1982.

Hawking, Stephen W. *A Brief History of Time*. New York: Bantam Books, 1988.

Hazlitt, W. Carew. *Faiths and Folklore of the British Isles*. Vols. I and II. New York: Benjamin Blom, 1965.

Herm, Gerhard. *The Celts*. New York: St. Martin's Press, 1975.

This is a solid, scholarly history of the Celtic people.

Holzer, Hans. *The Lively Ghosts of Ireland.* New York: The Bobbs-Merrill Company, Inc., 1967.

Hans Holzer is a widely published writer of metaphysical topics and his books are well worth reading for an intelligent insight into modern occult topics from a non-pagan point of view.

K'Eogh, John. *An Irish Herbal.* Suffolk, England: Aquarian Press, 1986.

Lerner, Gerda. *The Creation of Patriarchy.* New York: Oxford University Press, 1986.

Matthews, John. *The Elements of the Arthurian Tradition.* Shaftesbury, Dorset: Element Books Limited, 1989.

Though Arthur is considered part of the Celtic myth cycle, he belongs more in the Welsh Tradition than in the Irish. But he is a strong Celtic archetype upon which many other myths are based, and it is well worth any serious Wittan student's time to study Arthur's story.

The Oxford Illustrated History of Ireland. Ed. by R.F. Foster. New York: Oxford University Press, 1989.

Piggot, Stuart. *The Druids.* New York: Frederick A. Praeger, Inc., 1968.

Rees, Alwyn and Brinley Rees. *Celtic Heritage: Ancient Tradition in Ireland and Wales.* New York: Thames and Hudson, 1961.

This is one of the best books still in print on the myth cycles and old pagan beliefs of Ireland.

Reilly, Robert T. *Irish Saints.* New York: Avenel Books, 1964.

The Roche Collection of Traditional Irish Music. Ed. by Michael O'Suilleabhain. Cork, Ireland: Ossian Publications, 1982. (Distributed in the United States by Music Sales Corporation of New York.)

Rolleston. T.W. *Celtic Myths and Legends.* New York: Avenel Books, 1986.

This collection of myths, which are mostly Irish, has a helpful glossary in the back which can help the novice mythologist sort out the many characters and deities which populate these stories.

Ross, Anne. *The Pagan Celts.* Rockleigh, NJ: Barnes and Noble Publishers, 1986.

Ryall, Rhiannon. *West Country Wicca: A Journal of the Old Religion.* Custer, WA: Phoenix Publishing, Inc., 1989.

Written from a Cornish-Celtic perspective it is one of the only modern books on witchcraft written by someone who was a native practitioner before Gerald Gardner initiated the neo-pagan revival in the 1950s.

Stone, Merlin. *When God Was a Woman.* New York: Harcourt Brace Jovanovich, 1976.

The Enchanted World. Alexandria, VA: Time-Life Books.

Walker, Barbara G. *The Crone: Woman of Age, Wisdom and Power.* San Francisco, CA: HarperCollins, 1985.

Waring, Phillipa. *A Dictionary of Omens and Superstitions.* New York: Ballantine Books, 1979.

Wilde, Lady. *Irish Cures, Mystic Charms and Superstitions.* New York: Sterling Publishing Company, 1991.

This collection from Lady Wilde's larger mid-nineteenth century book makes interesting reading. Reading between the lines of each quaint entry clearly points out how Christianity adapted Wittan practice into modern Irish folk wisdom.

Women of the Celts. Trans. by Jean Markale. Rochester, VT: Inner Traditions International, Ltd., 1972.

This superb work uncovers the matricentric focus of the early Celtic myth cycles.

There are a number of pagan periodicals being published both in America and in Great Britain which offer readers not only thought provoking articles and recipes, but contacts with other pagans. Some of these are very good, others run from mediocre to horrible! You will have to read them and decide for yourself. However, there is one publication to which I urge all Wittans to subscribe. *Circle Network News* is published quarterly by Circle Sanctuary. This newspaper offers articles and contacts from all traditions. Circle has been involved in anti-defamation campaigns, and has recently begun a concerted effort to find ways to offer aid to pagans needing legal help arising from problems incurred because of their religious convictions. Circle Sanctuary offers meetings at each of the sabbats, and at Midsummer hosts the greatly attended Pagan Spirit Gathering.

The paper is written largely by the readership and offers insightful articles, ritual poetry, recipes, and the addresses of pagan contacts, publications, and organizations around the world. At present, a yearly subscription costs $13.00 for U.S. bulk mail; $17.00 for first class mail to the U.S., Canada, or Mexico; and $24.00 airmail to anywhere else. Circle can only accept payment in U.S. funds. Last I heard, a sample copy was $4.00. Send a self-addressed, stamped envelope for information:

Circle Sanctuary
Circle Network News
Box 219
Mt. Horeb, WI 53572
U.S.A.

❦ INDEX ❦

H

hair, 9, 50, 88, 92, 105-106, 173, 184
Halloween, 12, 32-33, 111, 167, 170-171
handfasting, 34, 52, 55-56
harp, 11, 44
hawthorn, 14, 160-161, 186
hazel, 14, 107, 138, 161
healing, 4, 13, 25, 42, 72, 74-77, 79, 81-85, 87, 118, 141-142, 155, 159, 161
heather, 81, 107, 197-198
herb, 33, 51, 74, 79-82, 85, 91-92, 94, 97, 101, 108, 110, 138, 142, 157, 162, 183, 193
high king, 8, 14, 18-21, 44, 54, 95, 183
holiday sugar cookies, 63
holly, 14, 81, 91, 102, 110, 116, 122-123, 126-127, 161, 175-177, 192
Holly King, 81, 126-127, 175, 192
Holy Grail, 10, 30
home (also see house), 6, 14, 25, 34, 37-38, 40, 42-43, 62, 66-67, 76, 81, 88, 93, 98-99, 102-103, 107-108, 119, 134-135, 137-139, 141-142, 161-162, 167, 169, 177-178, 180, 185, 193
honegar, 85-86
horse, 11, 88
house (also see home), 6, 14, 25, 34, 37-38, 40, 42-43, 58, 62, 66-67, 76, 81, 88, 93, 98-99, 102-103, 107-109, 119, 134-135, 137-139, 141-142, 144, 161-162, 167, 169, 174, 177-178, 180, 185, 193, 195
huckleberry, 108
hyssop, 51

I

Imbolg, 117, 166, 171, 177, 179-181, 197
Irish potato pie, 196
Irish soda bread, 63-64
iron, 2, 31, 73, 137, 151, 187
ivy, 14, 110, 158, 161

K

Kaballah, 17, 26, 38
Kele-De, 12, 150
King Arthur, 30
King Midhir, 132
King of Kinsale, 145
knife (also see athame), 28-29, 39, 71, 155
knot (also see cord), 25, 103-105, 191

L

Lammas (also see Lughnasadh), 194
lavender, 28, 50, 84, 92, 108, 193
leprechaun, 133-134
Lia Fail, 7
lilac, 50-51
love, 24-25, 42, 57, 61, 67, 72-73, 76, 80-82, 88, 91-94, 113, 121, 129, 133, 136-137, 141, 144-145, 158, 161, 176, 191, 193
Luchtain, 74
Lugh, 8, 11, 20, 74-75, 82, 87, 103, 124-125, 127, 171, 177, 184, 194-196
Lughnasadh (also see Lammas), 8, 11, 81, 165-166, 184, 194-195, 197

R

S

Stay in Touch. . .

Llewellyn publishes hundreds of books on your favorite subjects

On the following pages you will find listed some books now available on related subjects. Your local bookstore stocks most of these and will stock new Llewellyn titles as they become available. We urge your patronage.

Order by Phone

Call toll-free within the U.S. and Canada, 1–800–THE MOON.
In Minnesota call (612) 291–1970.
We accept Visa, MasterCard, and American Express.

Order by Mail

Send the full price of your order (MN residents add 7% sales tax) in U.S. funds to:
    Llewellyn Worldwide
    P.O. Box 64383, Dept. L732-4
    St. Paul, MN 55164–0383, U.S.A.

Postage and Handling

    ◆ $4.00 for orders $15.00 and under
    ◆ $5.00 for orders over $15.00
    ◆ No charge for orders over $100.00

We ship UPS in the continental United States. We cannot ship to P.O. boxes. Orders shipped to Alaska, Hawaii, Canada, Mexico, and Puerto Rico will be sent first-class mail. International orders: Airmail—add freight equal to price of each book to the total price of order, plus $5.00 for each non-book item (audiotapes, etc.). Surface mail—Add $1.00 per item.

Allow 4–6 weeks delivery on all orders. Postage and handling rates subject to change.

Group Discounts

We offer a 20% quantity discount to group leaders or agents. You must order a minimum of 5 copies of the same book to get our special quantity price.

Free Catalog

Get a free copy of our color catalog, *New Worlds of Mind and Spirit*. Subscribe for just $10.00 in the United States and Canada ($20.00 overseas, first class mail). Many bookstores carry *New Worlds*— ask for it!

ANCIENT WAYS
Reclaiming the Pagan Tradition
Pauline Campanelli, illustrated by Dan Campanelli

Ancient Ways is filled with magick and ritual that you can perform every day to capture the spirit of the seasons. It focuses on the celebration of the Sabbats of the Old Religion by giving you practical things to do while anticipating the Sabbat rites, and helping you harness the magickal energy for weeks afterward. The wealth of seasonal rituals and charms are drawn from ancient sources but are easily performed with materials readily available.

Learn how to look into your previous lives at Yule ... at Beltane, discover the places where you are most likely to see faeries ... make special jewelry to wear for your Lammas celebrations ... for the special animals in your life, paint a charm of protection at Midsummer.

Most Pagans and Wiccans feel that the Sabbat rituals are all too brief and wish for the magick to linger on. *Ancient Ways* can help you reclaim your own traditions and heighten the feeling of magick.
0-87542-090-7, 256 pp., 7 x 10, illus., softcover $14.95

CELTIC MAGIC
D. J. Conway

Many people, not all of Irish descent, have a great interest in the ancient Celts and the Celtic pantheon, and *Celtic Magic* is the map they need for exploring this ancient and fascinating magical culture.

Celtic Magic is for the reader who is either a beginner or intermediate in the field of magic. It provides an extensive "how-to" of practical spell-working. There are many books on the market dealing with the Celts and their beliefs, but none guide the reader to a practical application of magical knowledge for use in everyday life. There is also an in-depth discussion of Celtic deities and the Celtic way of life and worship, so that an intermediate practitioner can expand upon the spellwork to build a series of magical rituals. Presented in an easy-to-understand format, *Celtic Magic* is for anyone searching for new spells that can be worked immediately, without elaborate or rare materials, and with minimal time and preparation.
0-87542-136-9, 240 pp., mass market, illus., softcover $4.99

GLAMOURY
Magic of the Celtic Green World
Steve Blamires

Glamoury refers to an Irish Celtic magical tradition that is truly holistic, satisfying the needs of the practitioner on the physical, mental and spiritual levels. This guidebook offers practical exercises and modern versions of time-honored philosophies that will expand your potential into areas previously closed to you.

We have moved so far away from our ancestors' closeness to the Earth—the Green World—that we have nearly forgotten some very important truths about human nature that are still valid. Glamoury brings these truths to light so you can take your rightful place in the Green World. View and experience the world in a more balanced, meaningful way. Meet helpers and guides from the Otherworld who will become your valued friends. Live in tune with the seasons and gauge your inner growth in relation to the Green World around you.

1-56718-069-8, 6 x 9, 352 pp., illus., softcover $16.95

THE BOOK OF OGHAM
The Celtic Tree Oracle
Edred Thorsson

Drink deeply from the very source of the Druids' traditional lore. The oghamic Celtic tradition represents an important breakthrough in the practical study of Celtic religion and magick. Within the pages of *The Book of Ogham* you will find the complete and authentic system of divination based on the letters of the Celtic ogham alphabet (commonly designated by tree names), and a whole world of experiential Celtic spirituality.

Come to understand the Celtic Way to new depths, discover methodological secrets shared by the Druids and Drightens of old, receive complete instructions for the practice of ogham divination, and find objective inner truths concealed deep within yourself.

The true and inner learning of oghams is a pathway to awakening the deeply rooted structural patterns of the Celtic psyche or soul. Read, study and work with the ogham oracle ... open up the mysterious and hidden world within ... and become part of the eternal stream of tradition that transcends the individual self. Come, and drink directly from the true cauldron of inspiration: the secret lore and practices of the ancient Celtic Druids.

0-87542-783-9, 224 pp., 6 x 9, illus., glossary, softcover $12.95

WICCA
A Guide for the Solitary Practitioner
Scott Cunningham

Wicca is a book of life, and how to live magically, spiritually, and wholly attuned with Nature. It is a book not only about magic, but about religion and how to achieve a better relationship with our Earth. Wicca is presented as a gentle, Earth-oriented religion. This book fulfills a need for a practical guide to solitary Wicca—a need which no previous book has fulfilled.

Here is a positive, practical introduction to Wicca, designed so that anyone can learn to practice the religion alone, anywhere in the world. It presents Wicca honestly and clearly, without the pseudo-history that permeates other books. It shows that Wicca is a vital, satisfying part of twentieth century life.

This book presents the theory and practice of Wicca from an individual's perspective. The section on the Standing Stones Book of Shadows contains solitary rituals for the Esbats and Sabbats. The author's nearly two decades of Wiccan practice create an eclectic picture of various aspects of this religion. Included are exercises designed to develop magical proficiency, a self-dedication ritual, herb, crystal and rune magic, and recipes for Sabbat feasts.
0-87542-118-0, 240 pp., 6 x 9, illus., softcover $9.95

CUNNINGHAM'S ENCYCLOPEDIA OF MAGICAL HERBS
Scott Cunningham

This is the most comprehensive source of herbal data for magical uses ever printed! Almost every one of the over 400 herbs is illustrated, making this a great source for herb identification. Listed for each herb are magical properties, planetary rulerships, genders, associated deities, folk and Latin names and much more. This book also contains a folk name cross-reference and a full index. There is also a large annotated bibliography, and a list of mail order suppliers so you can find the books and herbs you need.

Like all of Cunningham's books, this one does not require you to use complicated rituals or expensive magical paraphernalia. Instead, it shares with you the intrinsic powers of the herbs. Thus, you will be able to discover which herbs, by their very nature, can be used for luck, love, success, money, divination, astral projection, safety, psychic self-defense and much more. Besides being interesting and educational it is also fun, and fully illustrated with unusual woodcuts from old herbals. This book has rapidly become the classic in its field. It enhances books such as *777* and is a must for all Wiccans.
0-87542-122-9, 336 pp., 6 x 9, illus., softcover $14.95

Prices subject to change without notice

THE MAGICAL HOUSEHOLD
Empower Your Home with Love, Protection, Health and Happiness
Scott Cunningham and David Harrington

Whether your home is a small apartment or a palatial mansion, you want it to be something special. Now it can be with *The Magical Household*. Learn how to make your home more than just a place to live. Turn it into a place of security, life, fun and magic. Here you will not find the complex magic of the ceremonial magician. Rather, you will learn simple, quick and effective magical spells that use nothing more than common items in your house: furniture, windows, doors, carpet, pets, etc. You will learn to take advantage of the intrinsic power and energy that is already in your home, waiting to be tapped. You will learn to make magic a part of your life. The result is a home that is safeguarded from harm and a place which will bring you happiness, health and more.

0-87542-124-5, 208 pp., 5¼ x 8, illus., softcover   **$9.95**

SPELL CRAFTS
Creating Magical Objects
Scott Cunningham and David Harrington

Since early times, crafts have been intimately linked with spirituality. When a woman carefully shaped a water jar from the clay she'd gathered from a river bank, she was performing a spiritual practice. When crafts were used to create objects intended for ritual or that symbolized the Divine, the connection between the craftsperson and divinity grew more intense. Today, handcrafts can still be more than a pastime—they can be rites of power and honor; a religious ritual. After all, hands were our first magical tools.

Spell Crafts is a modern guide to creating physical objects for the attainment of specific magical goals. It is far different from magic books that explain how to use purchased magical tools. You will learn how to fashion spell brooms, weave wheat, dip candles, sculpt clay, mix herbs, bead sacred symbols and much more, for a variety of purposes. Whatever your craft, you will experience the natural process of moving energy from within yourself (or within natural objects) to create positive change.

0-87542-185-7, 224 pp., 5¼ x 8, illus., photos, softcover   **$10.00**